The Rise and Fall of the *Saturday Globe*

The Rise and Fall of the *Saturday Globe*

Ralph Frasca

SUP

Selinsgrove: Susquehanna University Press
London and Toronto: Associated University Presses

Associated University Presses
440 Forsgate Drive
Cranbury, NJ 08512

Associated University Presses
25 Sicilian Avenue
London WC1A 2QH, England

Associated University Presses
P.O. Box 39, Clarkson Pstl. Stn.
Mississauga, Ontario,
L5J 3X9 Canada

The paper used in this publication meets the requirements of the American National Standard for Permanence of Paper for Printed Library Materials Z39.48-1984.

Library of Congress Cataloging-in-Publication Data

Frasca, Ralph, 1962-
The rise and fall of the Saturday globe/Ralph Frasca.
p. cm.
Includes bibliographical references (p.) and index.
ISBN 0-945636-16-4
1. Saturday globe (Utica: N.Y.) 2. American newspapers—New York—Utica—History. 3. American newspapers—History. 4. United States—History—Sources. 5. Journalism—United States—History—19th century. 6. Journalism—United States—History—20th century. I. Title.
PN4899.N42S264 1992 89-40761
071'.4762—dc20 CIP

PRINTED IN THE UNITED STATES OF AMERICA

Contents

Foreword

Clark R. Mollenhoff

Ralph Frasca has put together an interesting and well-researched book on the *Saturday Globe*, perhaps the first newspaper in the United States to have made some claim to being a truly national newspaper. Tom and Will Baker, from their publishing headquarters in Utica, New York, made the *Saturday Globe* a pioneer in news-gathering activities, in printing techniques, and in the methods used to build and hold circulation.

Although the *Saturday Globe* purported to avoid the sensationalism of the Pulitzer and Hearst brand of journalism, it registered its largest circulation in its colorful depth coverage of the most tragic events of the period between 1881 and about 1910. Frasca offers an interesting, detailed review of the newspaper coverage of such natural disasters as the Johnstown, Pennsylvania, flood of 1889, the tidal wave's destruction of Galveston, Texas, in 1890 and the San Francisco earthquake of 1906. There is also a provocative analysis of the coverage of such national tragedies as the assassination of Presidents James Garfield in 1881 and William McKinley two decades later, and an explanation of how the news and editorial coverage of McKinley by the Hearst organization probably encouraged McKinley's assassin.

Frasca provides a thorough analysis of the manner in which the *Saturday Globe*'s personalized coverage of these and other tragedies explained the newspaper's whopping circulation gains in a wide area, far removed from its home base in Utica.

From the standpoint of newspaper history, this work clearly chronicles the many "firsts" that were claimed by the *Saturday Globe* as it explored and experimented with a wide range of innovations to improve its product and expand the geographic scope

---

During his distinguished career, Clark Mollenhoff served as a Washington correspondent for Cowles Publications and the *Des Moines Register*, winning the Pulitzer Prize for national reporting in 1958. He has authored eleven books, including his recent *Atanasoff: Forgotten Father of the Computer*. He is a professor of journalism at Washington and Lee University.

of its audience. The *Saturday Globe* employed production devices and visual techniques that later became almost universally used by magazines and newspapers. The Baker brothers' aggressive desire to make use of the most imaginative innovations extended beyond the printing plant, as they were among the first to use newspaper carriers to make practical a home-delivery system that eventually stretched from coast to coast in the United States and into some parts of Canada. The editor and the publisher of the emerging Curtis Publishing Company studied and copied the *Saturday Globe*'s system, enabling them to provide successful distribution for the *Saturday Evening Post*.

While claiming opposition to the sensationalism of Pulitzer's *World* and Hearst's *Journal*, Will and Tom Baker did engage in a lower-key sensationalism, as manifested by the *Saturday Globe*'s extensive coverage of particularly brutal crimes. Some examples include particularly ghoulish illustrations depicting the headless corpse of a Kentucky girl who fell victim to a sex crime and a woman's head, which had been severed from a mutilated body.

Frasca gives a particularly interesting account of how the *Saturday Globe*'s managing editor, Albert M. Dickinson, was able to circumvent Hearst's massive checkbook journalism during the 1897 heavyweight title fight between James J. Corbett and Robert Fitzsimmons. The Corbett-Fitzsimmons fight was of great national interest, and the Hearst organization had made arrangements for the "exclusive" rights to "interviews, photographs, and signed statements." Dickinson overcame this obstacle by publishing personal observations, interviews with others connected with the fight and sketches of the fighters created by the *Saturday Globe*'s own artists. More than twenty-five sidebar stories on the fight were carried in the March 20 1897 issue of the newspaper, the day it reached its peak circulation of 294,000 copies. That the picture of the headless Kentucky girl was also prominently displayed in this issue may have contributed to that circulation zenith.

Ultimately, this book describes the establishment of a national newspaper in the nineteenth century. The *Saturday Globe* filled a need, but failed when better transmission of in-depth stories in local and regional newspapers became possible with technological advances.

In *The Rise and Fall of the Saturday Globe*, Ralph Frasca has focused on an important part of journalism's history, and at the same time has reviewed journalistic practices in the period before the profession adopted the various journalism codes of ethics that emerged in the 1920s.

Preface

The state of today's high-technology journalism and the press's constant struggle for freedom (some say carte blanche) on legal, political, economic, and technological fronts tend to obscure the advances made in journalism of the late nineteenth century. This was the period characterized by images of cigar-chomping editors, hard-boiled newspaper hacks trying to "scoop" each other on the big story, street-corner newsboys trumpeting the news of the day, and readers greedily devouring sensational and lurid accounts of politics, sex, and crime. Like so many stereotypes, these images had some basis in fact, but their one-dimensional simplicity obfuscates the reality of the press in the time period between the Civil War and World War I. Newspapers at that time were innovative, ambitious and fiercely competitive, battling the encroachment of magazines just as newspapers today are trying to ward off broadcast journalism and new information technologies.

This book's purpose is to resurrect the faded memory of a prominent newspaper that enjoyed its heyday a century ago. The *Saturday Globe*, first called the *Utica Saturday Globe*, was a unique newspaper, a child of its time. It achieved national circulation and prominence, but slipped into obscurity under the weight of fierce competition and feeble management. Telling the story entailed locating and examining documents in public and private collections, interviewing those who remember the *Saturday Globe*, and perusing more than 1,000 issues of the newspaper.

The *Saturday Globe* has been defunct since 1924. All that remains are an incomplete set of back issues, the memories of a few elderly citizens, and the building on Whitesboro Street in Utica that served as the newspaper's home for forty years, although this may soon perish, either due to its own structural instability or as a victim of urban renewal. As best as can be determined, all of its employees have died, and the equipment, newspaper morgue, and business records have vanished. According to Marietta von Bernuth, granddaughter of publisher Will Baker, "the lack of business records, correspondence, or diaries relative to the *Globe* and by or addressed to either of the Baker brothers'' is due to the fact that most primary-source material was ''stored in a barn behind my grandfather's house on Genessee Street'' in Utica. The barn was destroyed by fire in the 1920s.[1]

Another possibility is that some records were turned over to the Globe-Telegram Co. when it assumed control of the newspaper in 1920, but efforts to trace materials through descendants of this short-lived consortium's members proved unsuccessful. Thus, pleas of the difficulties of research and the ravages of time must be entered in instances when treatment of the *Saturday Globe* and its principals is not as extensive as would have been possible had more documentary evidence survived, along with the hope that others might take up the challenge to unearth more records and source material about this newspaper. In their stead, the contents of the *Saturday Globe* are heavily relied on, enabling the newspaper to tell its own story, as well as that of its era, for to do so answers G. Thomas Tanselle's call for historians ''to examine printed items—as specialists in other fields examine other kinds of artifacts—in an effort to see how much of their own history they can tell us.'' He decried that ''the examination of the artifacts is, oddly enough, the most neglected basic area in the historical study'' of the American media.[2]

Nonetheless, the question arises: Why exhume facts, recollections and anecdotes of a largely-forgotten newspaper whose only monument is a decrepit shell of a building that waits forlornly for the wrecker's ball? If there is an answer, it is this: all that is written is a record of its time. The *Saturday Globe* reflected the age in which it existed and became, for hundreds of thousands of people in the United States and abroad, an integral part of their lives. During its forty-three-year lifespan from 1881 to 1924, it chronicled for its international audience the bizarre, the tragic, the humorous, and the important. To quote British statesman Benjamin Disraeli: ''To preserve the past is half of immortality.''

This book is a cultural and sociological examination of a trailblazing newspaper and its place in the context of American journalism of the late nineteenth and early twentieth centuries. It is not a ''great man, great newspaper'' hagiography, but instead a view of how one unique newspaper, the practice of journalism, and developments in American society and technology were all inextricably intertwined. As the only comprehensive source on the *Saturday Globe*, this book fills a void in the history of mass communication. The story is intended to be interesting and informative for both general readers and scholars—a historiographic balance not easily achieved, according to historian Robert Jones

Shafer. "Critics sometimes chide the [historical] profession for excessive attention to scholarly analysis and too little production of stimulating narrative history," he noted. It is hoped this book will gratify "the apparently unslakable public appetite for good narrative history," which, Shafer wrote, "is important as a communication link between scholar and public."[3]

At the same time, scholars should find the story of the *Saturday Globe* useful. This landmark newspaper not only deserves recognition as a vital (and largely overlooked) element of local and state history, but also deserves recognition in the annals of social/cultural history and journalism history, for all that is published sheds light on the history of mass communication, especially the people who made and consumed the news. It is important to be mindful of the context into which the *Saturday Globe* fits, but it is equally requisite to pay vigilant attention to such individual cases and breakthroughs, because they are the foundation of the larger context. Exposing the *Saturday Globe* to scholarly light follows other recent works that have explored individual newspapers and their proprietors as social and cultural forces that helped shape the character of the American press in the postindustrial era.[4]

The more pieces that are added to the mosaic of journalism history, the more vivid the larger context will appear, for without the richness of detail and the clarity of focus on such newspapers as the *Saturday Globe*, there can be no broad generalizations about the American media. In *Measure for Measure*, Shakespeare succinctly expressed the importance of looking to the past for perspectives on problems of the present: "This news is old enough, yet it is every day's news." The same may be said for the rise and fall of the *Saturday Globe*.

I wish to express my appreciation for the research assistance of Douglas Preston and his staff, Oneida Historical Society; Gene Allen and Ronald Labuz, Bagg's Square Association; and the staff of the Utica Public Library.

My thanks also to *Saturday Globe* ex-newsboys Thomas Dodge, Ed Lee, and Gilbert Lee; Marietta von Bernuth, granddaughter of Will Baker; Sally Luther, daughter of artist Denis Howe; Thomas Spooner, who helped me make sense of an unwieldy miscellany of material; Ron and Fran Pytko, Utica historians who counseled me at several stages of this process; and the late Will and Tom Baker, whose fortitude and vision more than a century ago made this book both possible and necessary.

Special thanks to my mother, Rita Frasca, for her devotion and sagacity. It is to her this book is dedicated.

Lastly, if this chronicle contains any unforgivable errors, glaring omissions or heinous gaffes, the author will staunchly blame someone else.

Ralph Frasca

The Rise and Fall of the *Saturday Globe*

1
The Genesis

Since its inception, journalism has filled the persistent need for familiarity with one's surroundings and knowledge of the latest developments in one's environment. It offers superior fuel to stoke the fires of open, unrestrained communication that keep warm the libertarian concept of a "free marketplace of ideas." Journalism history is alternately a tale of wealth, profits, and power and a tale of efforts to keep open the lines of communication that keep a citizenry informed. The historical study of journalism shows that throughout the life of our nation the press has maintained a curious partnership, almost a symbiosis, with the nation itself. The press has wielded substantial influence over political, social, and economic developments—it has shaped the course of the nation. Reciprocally, the influences and characteristics of each period of our nation's history have molded the press.

The latter decades of the nineteenth century were a fertile era for both the press and the nation—both were in the midst of great periods of growth. For the press, this era marked a revolutionary change in journalism history. It was characterized by a pronounced increase in narrative, emotion-provoking treatment of arid "hard news" stories, prompting the pejoratives "sensationalism" and "yellow journalism" to be affixed to press efforts. There were advances in cooperative news-gathering; the development of editorial staffs; increased competition for circulation and advertising; the early uses of political cartoons, color, woodcuts, and photographs; upgraded production techniques; and an emphasis on presenting features and "human interest" news.

These press developments were inextricably linked to changes in American life—the rise of mechanization, the widespread development of factories; the growth of cities; the soaring population rate, especially in urban areas; the establishment of suburbs; new democratic, political, and economic movements; and new means of entertaining and informing the burgeoning populace. Newspapers of the day were spawned by these new conditions and, in turn, affected and influenced them.

In the midst of this heyday for the press and the nation was a newspaper, now virtually forgotten, which was a major force in its day. Its proprietors were Will and Tom Baker, and they guided the *Saturday Globe* for all but the denouement of its forty-three-year lifespan. The *Saturday Globe* was a mirror of people's deeds and a purveyor of information about their environment; but just as importantly, it served to unite a nation of communities that constantly were being redefined as population and industry expanded, and the populace moved westward. As the act of association is critical to considerations of community development, whether on a local, regional or national scale, it is instrumental to regard the process of association just as intently as its result. Newspapers effectively served this social role, and the *Saturday Globe* answered the call on a national and international scale.

With its splendid color artwork, the *Saturday Globe* became one of the most visually appealing newspapers of its day, and with its circulation and production innovations, it grew to a position of novel and influential status. In many ways, the *Saturday Globe* was a theoretical forerunner of *USA Today*. Although never a politically partisan newspaper, the *Saturday Globe* did emanate a morally conservative tenor, which was sometimes difficult to reconcile with the newspaper's tendency toward sensationalism. When not depicting severed heads and graphically describing the gruesome deaths of criminals in the electric chair, the *Saturday Globe* was a storehouse of social and literary miscellany, tending to offer editorial content more suited to the pages of a magazine than a newspaper. It opened the minds of its enormous readership to social and cultural trends while adhering to Benjamin Franklin's view that a newspaper serves the public best by communicating information and instruction in an entertaining and useful manner.[1]

*****

Thomas F. Baker grew up with newspapers. Born 5 April 1847, he and his family moved from Hartford, Connecticut, to St. Louis, Missouri, in 1849 and then to Utica, New York, in 1850.[2] After his school day at Assumption Academy was finished, Baker hawked the *Utica Observer* on street corners. It was this experience that filled his veins with printer's ink and his head with dreams of the newspaper business.

In 1863, the sixteen-year-old Baker became a printing apprentice at the *Utica Herald* in the waning years of that labor practice. The apprenticeship, in printing and many other trades, was a custom established to pass on occupational skills to male youths in America and in other nations. Apprentices were contractually bound laborers who performed duties intended to teach them a craft, thus insuring a steady and adequate supply of skilled labor within the trade. Apprenticeships usually lasted six or seven years, during which time the apprentice received no pay but lived and ate in the master's house. Another function of the apprenticeship, both in America and abroad, was more subtle—it served to reaffirm social class hierarchy. Masters in the most attractive trades sometimes demanded fees in order to take on apprentices. As impoverished parents could seldom afford this payment, their children were rarely apprenticed in trades that offered the prospect of climbing the social ladder. The heyday of the apprenticeship system was in the eighteenth century, but by the mid-nineteenth century the custom was waning due to the rise of mechanization and the practice of hiring "halfway journeymen," or boys who had not finished their apprenticeship, in place of full-fledged journeymen. Because many proprietors were satisfied to hire inadequately-trained help at lower wages than journeymen printers would normally require, the apprenticeship system gradually became superfluous.[3]

After his four-year apprenticeship, Baker advanced to the paid rank of journeyman printer with the *Herald*.[4] While there, Baker was struck with a desire that would nag him for the next ten years—he wanted to establish a weekly newspaper for the masses, uninfluenced by social classes or political parties, which would carry illustrations of not only the people in the news but the events themselves. The fulfillment of his ambition was the *Saturday Globe*, one of the largest newspapers in existence from the 1880s to the 1910s. Dynamic coverage of the assassination of President James Garfield, the Johnstown flood, and several prominent murder trials and executions brought the *Saturday Globe* to national prominence, enabling it to become the first national newspaper to print regional editions. Its international circulation reached a zenith of nearly 300,000. The *Saturday Globe* was one of the very first newspapers—possibly the first—to print illustrations on a cylinder press and to cast a halftone cut into a form instead of "matrixing" it. It also claimed to be the first five-cent newspaper to print a halftone cut. It was a pioneer in the use of color, cartoons, large front-page pictures, and a complex linotype system.

These developments were recounted in a front-page autobiography titled "A Glance Back to the Babyhood of the *Globe*," published in the waning days of the Baker regime. This historical sketch recounts the genesis of Tom Baker's embryonic vision of what was to become the *Saturday Globe*:

> There was nothing like it anywhere in the world—nothing to copy after, nothing to suggest it, nothing to improve upon. There was no blazed trail to follow, no failure to warn, no success to encourage.
>
> But the idea of it formed in the brain of a young man as he clicked the metal types into his "stick" in the old *Utica Herald* composing room. And the idea, once formed, would not down. It kept recurring, kept coming up for consideration and study and improvement, until finally in the brain of that young man the whole thing unfolded and he saw far into the future a monument of such success as to be well worth striving for. He knew it meant hard work and courage and persistency and an unending striving toward the goal which he saw so clearly in the future. But he had faith in his idea, faith that the people would respond.
>
> Briefly, his idea was a weekly paper in which the common people would see themselves represented, interpreted, understood; a newspaper clean in its morals but simple in its diction and printing just the things in which the masses were interested; a journal which would tell the plain people the news of themselves and of their equally plain neighbors; a publication which—marvel of marvels—would carry illustrations, pictures of the people who were in the news and pictures of the events in which they were interested.[5]

Baker first attempted to bring his plan to fruition after just three years as a printer, when he and Benjamin L. Douglas established the afternoon *Utica Daily Bee* in 1870. The newspaper did not fare well and was sold two years later to Seth W. Paine. It folded shortly thereafter, and Baker returned to the *Herald*'s composing room, but failed to shake the entrepreneurial urge. In 1877, he teamed with former *Utica Observer* employee Dennis T. Kelly to form the *Utica Sunday Tribune*, the first Sunday newspaper ever printed in Utica. The first issue of the four-page newspaper, printed in the heart of the city at Genesee and Broad streets, was 6 May 1877. There was substantial doubt that a Sunday newspaper would survive in the conservative, primarily Catholic city, but opposition to Sunday newspapers was subsiding in East-Coast cities due to the influx of European immigrants who arrived without the American conservatism regarding the Sabbath. Thus, by 1850, one in nine New York City residents bought a Sunday paper, and by 1889, one in two New Yorkers purchased one. This repudiation of a Judeo-Christian norm gradually spread inland, and the partners capitalized on the situation. Without any direct competition, the *Sunday Tribune* found a ready audience and thrived.[6]

Transportation problems frustrated the partners' attempts to distribute the newspaper outside of Utica until they borrowed a short-lived distribution method from the U.S. Post Office. Because few trains operated on Sunday, Baker and Kelly established a type of pony express from Utica to outlying towns as far as forty miles away. Subscribers received their newspapers from post riders, who made weekly trips along established routes and were either paid a quarterly sum by the printer or received a percentage of the money collected from subscribers. The plan was risky, as post riders had a history of irresponsibility and transience. In one case, two post riders in Poughkeepsie, New York, collected what was due to their employers and vanished. However, the system of post riders conveying newspapers to Little Falls, Rome, Waterville, and other outlying towns worked well for Baker and Kelly, according to Utica historian Moses Bagg, who wrote that the *Tribune*'s experiment had "never been met in the way of enterprise by any newspaper in this section."[7]

After five months of operation, Dennis Kelly sold his interest to his brother Patrick in order to begin publishing the short-lived *Daily Republican*. Patrick Kelly and Baker saw the *Sunday Tribune*'s circulation climb to 3,500 within a year. Within a few years the *Sunday Tribune* was distributed as far north as the Canadian border, in such Northern New York towns as Governeur, Canton, Philadelphia, Potsdam and Norwood. By 1892 its circulation had risen to between 7,000 and 8,000. Rural readers, particularly farmers, had greatly increased the *Sunday Tribune*'s circulation base, a fact Baker no doubt recalled when selecting the *Saturday Globe*'s target readership groups only a few years later.[8]

Reveling in his success, Baker sold his interest to Patrick Kelly in 1879 and persuaded his older brother, William T. Baker, to leave his job as a marble cutter and join him in publishing the *Binghamton Sunday Tribune* in Binghamton, New York. The younger Baker was drawing close to his dream newspaper; like the Utica version, Binghamton's *Sunday Tribune* was the only Sunday newspaper in the city, and despite the Bakers' risk of offending the citizenry's religious beliefs, their newspaper succeeded. The Bakers sold the Binghamton weekly in 1881 and returned to Utica intent on establishing a new Sunday newspaper.[9]

The Utica to which the Bakers relocated in 1881 was a thriving community of about 35,000 people, Within thirty years the population would more than double, and nearly triple within fifty years.[10] Utica had originally been called "Yah-nun-dah-sis," an Indian name meaning "around the hill." Colonists built Fort Schuyler about 1758 to protect themselves—and a lucrative fur trade along the nearby Mohawk River—from Indian and French-Canadian raids. A settlement grew up around the fort, and the area became a commodity-producing hinterland for the seaport of New York. Also, its fertile land enabled New York to surpass Boston (which relied on the less productive soil of interior New England) in the West Indian and southern European comestibles trade and generate more income, which translated into a higher volume of imported goods than New Englanders could afford. By 1793, the area boasted a post office, general store and tavern, all of which were run by early settler John Post. Five years later the Fort Schuyler community was incorporated as the village of Utica.[11]

Waterways dictated American demography in the eighteenth and early nineteenth centuries by providing a primary means of transportation and sustenance, and the Mohawk was instrumental in the development of Utica and other early communities in upstate New York. Boats of small tonnage navigated the Mohawk River from Utica east to the Albany area, where it joined with the Hudson River, which flowed south to New York. The Indians called the Mohawk "Te-non-an-at-che," or the river flowing through mountains. As with most Indian names it was a descriptive appellation, for the Mohawk is the only river that traverses the rock wall of the Appalachian plateau, which extents from Northern New York to Georgia.[12]

Problems with the movement of troops to interior lands during the War of 1812 underscored the need for improved transportation modes. In subsequent years, as trade in upstate New York flourished and settlers forged westward to populate inexpensive interior farmland, governmental officials decided to construct a canal independent of existing rivers and lakes from Albany to Lake Erie. Construction on the Erie Canal began in 1817 and was completed by 1825. For much of its distance, including the section that passes through Utica, the canal parallels the Mohawk River. Some sections of the Erie Canal have survived to this day.[13]

Along with canals, railroads were instrumental to the nation's growth, for they enabled more goods to reach more and wider markets in less time. In 1830, the United States had just twenty-three miles of railroad, but by 1840 it had 3,000 miles and would have ten times that amount by the Civil War. The first railroad to permeate central New York was the Utica and Schenectady line, completed by the summer of 1836. Trains were able to make the seventy-eight-mile trip in under seven hours. "For three or four years, at least, this city must be the termination of this great railroad, and the point farthest west that has direct communication with tidewater," Utica's *Oneida*

Whig noted. "We feel confident that in a short time this city will be a favorite residence for families of wealth and intelligence from the large cities and neighboring country. We think also that the various kinds of artisans and manufacturers will find this city a good place for carrying on their business." By 1880, at least seven railroads originated in or were built through Oneida Country.[14]

By the end of the eighteenth century, several roads had been built in Utica and the surrounding areas, notably the Great Western Turnpike and the Seneca Turnpike. Utica benefited from its location on the Seneca, as its population grew from 300 in 1800 to nearly 3,000 in 1820. The nearby city of Rome, which was not situated on the Turnpike, had seven times more people than Utica in 1800, but twenty years later had only increased to 3,500 residents.[15] The existence of such roads encouraged Jason Parker to start the area's first stagecoach line for the transportation of mail and passengers in 1795, traveling from Whitestown (near Utica) to Canajoharie, fifty miles east—a distance he could cover in twelve hours. That year he advertised in an area newspaper:

> Parker's mail stage from Whitestown to Canajoharie. The mail leaves Whitestown every Monday and Thursday, at 2 o'clock p.m., and proceeds to Old Fort Schuyler the same evening; the next morning starts at 4 o'clock and arrives at Canajoharie in the evening; exchanges passengers with the Albany and Cooperstown stages and the next day returns to Old Fort Schuyler. Fare for passengers $2.00, way passengers four cents per mile. Fourteen pounds of baggage gratis—150 weight rated the same as a passenger. Seats may be had by applying at the post office, Whitestown, at the house of the subscriber, Old Fort Schuyler, or at Captain Roof's, Canajoharie. August 1795. Jason Parker.[16]

By 1811 Parker had extended the stage line the length of the state, from Albany on the east to Buffalo and Niagara Falls on the west. Advertising a Utica-to-Albany route, Parker noted:

> Eight changes of horses. The mail stage now leaves Bagg's, Utica, every morning at 4 o'clock. Passengers will breakfast at Maynard's, Herkimer, dine at Josiah Shepard's, Palatine, and sup (on oysters) at Thomas Powell's Tontaine Coffee House, Schenectady. Those ladies and gentlemen who will favor this line with their patronage may be assured of having good horses, attentive drivers, warm carriages, and that there shall not be any running or racing of horses on the line.[17]

At the time of Parker's death in 1830, eight stagecoaches passed through Utica on daily east-west lines and twelve daily and semiweekly passed through on north-south routes. Shortly before Parker died, he took on a young man named John Butterfield as a partner. Butterfield greatly expanded the stagecoach business, at one time operating forty lines running from Utica north and south, until railroads proved a more expedient mode of transportation, the first of which ran in the city on 27 July 1839 on the Utica and Schenectady line.[18]

A wealthy man by 1863, the sixty-two-year-old Butterfield believed that Utica's growing population (by this time more than 20,000) necessitated construction of a street railway system that would connect the city with the neighboring communities of New Hartford and Whitesboro. Only four U.S. cities (New York, Boston, Philadelphia, and New Orleans) had streetcar service at the time; Butterfield was determined to make Utica the fifth.[19] He organized a company, laid tracks along Genesee Street and commenced transportation in the fall of 1863, as the *Utica Herald* reported:

> Opening of the Street Railroad. The thing is done! The horse cars move up and down Genesee street at last. Yesterday, about 2 p.m. three of them were in position on the lower end of the track, and filled with gentry who had been invited to share the pleasures and perils of the first ride. John Butterfield, Esq., President of the Company appeared and took the lines of the horses attached to the first car. "Go" and they went up Genesee street on a swift trot, with their car and its dignitaries, followed by the two cars behind. The delighted people that lined the street and stood at the doors and windows smiled and shouted. The passengers were not less delighted and enthusiastic. The horses trotted all the way up Genesee street hill and proved that the grade, about which some doubt had been expressed, would answer the purpose. It was necessary to stop about 50 rods north of the Orphan Asylum, as the rails had been laid no farther. The horses were immediately transferred to the other ends of the cars and went back at the same rapid pace. The treat trip was ended and the practical operation of the Utica Street railroad inaugurated. Henceforth we may ride and smile on street cars to our heart's content.[20]

Utica businesses in the last half of the nineteenth century were booming, but none more so than the knitting industry. Fluctuating agricultural conditions in the early decades of the nineteenth century prompted area farmers to diversify their agricultural production by turning to dairy farming and sheep raising. The first woolen textile mill was established in Oriskany, about fifteen miles from Utica, in 1811, providing an area market for wool. In 1845, Oneida County, of which Utica is the county seat, reported 200,000 sheep, or ten percent of the state total.[21]

By mid-century, numerous knitting mills were operating in the Utica area. Two Lowery brothers of Belfast, Ireland, established the Utica Knitting Factory in 1863 to manufacture socks. Two years later one of the brothers teamed with his brother-in-law, James L. Williams, to found the Lowery and Williams Knitting Mills at the corner of Franklin and Fulton streets. The mill later relocated to an area known as the Utica Highlands, changed its name to the Utica Knitting Co., spread to other plants in the city and surrounding communities and became the largest knitting company in the world, producing between 35,000 and 40,000 knit garments a day. Much of the success of the Utica Knitting Co. was due to the *Saturday Globe*'s Will Baker, who became a director of the company in 1898 and in later years served as chairman of the board.[22]

Utica's knitting industry died in the mid-1900s as textile mills throughout the region migrated to the South after World War II. Little remains to commemorate their departure except a few decaying and vacant mills and the names of such area villages and hamlets as New York Mills, Clark Mills, Coleman Mills and Washington Mills.

The later years of the nineteenth century saw many economic developments. The Mohawk Valley Cotton Mills firm doubled its capital and the size of its operation; the Kernan Furnace Co. boosted its capital 150 percent and erected a new building in East Utica; a Utican, Colonel Arthur Savage, invented the Savage Rifle and initiated its production under the name Savage Arms Co.; the shoe factories were booming and employed hundreds of Uticans and the Utica Electric Light and Power Co. was created to harness the water power at Trenton Falls and supply Utica with electricity.[23]

Utica was one of the main population centers in Upstate New York and the seat of rapidly-growing Oneida County, but perhaps more importantly, it was a crucible of social change. Utica had grown quickly into a city, not only economically and demographically, but also sociologically. According to two sociologists, a city is "a state of mind, a body of customs and traditions" that are transmitted as organized attitudes. "The city is not, in other words, merely a physical mechanism and an artificial construction. It is involved in the vital processes of the people who compose it; it is a product of nature, and particularly of human nature."[24]

With each passing decade of the nineteenth century, America's cities increasingly became a pastiche of racial and ethnic heritage, its citizens awash in a whirlpool of social and geographic change. Utica was no exception. Utica and the surrounding area developed into both a social construction of human nature and a thriving business and transportation hub, characterized by cultural, political, economic, and religious diversity. The region's cheap land, fertile soil and good transportation attracted many immigrants from northern and western Europe. The chief ethnic groups were the Germans, Irish and Welsh, with a growing number of Italians in the latter decades of the century. The settlers predominantly were Catholics, Presbyterians, Episcopalians, Congregationalists, Methodists, and Welsh Baptists. According to one cleric, however, many denizens were agnostic. According to the Rev. John Taylor in 1802, Utica was "a mixed mass of discordant materials. Here may be found people of ten or twelve different nations and of almost all religions and sects, but the great part are of no religion."[25]

The area also witnessed the development of several utopian societies, such as the Oneida Community, a group of ex-Calvinists who believed that Christ had already come a second time, so that people could no longer afford to alternate sinning and repenting. As a result, they believed in the avoidance of sin and selfishness, manifested by the establishment of communal living. Establishing itself in Sherrill, New York, in 1848, the Oneida Community developed a socialized society in which children were raised en masse by selected guardians once they reached one year of age. The Oneida Community disbanded in the 1880s, but not before establishing Oneida Ltd. Silversmiths, present-day maker of Oneida silverware.[26]

The increasing diversity and expansion seemed to come too fast for the area, however, threatening economic stability with the prospect of a variegated citizenry becoming increasingly factious and contentedly indolent in celebration of the region's economic growth. According to Douglas B. Adams, "industrialism created a frontier, even in established eastern cities, for society had been changed and the citizens were exploring new attitudes and behaviors." To provide cross-cultural goals and maintain high levels of productivity, employers expounded the Franklinesque virtues of honesty, sobriety, punctuality, and hard work, and reinforced these values with financial incentives and the encouragement of religious teachings. In an eastern city comparable to Utica, upper-class leaders encouraged participation in the Second Great Awakening revivalist movement to promote "self-discipline, industry, sobriety, self-denial, and respect for authority," according to Paul G. Faler. In Rochester, another upstate New York city, the revival of religion was viewed largely in response to a breakdown in society created by industrialization and rapid growth. In Faler's estimation, "it was the growth of manufacturing that provoked profound changes in social customs, institutions, and standards of moral conduct. There was a concerted effort to destroy or alter any practice that was deemed incompatible with the emerging capitalist order."[27]

The Godlessness that the Rev. Taylor noted at the beginning of the century was attacked by Revivalist publications. "Of all the multifarious *isms* which distract the morals, or excruciate the human system—either in a metaphysical or physical point of view, there is none more astonishing to the reflecting mind ... than *Atheism*," according to "J.K.," a writer in one Utica-based religious magazine. The Rev. Isaac B. Pierce preached that all goodness comes not from man but from God. "The empire of virtue is based, in the human heart, upon [God's] goodness and rectitude."[28]

The blossoming of Utica's economy was partly responsible for its social changes, which paralleled a rise of mass culture at the beginning of the nineteenth century. The expansion of political democracy and popular education eroded the upper-class monopoly on culture at about the same time technology was making mass production possible. Consequently, business entrepreneurs reaped the profits of satisfying the cultural desires of the multitudes with pictures, music, furniture, books, magazines, and newspapers.[29]

As inland population swelled with communities forming along waterways and dirt roads, and as printing presses became cheaper and more accessible, country presses sprang up to serve these new markets. This represented a substantial change from journalistic norms of the eighteenth century, when newspapers were customarily confined to the largest population areas, usually in port cities. The spread of the press to the interior reflected the expansionist interests of the nation, as well as the facility for using waterways as the highways into this region. Newspapers did more than any other social institution to unify pioneers and bring a community spirit to the wilderness settlements which served as trading centers. Also, their presence lent prestige, for it was akin to a status symbol for a rural hamlet to have a printer, as such areas could set themselves apart from others by boasting of the power of mass communication, even if the elevated status did not always accrue to the printers themselves.

Printers serving these remote areas in the antebellum nineteenth century conceived of themselves as more than mere mechanics who performed work that taxed the hands and body but seldom engaged the mind. They inherited from their colonial predecessors a fiercely independent spirit that inspired them to devote their presses to discussions of social issues and assume the role of chief molder and fomenter of public opinion.[30] Writing of himself in the third person, printer Thomas Kirk asserted, "Disdaining all servile attachment to any man, or set of men whatever, his support will be afforded only to those whose conduct he conceives entitle them to his approbation and esteem." Printers fancied themselves as guardians of public interest, calling themselves "independent in spirit," noting that the press was "the ark of our public safety" and claiming that their publications were designed "to diffuse among the people correct information of all interesting subjects; to inculcate just principles in religion, morals, and politics; and to cultivate a taste for sound literature."[31]

Printers occupied a significant place in two distinct social strata. On the one hand, they were common laborers who worked with their hands, ploddingly plying their trade as they became stained and sweaty. On the other hand, printers were both purveyors of and contributors to the greatest writings of the age. They maintained a vital relationship to the highest thoughts and most brilliant ideas then known to mankind. Printers were often community leaders, prominently involved in the most important social and political issues of the day. They were just as influential and vital to a community as lawyers, religious leaders and politicians; perhaps more so, because they controlled what was commonly the sole means of mass communication in an era before telephones, radio, and television at a time when every book was valued and literacy was esteemed. Printers assumed this role less through community mandate than through the good fortune and connections required to set up and maintain a print shop. This contrasts with the romanticized notion of itinerant printers wandering the countryside, requiring nothing more than a case of type, a press, and a community in which to print. This interpretation is naive, as it does not take into account such prudential and economic factors as marshalling community support and the financial wherewithal to set up and maintain a print shop.[32]

Printers often relied on patrons to subsidize their presses, simultaneously becoming obligated to represent the political principles of those benefactors. The early nineteenth century was characterized by fierce partisan journalism, as party papers pummelled opposition politicians and each other with invective and defamation, prompting historian Frank Luther Mott to label this era the "dark ages" of journalism. Calling the party press "disgraceful," Mott wrote that such newspapers "reflected the crassness of the American society of the times. Scurrility, assaults, corruption, blatancy were commonplace. Journalism had grown too fast." Milton W. Hamilton concurs, citing examples of the influence on the press exerted by political factions and noting that partisan printers abandoned a substantial part of the press freedom fought for by eighteenth-century printers.[33]

Many readers of the "dark ages" newspapers grew weary of the overt political slant and longed for a more balanced and impartial presentation of information and opinion. Once, when a western New York newspaper surrendered its neutrality, fifty patrons canceled their subscriptions, some "declaring their unwillingness to have anything to do with politics, not even so much as to take a political paper."[34]

By mid-century, American newspapers began spurning the editorial dictates of political patronage and embracing eclecticism in the hope of attracting a mass audience with an omnibus product. This gradual shift in loyalty broke the economic grip of parties and provided new freedom by enabling the press to replace the political faction with the mass audience as the object of its dependency and allegiance. This change "re-synthesized the newspaper-reading audience by appealing in a single paper to a wide range of interests," Bernard A. Weisberger wrote. "This new journalism would set its own boundaries, evoke its own professional loyalties, and tailor its own style of expression. As a form of communication, it would not be a passive channel between segments of the public but would to some degree change the nature of the public in the very act of limiting it."[35]

Before the era of party patronage, another type of political dependence existed in the American press. Many of the earliest newspapers on the frontier were established by publishers who hoped to parlay their precedence into governmental printing contracts. Some were motivated by the prospect of wealth, some by the vanity of seeing their thoughts communicated via print to a mass audience and some by the desire to advocate particular political, social, or religious principles. However, all were concerned, in varying degrees, with making a living and serving the public.

The first newspaper printed west of Albany was based in the Utica area. On 11 July 1793, the *Whitestown Gazette* commenced publication a few miles west of Utica, under the proprietorship of several town fathers and printed by Richard Vosburg. It folded before Christmas, and was replaced the following January by *The Western Centinel*, of which Oliver Eaton was the printer. In the ensuing years, Utica and environs became home to many newspapers, some of which survived less than a year.[32]

The advent of the telegraph signaled a radical change for the American press, because it allowed small newspapers not only to acquire the same news as their big-city counterparts, but also much faster than had previously been possible. The first telegraphic wire was stretched from Albany to Utica in January 1846, enabling the Utica *Daily Gazette* to report, "The Electric-Magnetic Telegraph between Albany and Utica was put in operation Saturday forenoon, and worked all day to a charm. Various items of news from Albany and New York were transmitted, the proceedings of the legislature as they transpired, and innumerable messages between individuals. The greatest excitement prevailed along the street for the whole day, and the operations of the wonderful instrument were witnessed in silent astonishment by a continually changing crowd at the telegraph office."[37]

The telegraph lent itself to the prospect of cooperative newsgathering, and in 1848 a group of nineteen New York newspapers, including the *Daily Gazette*, organized the New York State Associated Press to share costs and take advantage of its prompt transmission of information. This wire service, the first in the nation, evolved into the modern-day Associated Press. Because this cooperative amassed news intended for publication in newspapers with a variety of political allegiances, its writing was, by necessity, neutral and fact-oriented.[38]

It has been argued that this technology signaled the beginning of journalistic objectivity, which Walter Lippman wrote was essential "in matters affecting the liberty of opinion," because objectivity alone makes it possible to understand facts by ensuring an impartial presentation. Lippman repudiated the libertarian notion, first advanced by John Milton in *Areopagitica*, that truth will always prevail over falsehood, contending that truth "can prevail only if the facts to which they refer are known; if they are not known, false ideas are just as effective as true ones, if not a little more effective."[39]

While the nineteenth-century press experienced varying degrees of economic freedom, depending on the political climate, it enjoyed considerable legal freedom. However, sometimes the exertion of this liberty angered readers and encouraged extralegal sanctions, which were often violent. A mob vandalized the office and assaulted the proprietors of the *Anti-Masonic Free Press* in Oswego, New York, in 1830 for printing an article critical of the local fire company. In Utica, the *Standard and Democrat*'s office received the same treatment five years later for that newspaper's abolitionist slant. However, the ultimate penalty for free expression was paid by an abolitionist editor in Alton, Illinois. After his office was wrecked three times, he was shot to death in 1837 by an irate mob opposed to his antislavery stance. It is interesting to note that the violence at the Utica and Alton antislavery presses occurred in Northern states.[40]

Despite these setbacks, newspapers continued to grow in numbers and social importance, and with them printers enjoyed considerable public esteem. By the mid-nineteenth century, they were among the highest-paid wage-earners and were able to "live comfortably and in not a few instances in a certain style of gentility," according to the *New York Tribune*.[41] Journalists were commonly counted among the city's most influential people, with many holding public office and one, Horace Greeley, even running for president. This elevated status was a far cry from the early eighteenth century, when printing was regarded as a mere craft and its practitioners esteemed as little more than common laborers. In the later 1720s, Benjamin Franklin suffered from the low-status nature of printing when he desired to marry the niece of Thomas Godfrey, a glazier and self-taught mathematician who boarded with Franklin and set up his shop in the same building as Franklin's printing business. The match was forbidden by her parents, who had been told by printer Andrew Bradford that "the Printing Business was not a profitable one." As a result, Franklin "was forbidden the House, & the Daughter shut up." Noting "this Affair having turn'd my Thoughts to Marriage," Franklin "made Overtures of Acquaintance in other Places," believing, as Franklin's "Poor Richard" character would later write, "He that has not got a Wife, is not yet a compleat Man." However, Franklin was repeatedly scorned, "the Business of a Printer being generally thought a poor one."[42]

Just as the nineteenth-century press was prospering, so was Utica, which by the end of the century had become a "boom town." Eight railroads ran through the thriving city, along the Erie Canal and Mohawk River, and city and county roads were modern for the time. As a business and transportation hub, Utica had few rivals in the region, the *Oneida County Gazetteer and Business Directory* noted:

> The present business outlook of the city is most gratifying. During the past three or four years very large amounts have been invested in manufacturing enterprises in or about the city. Among the new industries are the Savage Arms Co., Remington Automobile & Motor Co., Weston Mott Wheel Works, Bossert Electric Construction Co., Utica Pipe Foundry, and companies interested in the knit goods trade. Utica is now using 19,681 horse power and has an annual pay roll of $5,286,600. It has more than 15,000 people at work in its mills, and manufactures over $24,000,000 worth of goods yearly. The city uses at present 7,000 horse power from Trenton Falls, and twice that amount will be ready whenever

> needed. The large factories recently erected in East and West Utica, have caused many to build comfortable and attractive homes in that vicinity. What seemed but a short time ago to be an expanse of commons is rapidly becoming an enterprising part of the city. With railroad competition in every direction, its facilities for cheap transportation rival those of any other city in Central or Western New York. Utica is becoming decidedly a progressive city and promises ere long to outstrip her sister cities in thrift, enterprise and population. The city is the central and trading point, both wholesale and retail, of the most prosperous and populous towns of the famous Mohawk valley and is connected by electric road with a rich suburban district many miles in extent.[43]

Both locally and nationally, society was experiencing considerable growth and change. These nineteenth-century social, commercial, technological and transportation revolutions, coupled with the erosion of the party press, created a suitable environment for the *Saturday Globe*'s debut in 1881 and its rise to international circulation. The Utica area's advanced and diverse modes of transportation enabled the newspaper to be widely and promptly distributed and permitted its reporters to travel considerable distances to gather news. The region's economic status was additionally attractive. Because newspapers of the era were dependent on the financial fortunes of their communities, and because a healthy local economy translated into more subscribers and more advertising revenue, the Bakers had every reason to believe their plan for establishing a new newspaper in Utica would meet with success.

2

The *Globe* Begins to Turn

While other Uticans were enjoying the spring weather on 21 May 1881, the Baker brothers were huddled with fifty boys on the third floor of the Thomas building on Bleecker Street, just a toss of a rolled-up newspaper from the modern hub of the city, "The Busy Corner," at Genesee and Bleecker streets. The Bakers were giving the newsboys a pep talk on selling the *Utica Saturday Globe*, as it was then called, which was slated to hit the streets for the first time that afternoon. Tom Baker was listed on the company payroll as the editor, while older brother Will was the publisher.[1]

The Bakers had decided that Utica, one of the largest cities in Upstate New York with an 1880 population of 33,914, would be an ideal site for their weekly newspaper. However, the local competition was stiff. On a daily basis, Utica-area readers could choose the *Herald* or the *Observer*. In addition to the *Sunday Tribune*, which Tom Baker had helped establish four years earlier, weekly fare included the *Oneida Weekly Herald*, which was published on Tuesday.[2]

The *Saturday Globe* staff was small, and operated out of the two rooms that comprised the newspaper office. The presswork was done by Curtiss and Childs, a job-printing firm at 167 Genesee Street. The *Saturday Globe*'s composing-room men had to carry the lead print plates, each of which weighed more than a hundred pounds, from the third story of the Thomas building around the corner to the Curtiss and Childs pressroom.[3]

The Bakers decided to publish their weekly on Saturday for several reasons. They were doubtless motivated by a desire to avoid head-to-head competition with the successful *Sunday Tribune* Tom had helped create, and to avoid Sabbatarian opposition. Perhaps more pragmatically, they chose Saturday because that was the day laborers were usually paid at the end of their six-day work week, and thus would have money in their pockets when they got off work in late afternoon. It was about this time of day when the *Saturday Globe*'s street sales started. Because many workers could afford only one newspaper per week, they were more inclined to buy it Saturday for weekend reading.[4]

The optimistic brothers ordered 2,000 copies of the first issue printed, which sold for five cents, fairly expensive for the times. Only 700 sold, so after the newsboys took their two-cent profit, the paper netted just $21 in street sales for its first issue.[5]

That 21 May issue consisted of eight pages with six twenty-inch columns per page. Four of the eight pages were of the "ready print" variety, an assortment of feature articles purchased in preprinted form. The remaining pages consisted of national and local news. Additionally, there was a column of one-sentence notes on page five. Among the nuggets of general information such as one might find on a sugar packet or the back of a cereal box were these amusingly self-serving ditties: "The Globe revolves for all," "Our cardinal banner bearing the words 'Saturday Globe' evokes praise from those who have an eye for the attractive" and "The Saturday Globe is independent in everything. Make a note of it."[6]

There were just a few advertisements in the first issue, a quarter-page (three columns by ten inches) ad for the Buckley, Myers and Co. department store, 81 and 83 Genesee Street, Utica, on page five and several one-column ads, none more than four inches high, for such local establishments as a boarding house, a ladies' department store and a plumber. These appeared on page eight.

The two pages on which the ads appeared were the only ones devoted to local copy. The primary story of local relevance listed the numerous reasons for Utica's growth and prosperity. This was a variation on the frontier journalistic practice of boosterism: instead of selling the community to potential residents as a means of stimulating population growth, it sold the community to itself, presenting middle-class views that supported the efforts of the municipality's economic and political interests. In the process, the *Saturday Globe* proprietors likely accomplished their obvious goal of ingratiating the fledgling newspaper into the good graces of proud Uticans.[7]

However, there may have been a subtler intention behind the glowing essay on the city's progress and virtues. The urban and mobile society created in the nineteenth century and the rapid growth of both their city and their country left many Americans feeling isolated and distant, viewing others as objects rather than neighbors and placing more faith in institutions than individuals. Living in a city that seemed to typify this turbulent surge, Uticans were just as likely as anyone else to feel slowly but inexorably cut off from their eighteenth-century heritage that emphasized family, kinship, neighborhood, church and personal connections. The Bakers' essay underscored the values of community and civic pride in this era when many felt adrift in an impersonal society.[8]

From the outset, the *Saturday Globe* eschewed the heavy doses of political and commercial fodder common in newspapers for most of the century, opting instead for a smorgasbord of light reading, which made it more similar to magazines than newspapers. As the Bakers envisioned the *Saturday Globe* as the only newspaper in many homes, and in some virtually the only literature, they felt obliged to provide some literary fare each week. Thus, it was not uncommon for sentimental poems and inspirational biographies to abut accounts of gruesome murders or weighty political affairs.

The maiden issue contained a miscellany of both national and local interest, including fiction; poetry; social notes; short baseball items written in opinion form; several obituaries, most of which were fashioned in glowing praise of the deceased; and several lines of folksy humor and corn-pone wisdom, such as "if New York does not soon collar a street-cleaning process, she will cholera pestilence" and "a farmer friend calls one of his early vegetables 'Waterloo' because it is a big beet." Front-page news included reports of a mine cave-in in Deadwood, Dakota; the roller-skating craze in New York City; the resolution of a twenty-year-old murder mystery; the adverse effect of Chinese immigration on San Francisco laborers; and the deaths and property damage caused when a passenger train hit a herd of cows on the track in Templeton, Indiana, careened down the embankment and burned.[9]

The Bakers designed this melange to be of the broadest possible interest, free of partisanship and doctrine, in an effort to attract an eclectic audience of laborers, merchants, professionals, women, and children. This potential readership was culturally and ethnically heterogenous and included many immigrants for whom English was a second language, if they spoke it at all. Recognizing the diversity of their mass market, the Bakers tried to make their newspaper interesting and attractive, with vivid yet simple writing and a liberal use of illustrations.

The Bakers' desire to be ecumenical is reflected in their inaugural statement:

> The *Utica Saturday Globe* enters the field of journalism with no axe to grind, in the interest of no party, faction of a party or an individual. In matters political it will strive to be impartial, conscious that whatever support it receives comes from all classes and shades of political belief. As the wishes of our readers will be paramount to all other con-

> siderations, intelligent patrons can perceive that their tastes will be best suited by pursuing a thoroughly independent course.
>
> Divorced from party support, every public measure arising will be discussed fairly and with the sole purpose of reaching just conclusions . . .[10]

The *Saturday Globe*'s editorial policy emphasizes the public-service ideology that emerged in journalism of the previous century, along with the later phenomenon of impartiality. The eighteenth-century press traditionally had been the faithful servant of the masses, but particularly the laboring classes, which viewed the press as a form of social equalizer, revealing as much information to carpenters and blacksmiths as to the colonial gentry. Artisans and laborers were part of a burgeoning middle class and constituted a large portion of advertisers' clientele. As a result, the interests of the common folk were usually the interests of the press, which became the chief fomenter and molder of public opinion. As their social importance and status increased, printers came to fancy themselves as guardians of the public interest, purveying information, education and entertainment in keeping with their ideology of public utility.[11]

However, in the highly factional period that followed American independence, political leaders began the process of financing newspapers to serve as mouthpieces of their parties' dogma. The first serious political division occurred over passage of the Constitution in 1787 and escalated into the bitter newspaper war between Federalist supporters of John Adams and Alexander Hamilton and Republican adherents of Thomas Jefferson and James Madison. Federalist editors like John Fenno and Noah Webster propounded arguments for a strong central government that would aid commerce and orchestrate national defense, while Republican counterparts Philip Freneau and Benjamin Franklin Bache advocated a decentralized government based on state sovereignty and an agrarian economy. This established a pattern of political conduct which was to characterize the press for much of the nineteenth century.[12]

As the nation became more complex and diverse in the nineteenth century, governmental leaders concluded that the printed word was an indispensible tool for political success. They found that a financially dependent newspaper could outline political philosophy, present information and opinion that reflected favorably on party candidates, and pressure fence-straddling officeholders into particular actions. Newspapers also benefited from this arrangement, as party affiliation offered a guaranteed readership and financial support. Numerous frontier newspapers were established with funding from politicians who wanted a platform to advance their political ambitions. Thus the number of newspapers swelled in the party-press era from 1,200 in 1833 to 3,000 in 1860. Many printers, such as James Bogert, had no qualms about confessing their partisanship. In retracting some potentially libelous statements printed about a political adversary in his newspaper, Bogert excused the libel by noting that it was in the spirit of factionalism and that "political considerations were our sole object."[13]

The influence of party affiliations mandated that newspaper staff have the "correct" political principles. It was common for newspaper editors to be hired on the basis of their political affiliations. When Elihu Geer decided to start a daily newspaper in 1843 called *The Athenian*, he asked the advice of political insider James F. Babcock regarding several prospective editors. Of one candidate, Babcock wrote "he is quite a politician," although "on the whole [his political outlook] was not as judicious as it might have been." Of the other prospect, Babcock noted his good character and excellent writing skills, but suggested Geer "learn in a round a bout way, what interest he takes in politics, & how he stands generally."[14]

Although they viewed it as essential, many politicians disdained the party press because they feared it had a "hypodermic needle" effect on the majority of the populace, which could be stirred to violent passion by a newspaper "injection" of virulent political rhetoric. Their suspicions were not unfounded, because the development of the party press heralded the decline of deference to the elite and the broad dissemination of political concerns among the lower and middle classes.[15]

The party press throughout the nineteenth century could be especially vituperative when assailing opponents. No forms of scurrility were spared, including name-calling and accusations of greed, religious intolerance, dementia, and even sexual immorality. Early in the century, Republican editors delighted in branding Hamilton as an "adulterer," while Federalists accused Jefferson of fathering children by one of his slaves. The same acerbity characterized the political press in the later decades. During the 1884 Presidential campaign, the Buffalo *Evening Telegraph* published "A Terrible Tale," revealing hometown candidate Grover Cleveland's paternity of an illegitimate son. Republican cartoonists had a field day with Cleveland, a Democrat, portraying such scenes as a small boy crying, "Ma, Ma, Where's My Pa?" The Democrats had the last laugh, though, adding the line "Gone to the White House, Ha Ha Ha!" after Cleveland's election.[16]

This vicious form of journalism did not seem to trouble the consciences of many editors, who recognized that they were political functionaries and their newspapers organs of doctrine. In fact, some, like Horace Greeley and Thurlow Weed, took advantage of their political connections and the elevated social status accruing to journalists by parlaying their political roles into public office.

The party affiliations of the press supplanted balanced discussion of public issues and calls for the election of sagacious leaders with personal attacks on the motives, intelligence, and even sanity of opposition members. However, by mid-century, some newspapers were beginning to decry the subjective, partisan nature of news reports and call for ideological independence. The *New York Times* asserted its intention "to publish *facts*, in such a form and temper as to lead men of all parties to rely upon its statements of facts, and then to discuss them in the light of truth and justice, and not of party interest." The *New York Tribune* declared "the public wants of [newspapers] nothing but the publication of news and temperate, dignified, gentlemanly explanation and criticism of current events."[17]

This move away from partisanship and toward factuality constituted a radical change of the press's role. The alteration took nearly half a century to evolve, but it changed American journalism forever. The press's break with its politically controlled tradition was partially due to the public's financial support, which enabled newspapers to sever their dependence on party pursestrings, but was also attributable to the nineteenth-century rise of science and technology, in which exactitude and pristine facts were the highest pursuits. These developments bred objectivity, in which "a person's statements about the world can be trusted if they are submitted to established rules deemed legitimate by a professional community," sociologist Michael Schudson wrote. Historian Frank L. Mott claimed that news became more valuable than opinion when "the great advances in news-gathering techniques joined with a certain relaxation in party lines and loyalties to put news far ahead of editorials in popular interest."[18]

Partisan journalism was waning when the *Saturday Globe* commenced publication in 1881, and the Bakers made it clear in the inaugural statement that their newspaper would be impartial, not only to serve the public's desire for news unfettered by opinion or bias, but also as a sound business measure to attract as many readers and advertisers as possible. Although the philosophy of objectivity surely impressed many readers, the newspaper's physical appearance did not. The pages of the first issue, particularly the four the *Saturday Globe* staff printed itself, were riddled with typographical errors. Despite their later success with the weekly, the Bakers never forgot the many flaws of that maiden issue. The *Saturday Globe* published a twelve-year history of its operation in 1893, in which that first edition was recalled. The newspaper self-deprecatingly noted:

> On May 21 1881, the first number of the Utica *SATURDAY GLOBE* was sent out for inspection and criticism by the public. Such a paper issued to-day would seem a caricature of the printer's art. There were 48 short columns to the little sheet, four of the eight pages being 'ready print.' This part of the paper was unquestionably the more attractive and meritorius half of it. No one who saw that first number believed the paper could survive three months. In fact, if there had not been a rapid and constant improvement it would not have deserved so long an existence as even the most uncharitable predicted for it. And yet the projectors had sufficient confidence to print 2,000 copies of that first issue, and perhaps from curiosity, the public purchased 700 of them.[19]

That premier edition also carried an apology. The Bakers had hoped the first issue would feature an illustration of former New York Governor Horatio Seymour, a native Utican, and hired a New York City cngraver to cut the image into a wood block. With the advent of electrotyping, wood engraving had become a practical means of publishing illustrations in long press runs, replacing steel and copper-plate engraving after the Civil War. However, woodcuts were expensive, generally within the financial means of only the largest dailies and magazines. Illustrations were the exception rather than the rule for most American newspapers at the time, because the insertion of one picture involved an enormous amount of money and time. Despite the Bakers' outlay of money, time proved to be an insurmountable obstacle, and the artist missed the deadline for the first issue.[20] Embarrassed after having conducted an extensive publicity campaign in which they promised that the first issue would contain the illustration of Seymour, the Bakers printed this apology on page 5 under the heading "Our Disappointment!"

> The *Saturday Globe* intended to present the portrait of Governor Horatio Seymour in its first issue. In this we are disappointed, as the engraver who has had the work in charge in New York has failed to send us the cut on time. Next Saturday we will be able to produce it. We intend to follow it up with the portraits of other distinguished men in Central New York. In the meantime look out for the portrait of Horatio Seymour in our next issue.[21]

However, whether the Baker brothers had enough money to produce another issue was in doubt. The *Saturday Globe*'s existence was precarious from the outset. The newspaper's entire capital had been expended producing the first number and it was not certain the Bakers could produce further issues. They were able to print the second edition, though, probably thanks to loans, although no business records exist to confirm this theory. That edition featured the promised woodcut of ex-Governor Seymour, three columns wide on page 1.[22]

Although a week late, the expensive woodcut caused quite a stir in Utica, for illustrations were seldom seen in newspapers of the period, particularly in such a small, fledgling weekly as the *Saturday Globe*. All 2,000 copies of the second issue were sold, largely on the strength of the picture. In fact, some readers showed sufficient confidence in the newspaper's solvency and fortitude to pay in advance for subscriptions. This, plus second-issue street sales, enabled the Bakers to produce the third issue, which featured a woodcut of the U.S. senator from New York, Francis Kernan, a native Utican. The fourth issue carried a picture of Utica businessman and philanthropist Theodore Faxton.[23]

Although a breakthrough in illustration when first devised, woodcuts soon became obsolete in an era of rapid technological advances. Just twelve years later, the *Saturday Globe* recalled this illustration method as crude:

> In the early days of the *Globe*, as at the present time, illustration was a leading feature of the paper. But newspaper illustration was then in its infancy. In fact the *Globe* was a pioneer in that direction. The consciences of the publishers are still harassed with the recollection of the awful wood-cut productions which were published among the earlier efforts as likenesses of some of our most eminent men. It has ever since been a matter of deepest mystery why the victims of this chopping-block method of illustration never wreaked a bloody but just vengeance. But they never even sued for damages. In fact, in a later and brighter era of the *Globe*'s career, many of them consented to help wipe out the memory of those early horrors by having really good likenesses of themselves in the paper. The forbearance, we may say fortitude, of these gentlemen in those days of the *Globe*'s infancy will always be remembered with gratitude.[24]

In addition to the woodcuts, the *Saturday Globe* instituted another practice with the second issue which was also to make it a celebrated newspaper of its day—it began publishing multiple editions. In an effort to introduce readers outside of the Utica area to the 28 May issue of the *Saturday Globe*, one edition was printed especially for

Utica readers and another for those in outlying regions. By the third issue the *Saturday Globe* had agents peddling the newspaper in four Oneida County towns. Shortly thereafter the first zoned edition for a neighboring community was produced, as the *Saturday Globe* introduced itself to residents of the Herkimer County village (now city) of Little Falls, twenty-five miles east. Other regional editions soon followed, and by 16 July, less than two months after the first issue, the newspaper was sold as far away as Carthage, a Northern New York town near the Canadian border, about eighty miles north of Utica.[25]

A newspaper's readership is only as wide as its distribution methods are effective. In the early years of American journalism, newspapers were commonly distributed by carriers—often one of the printer's apprentices—in town, and by post riders in outlying areas. Since apprentices received no pay and only room and board for their years of service, it became customary that each New Year's Day these carriers were allowed to solicit gifts from readers by reciting poems, usually written by local literati. Many printers supported this practice by publishing an appeal on behalf of the carriers, or even one of the poems, in that day's newspaper. The first known "Carrier's Address" appeared in Andrew Bradford's *American Weekly Mercury* in 1720. Twenty-six years later, his former employee Benjamin Franklin published "The Yearly-Verses of the Printer's Boy" in his *Pennsylvania Gazette*, which began:

> Since 'tis a Custom ev'ry Year
> When it begins, for to appear
> In an emphatic Rhimish Mode
> To great you at your own Abode,

and ended:

> Hoping you will not think it strange
> That Something's wanting in Exchange
> Kind Sirs:—I do not name the Sum;
> But what you please; and I'll be gone.[26]

The tradition of carrier's addresses continued well into the nineteenth century. The 1820 New Year's Day edition of the *Cayuga Republican* noted:

> The Printer's Boy will ne'er refuse,
> To bring you papers fresh with news,
> From ev'ry country, ev'ry where,
> Whate'er is wonderful and rare,

From Georgia to the northern Maine,
Who fought, who fell and who was slain,
Who nab'd a horse, and who hath stole—
Who broke into or out of gaol.
Beside ten thousand other things,
From blackguards up to dukes and kings,
All marriages we shall relate,
As well as great affairs of state,
In fact our columns shall abound,
With all things rare that can be found.[27]

Five years later, the *New England Galaxy* proclaimed the true purpose of the "Carrier's Addresses":

Songs of printers, in annual roundelays,
Formed in fancy and uttered in rhyme,
Are sung, not to please young nymphs on holidays,
But to win for the carrier dollar and dime.[28]

Post riders, discussed in the previous chapter, delivered newspapers to distant areas. Since publishers often doubled as postmasters, particularly in the eighteenth and early nineteenth centuries, they had the authority to arrange for their newspapers to be carried free to other post offices, where subscribers could acquire them.[29]

With the advent of the penny press in the 1830s it became possible for patrons to purchase single copies of a newspaper from street-corner newsboys, instead of the earlier custom of subscribing for six months or one year. This method was normally used just in the newspaper's home city, enabling the proprietors to oversee the revenue but also reducing the geographic circulation area of most newspapers. The Bakers circumvented this problem by employing an uncommon method of selling newspapers that has since been extensively used by leading publications—they gave complete financial responsibility to a network of children, nearly all of whom were boys, which eventually stretched across the country and into other nations. These newsboys were given the duties of ordering and selling the newspapers and returning unsold copies. The Bakers once boasted of having two six-year-olds selling *Saturday Globe*s in Nebraska City, Nebraska. Other newspapers, particularly local ones, decried this faith in youth as "the greatest risk in journalism," but the system worked and circulation grew.[30]

Octogenarian Tom Dodge remembered being a *Saturday Globe* newsboy from about 1916 to 1922. One of nineteen children, he was expected to make a financial contribution to the family as soon as he was old enough, he recalled while strolling the grounds of the *Saturday Globe*'s final home, a crumbling, three-story brick building on Whitesboro Street.

"See that?" he asked me, while pointing across the railroad tracks to a row of drab oil tanks. "Where those tanks are used to be Meadow Street, where I lived. There were thirteen houses on one side, twelve on the other, and I remember the names of all the families. Now there ain't nothing there but them tanks," he said wistfully.

Every Saturday Dodge used to cross the railroad tracks at about 8:45 A.M. and get in line at the rear of the *Saturday Globe* building to receive his allotment of newspapers. "We used to be at the back of the building and they would open up this big garage door and we would line up for our papers," Dodge said, while tugging on the heavy wooden door. It barely budges. "We would buy them for three-and-a-half cents and sell them for five. So, you had to buy an even number of papers because you couldn't pay half a cent," he chuckled. "I remember there was always one big kid—you know, a bully—who would let you stay at the front of the line if you gave him two or three cents. Of course, that was a lot back then, because you could go to the picture shows for a nickel. If you didn't pay this fellow, he'd push you to the back of the line. One day I was at the head of the line and he tried to make me pay to stay there. I wouldn't give him nothing, so he wanted to send me back. I wouldn't go, so he said he'd hit me. I said, 'Go ahead,' but he never did nothing, and never gave me any trouble after that," Dodge recalled.

Dodge used to deliver about twenty newspapers to regular home subscribers and then sell about twenty more at the Bagg's Square Hotel, the railroad station and to employees at the H.D. Pixley Clothing Co., the John G. Thomas Clothing Co. and the Williams and Morgan furniture store.

Dodge and I strolled through the litter-strewn interior of the decaying building. It was the first time in Dodge's life he had entered the structure. "From the outside, this was quite an impressive building back then," he said. "They never let us kids go in the building, but I used to look through the windows at 'em in there."[31]

Ed and Gilbert Lee also are alumni of the *Saturday Globe*'s newsboy corps. The brothers delivered the newspaper in 1916 and 1917. They used to line up at Mrs. Wolfe's store on Eagle Street, five doors west of Mohawk Street, and receive about fifteen papers each, which they either delivered to homes or sold on street corners. "We bought the papers from Mrs. Wolfe, and we had to pay cash," Gilbert Lee remembered. "We used to push and shove to be first on line, because if you got your papers first, you could take off on a run and get the best corner.''

Gilbert preferred the intersection of Mohawk and Bleecker streets, while brother Ed usually tried to sell his weekly bundle of newspapers via the less stressful—but often more time-consuming—method of cultivating regular home customers and simply delivering their newspapers every Saturday. ''It was a large paper, a heavy paper to deliver,'' Ed Lee said. ''It was filled with news, with lots of pictures that went with the stories. There were lots of pictures in the paper for those days.''

Ed drifted from delivering milk to printing and bookbinding at the Utica State Hospital to professional boxing before taking a job at Utica's Graffenberg Dairy, where he worked for thirty-four years, retiring in 1970. Gilbert graduated from the *Saturday Globe* to a career as a painter and paper-hanger.[32]

The *Saturday Globe*'s circulation method proved remarkably successful. Their carriers worked for less money than adults might have wanted, were industrious and possessed the energy and fortitude needed to hawk newspapers on street corners. The boys profited too, gaining practical insight into business, salesmanship, and journalism. As Frank L. Mott wrote, ''Many a hustling boy found his first interest in business or journalism or both through selling (newspapers and magazines) after school.''[33]

The *Saturday Globe*'s method of giving complete responsibility to a network of boys proved so successful that other newspapers and magazines with wide distribution areas took note and used the technique to their advantage. William D. Boyce, who founded the *Saturday Blade*, an eight-page folio combining news with fiction and miscellaneous items, in Chicago during 1887, immediately constructed a distribution system of boy agents in outlying areas. By offering prizes and the same liberal payment the *Saturday Globe* offered its boys, two cents on every five-cent issue, Boyce succeeded in recruiting more than 6,000 newsboys by 1890, mostly in the Midwest. Like the *Saturday Globe*, Boyce's product was a Saturday afternoon publication, and like the *Saturday Globe*, the Chicago paper allowed its young distributors to return unsold copies.[34]

In 1891, Boyce purchased the foundering *Chicago Ledger*, a mail-order newspaper that had specialized in miscellany since its inception in 1872. Boyce promptly changed the editorial focus to sensationalism and the circulation method to youthful agents. Circulation for both of Boyce's publications skyrocketed, until by 1924 they had a combined circulation of about 500,000.[35]

Grit magazine used the same circulation method to help save it from extinction. Published in Williamsport, Pennsylvania, it began as a weekend newspaper on 10 December 1882 as the *Williamsport Grit* because of its strictly local circulation. It was on the verge of extinction within two years but was saved by Dietrick Lamade and partners, who purchased it and changed its format to a feature-laden family newspaper. With increased circulation by 1887, the publication's name was changed to *Pennsylvania Grit* and a network of boys was recruited to distribute the weekly, using the same plan the Baker brothers formulated for the *Saturday Globe* six years earlier. By 1890 *Pennsylvania Grit* sported a circulation of 50,000, and increased that at least fourfold by 1905. In 1907 its national circulation demanded that the word *Pennsylvania* be dropped from the nameplate. It enjoys considerable success to this day, particularly among rural and small-town readers.[36]

An especially interesting appropriation of the *Saturday Globe*'s circulation method occurred when Cyrus H. Curtis, publisher of the successful *Ladies' Home Journal*, sent its editor, Edward W. Bok, to Utica to investigate the *Saturday Globe*'s remarkable circulation success with the intention of boosting the circulation of Curtis's most recent acquisition, the *Saturday Evening Post*. Curtis bought the weekly publication, which traced its lineage to Benjamin Franklin's short-lived magazine in the early eighteenth century, from the estate of deceased owner and editor Andrew Smythe in October 1897, a week before it was to become defunct. Curtis acquired the *Saturday Evening Post* for $1,000, an insignificant amount to him, considering that he was averaging $2,000 a day that year in subscription revenue for the monthly *Ladies' Home Journal*.[37]

Curtis inherited a publication with a paltry 2,000 circulation, which dropped to 1,200 by June 1898. Shortly thereafter, Curtis sent Bok to the *Saturday Globe* offices for three days, where he observed the newspaper's methods of circulation and printing multiple editions. He also tried, unsuccessfully, to hire the *Saturday Globe*'s veteran managing editor and right-hand man to Tom Baker, Albert M. Dickinson, to work at the *Ladies' Home Journal*.[38]

No sooner had Bok returned from his trip to Utica than the *Saturday Evening Post* began to use the method of employing boy agents. The publication met with unparalleled success. Offering such incentives as a free first week's supply of ten copies and prizes of cash and bicycles, with college scholarships for the older boys (more than 1,000 such scholarships were awarded for the 1903–04 school year), the *Saturday Evening Post* recruited 6,000 boys across the country and even lured newsboy distributors from the *Saturday Globe* by running frequent eighth-page ads in the Utica weekly, promising money and prizes to the young entrepreneurs. Surely the Bakers must have realized that they were aiding what would prove to be one of their fiercest competitors by printing the advertisements, but perhaps their patrician inclinations overruled any thought of refusing the ads. In any case, this choice, coupled with the decision to host Bok, proved in time to be a grave commercial blunder, as the *Saturday Evening Post* began to siphon much off the *Saturday Globe*'s readership at the turn of the century. By December 1898, just six months after its circulation had reached the 1,200 nadir, the *Saturday Evening Post* had made the incredible leap to 250,000 copies each week. It reached the 500,000 mark in 1903 and the 1 million plateau by 19 December 1908.[39]

The *Saturday Globe*'s first major story was printed 2 July 1881, only its seventh issue. As President James Garfield stood in the Baltimore and Potomac Railroad Station in Washington, he was shot by Charles Julius Guiteau, a disappointed office-seeker. This event occurred on a Saturday morning, during which time a large crowd had gathered in Utica to attend Barnum's Circus.[40]

Through an incredible stroke of luck for the *Saturday Globe*, news of the shooting flashed across telegraph wires after the morning *Herald* had hit the streets, and inexplicably that Utica daily did not print an "extra." The press at the afternoon *Observer* had broken down, leaving the *Saturday Globe* as the only newspaper in the city in which the excited residents and visitors could read the bulletins from Washington that day. The papers sold as fast as they were printed. Local interest was heightened by the fact that Guiteau had once lived in Barneveld, New York, just ten miles north of Utica.[41]

That 2 July *Saturday Globe* featured seven tiers of headlines, a total of eight inches high and in one column, each tier separated by a black hairline:

> *The President Shot*
> *As He is Boarding a railroad train to Washington*
> *The Country Fearfully Excited*
> *Suspension of Business Everywhere*
> The Nation Mourns the Murderous Assault
> *upon its Beloved President*
> Charles Guiteau, A Chicago Lawyer,
> the Murderer
> The President Reported In A Sinking
> Condition

Anticipating the public fervor, the *Saturday Globe* reporter began the story, "This city is wild with excitement over the report that

President Garfield, while alighting from the Limited Express of the Baltimore and Potomac Railroad, this morning, was shot and killed by an unknown man who, after firing the shot, escaped through the crowd."[42]

The story runs for twenty-seven inches in a manner that strikes the modern reader as bizarre, but which underscored the reliance on the telegraph as a means of transmitting news. After the lead, succeeding paragraphs presented facts piecemeal and seemingly in the order they were received by telegraph. In what amounts to little more than a chronological list of information shards, the reader first learned that the suspect's name is Dotty, which was changed lower in the story to Gatto and finally corrected to Guiteau. After having been informed in the lead that Garfield was killed, it is not until the last paragraphs of the article that the reader learned that Garfield was still alive.[43]

This style surely appears odd to readers accustomed to the modern, pragmatic newspaper style of the "inverted pyramid," in which the most important facts are presented at the beginning of a story and subsequent information provided in a gradually diminishing order of importance. However, the *Saturday Globe*'s peculiar story was due to the Bakers' desire to get the newspaper on the streets as fast as possible, even if it meant not taking time to rewrite the telegraph dispatches so that facts were presented in logical order.[44]

The following week's issue featured a large woodcut of the wounded leader, one of the first printed in upstate New York, along with the headline "Much Better." Bearing a dateline of "Washington, July 9, 7 a.m.," the story noted that attending physician D. W. Bliss "is well satisfied with the President's condition this morning" and that Garfield "passed a comparatively comfortable night, and feels quite refreshed." The encouraging report noted that Garfield's appetite was improving and the "discharge of pus continues."[45]

At the bottom of the placid, optimistic story the *Saturday Globe* upbraided some unnamed newspapers for what it regarded as unethical and unpatriotic coverage. "Much indignation is felt towards parties who are misrepresenting the condition of the President and who manufacture news to keep the public unduly excited," according to the report. "The rivalry between newspapers to obtain the latest news has resulted in all sorts of stories, generally of a character tending to prove that the President's recovery is impossible."[46]

One of the foremost purveyors of pessimism was Joseph Pulitzer's

St. Louis Post-Dispatch, which cast a suspicious eye toward the rosy reports regularly supplied to the press. One story bore the headline "The Doctors' Bulletin and Talk, as Usual, Rose-Colored," while on the editorial page the newspaper commented, "The condition of President GARFIELD is serious, if not critical . . . Those who accept the predictions of the President's physicians and believe the hundred-times repeated tale of his certain recovery should remember that even great physicians may deliberately conclude to tell white lies to save a mortally wounded patient. It is well understood that the bulletins are watched and read by the President." The *Post-Dispatch* cast a cynical eye on these bulletins, either for the sake of brutal honesty, as it claimed, or as a means of pandering to sensationalism in order to boost circulation, as its critics alleged.[47]

The same 9 July issue of the *Saturday Globe* that chastised nay-saying newspaper prophets of doom also featured a picture of Guiteau, looking sinister and smug, symbolically situated on the back page. This issue was the first of nearly 500 in the *Saturday Globe*'s history to present more than one illustration.

News the following week contended that Garfield was out of danger. The *Saturday Globe*'s telegraph dispatch was accompanied by a picture of Garfield's wife, Lucretia. However, beginning 23 July and lasting until September, the reports worsened. As Garfield lingered through the hot summer with a bullet lodged so deep in his pancreas that an operation to remove it was unsuccessful, the *Saturday Globe* printed pictures of Garfield's doctors in its 6 August issue, Garfield's mother in the 3 September issue and the President's children the following week.

Finally Garfield died of an abdominal hemorrhage caused by an aneurism. An enormous portrait of the deceased President covered the top half of the *Saturday Globe*'s front page, while the six columns of type beneath it were separated by thick black lines, giving the page a somber appearance. As was often the case in major stories, the headline consisted of numerous decks, which provided basic information (much as the lead paragraph docs in modern news stories) while it cataracted down the page.

> *FINIS!*
> President Garfield Dies
> *Monday Night*
> His Funeral Occurs in
> *Cleveland Monday*
> Sketch of His Life
> and the Scenes Around
> His Death Bed—
> *Profound Grief Everywhere*

The story began: "President James Abram Garfield died at the Franclyn Cottage, Long Branch (N.J.) Monday evening last at 10:35. Mrs. Garfield had retired for the night, and everything looked favorable for the President." The chronicle then touchingly describes the last few minutes of Garfield's life as told by General David Swaim, who was at Garfield's side.[48]

The dramatic circulation hike during the weeks of Garfield's suffering and subsequent death had brought out the *Saturday Globe*'s possibilities and given it a boost on the ladder to success. The pictures and vivid writing proved appealing and enabled the *Saturday Globe* to establish a toehold as a weekly supplement or alternative to the more staid central New York dailies.

The fortunate absence of competition on the day Garfield was shot didn't hurt either. "This was the event which turned the tide for the *Saturday Globe*, and while there were later days when it seemed as though the battle was well nigh hopeless, the skies grew constantly brighter and it was not long before the *Globe* was a recognized institution in Utica," the *Saturday Globe* noted in an autobiographical article. "Meantime, up and down the Mohawk valley and in the towns to the north and the south agents had been secured and the little weekly grew in strength throughout a constantly widening territory."[49]

Frank and Will Baker had seen what their readers wanted, and they looked for unusual or touching stories that could be written in a manner that would appeal to men and women alike and provide fuel for conversation. In addition to seeking an encore to the Garfield stories, a news story that could be presented as something just this side of an emotional drama, the Bakers sought to expand their coverage area. They found a story that accomplished both.

Sharing top billing with another gloomy report of the fading Garfield's condition in the 3 September issue was the saga of Jennie Cramer, daughter of a German cigar maker from New Haven, Connecticut. So that the menfolk did not mistake the story as being "women's news" and pass over it, the opening sentences described Cramer's beauty and physique and noted that she had many friends. She was identified as "perhaps the best-known girl in New Haven streets, and had universally the reputation of being the prettiest."[50]

Among her acquaintances were cousins James and Walter Malley, and through them she met Blanche Douglas. The quartet stayed overnight at Walter's mansion 3 August. When Cramer returned home the following day, her mother flew into a rage (probably because of the unseemly nature of the overnight stay, which the story suggests) and told Jennie to leave. She was last seen by her sister Blanche in the town square.

On 6 August, fisherman Asa Curtis found the girl's body in a one-foot pool of water at Savin Rock, six miles south of New Haven. The autopsy showed arsenic was the cause of death. James Malley was arrested and charged with her murder, while Walter Malley and Douglas were held as accomplices, but all were later released. No culprit was ever found, and Cramer's death became generally regarded as an accident or suicide.[51]

Jennie Cramer's case was obscure, and a month old by the time the *Saturday Globe* got wind of it, but through a series of sympathetic stories and vivid illustrations, she became a prominent figure. This status was exacerbated as other newspapers, seeing the *Saturday Globe* outselling them in their own towns, began to chronicle the saga for their readers, and Cramer was elevated to national recognition. She was eulogized in several songs, and her case was remembered for years.[52]

Cramer's case also provided the starting point for the first in a series of famous dime novels, a nineteenth-century literary genre of cheap, sensational fiction that appealed to the lower social classes. In the pages of dime novels, "tons of gunpowder were to be burned; human blood was to flow in rivers; and the list of dead men was to mount to the sky," Edmund Pearson wrote. "They dealt in violent action; in sudden death and its terrors."[53]

Dime novels were small and could easily be carried in a pocket, and thus were easy to conceal and transport. They conflicted with Victorian gentility by offering tales of adventure and combat, thus attracting scores of juvenile readers (and resulting in proportionate spankings), but were surprisingly strict in their moral standards, exalting masculine bravery and honesty and feminine virtue and purity. Nonetheless, dime novels were a literary movement distinct from other types of fiction, and in fact were more similar to sensational penny-press newspapers. According to Michael Denning, "The world of dime fiction was a separate world—in terms of production, reading public, and conventions—not only from the literary fiction of the nineteenth century, but from the popular fiction of genteel culture." This is the fiction that appeared in such popular magazines of the day as the *Atlantic* and *Harper's*.[54]

Dime novels were sometimes inspired by sensational stories in the press, as in Jennie Cramer's case. The hero of her fictionalized story was a detective named Old Cap Collier, and in the first episode he is called in to solve the murder. In a dialogue with the police chief, Collier learns that Blanche Douglas was "a woman of bad morals [who] introduced herself to the girl [Cramer], and it is thought, inculcated dangerous doctrines against morality into her mind." As a result of the overnight stay at Walter Malley's home, Collier learns, Cramer "was ruined."[55]

By the close of its first year, the *Saturday Globe* was enjoying a meteoric rise to success. Average circulation had climbed to 8,000, and the newspaper staff felt cramped in the two small rooms of the Thomas Block. So, the operation was relocated to an old building at 40 Charlotte Street, just a block and a half away.[56]

Underscoring the symbiotic relationships of city and newspaper, Utica was also experiencing rapid growth. Utica's population was growing so fast that in its first year the *Saturday Globe* printed a prognostication, based on a projection of the city's growth and immigrant influx, which concluded that the city would have 160,000 residents by 1911. The city never approached that figure. Its population peaked in 1930 at 101,740 and since has steadily declined—along with its economic fortunes.

3

Murders, Mass Distribution, and the Rise to National Prominence

Soon after the *Saturday Globe* moved to its new home on Charlotte Street, several structural flaws were discovered. "The new home was not all that could be desired," the *Saturday Globe* reported. "The roof leaked so that the printers had to move their cases every time it rained, and the rickety old outside stairs leading to the composing room endangered the limbs of those who every week carried the forms to the job office where the printing was done. But there was at least room to grow. And that was just what the lusty youngster most wanted."[1]

It was not long after the "lusty youngster's" first birthday that the next circulation surge occurred. In July 1882, Garfield's assassin Charles Guiteau was executed. Guiteau, a Freeport, Illinois, native, came from a family with a history of delusion and mental illness, and he appears to have received his share. Believing in his own perfection, which often manifested itself as egotism, Guiteau wandered to central New York, where he joined John Humphrey Noyes's Oneida Community until he was ostracized and ultimately harangued out of the flock. After failing in an attempt to establish a religious newspaper in New York, Guiteau passed the Chicago bar and became a lawyer. His practice consisted chiefly of chasing bad debts for clients. His perseverance, craftiness, and abundant self-confidence made him successful at this pursuit, but he developed a penchant for pocketing the debts.

Guiteau drifted aimlessly for years, marrying and divorcing, writing a cumbersome treatise on Biblical interpretation and serving as an itinerant evangelist before finally deciding to seek a political-patronage office. He pestered Garfield, James G. Blaine, Benjamin Harrison, Roscoe Conkling, and other Republican leaders for months, desiring employment as consul general in Paris, but was dismissed as a crank. Finally the waiting and hoping became too much for Guiteau. He saw his failure to benefit from the political "spoils system" as evidence of Garfield's treachery, and decided the Republican Party would enjoy more unity under Vice President Chester Arthur.

After tracking him for months, during which time he had numerous opportunities, Guiteau shot Garfield in the Washington train station. The wound was not immediately fatal, as Garfield survived eleven weeks before succumbing. Guiteau's trial lasted ten weeks, chiefly due to debate about his sanity, but he was finally hanged on 30 June 1882.[2]

Circulation of the *Saturday Globe*'s 1 July issue, which contained full coverage of Guiteau's execution, soared to 22,000. Although this dramatic increase was temporary, the additional sales afforded the newspaper widespread exposure, which yielded many new readers. By spring 1883, the *Saturday Globe* boasted an average circulation of nearly 15,000.[3]

By the time of Guiteau's demise the *Saturday Globe* had begun to expand its circulation area. Displaying five or six pictures per issue, the newspaper was reaching homes in northern Pennsylvania and throughout upstate New York.[4] To carry so many pictures, which were engraved and published at considerable expense to the Bakers, required complete faith in the two-year-old newspaper. Will and Tom Baker must have believed that circulation revenue would leap to cover such a cost, and gambled that the illustrations would serve as an attractive lure to potential customers, particularly the common folk—the farmer, the laborer, the merchant, the housewife— who soon emerged as the *Saturday Globe*'s chief constituency. Tom Baker remembered the lesson he had learned during his *Sunday Tribune* days and targeted the newspaper to rural residents more than city denizens, with the intention of presenting feature stories centering around the scandalous, sensational, or bizarre. It was this weekly presentation of unusual occurrences and social aberrations that provided fuel for mealtime conversation among the common folk and that formed the foundation of the *Saturday Globe*'s highly successful existence.

With such an arsenal of editorial fare, the Bakers had good reason to count on widespread readership, for in the late nineteenth century, after the party-press era and prior to the advent of radio and television, newspapers filled as much, if not more of, an entertainment function than an information function. Newspapers were benefiting from rapidly increasing literacy rates, which resulted from improved schooling, and were encouraged by the growing importance of newspapers and other printed matter in society. This fact, coupled with the decline of Victorian delicacy, prompted people to place greater reliance on the newspaper to amuse and entertain while it informed. Thus, the *Saturday Globe* offered stories of general interest, written in simple yet vivid language that would be appealing and understandable to readers lacking linguistic erudition, or for whom English was a second language.[5]

The Bakers clearly designed the *Saturday Globe* to be as entertaining as it was informative. Like many newspaper proprietors of the postbellum era, they were businessmen and administrators more than pseudo-politicians and opinion leaders, more concerned with making a profit by appealing to public desires than in shaping economic trends and political thought. After a century of party-controlled journalism inundated with slanted commercial and political information, readers wanted to be entertained, charmed, and shocked, and were inclined to reward with their patronage those newspapers that trafficked in these commodities.

The axiom that history repeats itself is evident in this demand placed on newspapers, as it signaled a return to the pre-Revolutionary journalism of the eighteenth century, which was characterized by printer-editors purveying occupational and moral instruction, along with ample doses of entertainment. Benjamin Franklin was the first and most influential in disseminating this doctrine of public service, contending that the press should function in an "entertaining and useful" manner. A return to this augmented entertainment function is evident today, as newspapers struggle to retain readership amid an explosion of competing media.[6]

The entertainment function in the nineteenth-century press was primarily the province of Saturday and Sunday newspapers, until dailies began to print comic strips, more illustrations, and more feature stories in the century's later decades. This led legendary publisher William Randolph Hearst to proclaim of one of his newspapers, "It is the *Journal*'s policy to engage brains as well as to get the news, for the public is even more fond of entertainment than it is of information."[7] Clearly the Bakers understood that readers had grown weary of partisan journalism and desired a breed of newspaper that would be relatively free of factional biases and mixed entertainment with information. No longer dependent on the assured but limited readership of the party press, postbellum publishers exercised their freedom (and financial prudence) to appeal to the widest possible audience.

This freedom was manifested in several ways in the pages of the *Saturday Globe*. One was to relate stories of the bizarre or amazing, such as tales of mountaineer Clark North, blind since birth, who delivered mail in the Catskill Mountains of upstate New York for thirty years by traversing his twenty-one-mile route on foot; and five-year-old East St. Louis girl Maggie Clark, who had a head the circumference of two feet, three inches. She was three years old before she could sit up and had never been able to walk.

Another *Saturday Globe* tactic was to expand its audience by printing items of interest to women: poetry, romance serials, fashion and etiquette essays, and informational articles such as how bread is manufactured and the mission of the Salvation Army. This material was designed to recognize the growing importance of women in society while endorsing the importance of their traditional roles of wife, mother, and homemaker. The *Saturday Globe* lauded "an increase of nervous power" in women. "The woman who works for her living to-day has far stronger nerves than her predecessors ever possessed," a front-page editorial proclaimed. "The most competent authorities declare that never in the history of the race has so excellent a type of women been evolved as the average woman of to-day."[8]

The third, and most successful, method of appealing to the widest audience—and simultaneously building circulation—was to engage in sensationalism, also known in the era as "yellow journalism." This form of reporting and writing emphasizes emotion for emotion's sake, or as Mott defined it, "the detailed newspaper treatment of crimes, disasters, sex scandals, and monstrosities." In contrast to the theory of objectivity, in which newspapers provide facts about the world that readers can use to form their own views, sensationalism meant newspapers were free to think and decide for their readers through the choice of which stories to cover and which words should be used to describe them.[9]

Sensationalism was not new to journalism. It existed in the penny-press era of the 1830s, and even before, in the late eighteenth and early nineteenth centuries. However, it was normally restricted to the editorial staples of sensationalism—the reporting of crime news, scandal, gossip, sex, divorces, and disasters. However, the sensationalism of the 1880s and 1890s added a dimension of editorial excitement, as evidenced by the way the news was displayed via such graphic devices as vertical and horizontal size of headlines, dimensions and type of illustrations, and darkness and colors of ink. The screaming headline and the shocking picture became synonymous with the sensationalist journalism of the late nineteenth century. In short, sensationalism became a method for newspapers to promote themselves through their commodity—information. This "self-advertisement," as Schudson called it, meant that "everything, including news, could and should be advertising for the newspapers." This explains the *Saturday Globe*'s penchant for printing its circulation figures.[10]

Critics launched literary assaults on sensationalism, calling it "social sewage that is allowed to stream in open sight" which is directed to "the lower order of mankind." Sensational newspapers "present a largely distorted view of society" to the average reader, who is "entertained with the swindles, the vices, and the crimes of the earth; his paper immerses him in all sorts of abnormal things. Such reading can only cease to pain him by hardening his heart and taking off the edge of his conscience."[11]

One scholar attributed the rise of sensationalism to the increased importance placed on securing telegraphic news, while a turn-of-the-century observer noted that as the press appealed to an ever-growing audience, it regressed to the lowest common denominator. Large newspapers "have far too many readers for the good of the social order in which they circulate."[12]

Newspapers defended sensationalism by linking it with the public-service ideology of crusading, but in reality it was providing a commodity the public hungrily devoured. Readers demonstrated a ravenous appetite for the scandalous, the prurient, and the horrific. The profit motive dictated the content of most newspapers, and it became evident that sensationalism sold well. According to one magazine, "The public which loudly condemns sensationalism ought not to like it, ought to put the seal of its condemnation on sensationalism by not reading the papers which engage in it .... But this is what they do not do, and the course of events clearly shows that if there is any guilt in sensationalism the public are more than guilty accomplices of it," for it is "the sensational papers which are most widely read."[13]

The most notorious merchants of sensationalism were Hearst and Pulitzer. Hearst is famous for his circulation-building tactic of whipping the United States into a frenzy by placing blame for the destruction of the battleship *Maine* on the Spanish, leading to the Spanish-American War. As one Pulitzer biographer noted of his *St. Louis Post-Dispatch*, "The element of sensationalism was never absent .... The paper launched into a systematic policy of publishing prying, gossip-mongering, frequently salacious 'news' which a modern journal would ignore," giving the *Post-Dispatch* "a reputation for indecency which lingered well into the twentieth century."[4]

On the subject of sensationalism, the *Saturday Globe* was a monument to contradiction. According to a *Saturday Globe* editorial, editor Tom Baker "never put pen to paper, nor permitted a subordinate to do so, except for words which could bring no blush to the cheeks of the most innocent." While conceding that sometimes tales of vice were necessary, the *Saturday Globe* asserted that "such recounting must be in language which could be interpreted only by the sophisticated and which suggested nothing to the unformed intellect. Write nothing, was [Baker's] order, which could not be read aloud at the breakfast table."[15] However, the newspaper regularly printed sensational stories that would raise eyebrows even today, and were surely considered shocking a century ago. By the mid-1880s, scandalous stories calculated to produce astonishment regularly found front-page space in the *Saturday Globe*. One, "A FIENDISH FATHER," noted in a subhead, "He Ruins Two of His Own Children, One of Whom is Only 12 Years Old."

> Alice Hughes, aged 12, living in Franklin Township, Gloucester County, N.J., became a mother on Monday, of a female infant, weighing eight pounds, the father of which is the girl's own father, Henry Hughes, a laboring man. Investigation revealed that the father had committed the same crime against an older daughter three years ago. Both children are still living.[16]

Another *Saturday Globe* story detailed the revolting episode of a woman "Eaten Alive By Hogs."

> Mt. Sterling, Ill.—Mrs. Greenwell, a widow aged 80, left her home Tuesday afternoon to visit a neighbor. She had not returned up to Wednesday, and search was made for her. After a time the bones and pieces of her bloody flesh were found surrounded by a drove of hogs, who were fighting over the remains, which were identified by scraps of clothing. It is supposed that the old lady fainted and that the hogs attacked her before she had regained consciousness.[17]

In another story, which bore the headline "Torturing a Child," the *Saturday Globe* reported that the Swiss parents of a ten-year-old boy burned him, froze him, and beat him savagely for trivial offenses. The writer concluded, "The authorities have taken steps to arrest [the parents], but a lynching may save the trouble."[18]

Other *Saturday Globe* stories during its early years carried such provocative and sensational headlines as "Mutilated Dead," "Why He Killed His Wife," "Young and Pretty, But Wicked," "Death Amid the Flames," "A Chamber of Horrors," "Possessed of a

Devil," "An 11-Year-Old Child Without Any Bones" and "New Zealand Cannibals—They Did Not Like the White Man Because He Was Too Salty."

In spring 1883 the *Saturday Globe* was again pressed for room and moved into a temporary home in a frame building on the northeast corner of Charlotte and Post streets while its new home, a brick, three-story structure, was being built by T. E. Kinney on the Bakers' Charlotte Street site. The *Saturday Globe* moved in during November 1883 and brought with it an addition to the family—a double-cylinder press, which ended the pressmen's strenuous trek to the Curtiss and Childs printing office. The next year, a downtown fire claimed the home of the *Utica Observer*, necessitating an arrangement that allowed the daily to publish its issues on the *Saturday Globe*'s press. The arrangement lasted until a new building was constructed to house the *Observer*.[19]

The *Saturday Globe*'s weekly circulation climbed to about 25,000 on its third birthday in May 1884, and to about 35,000 a year later. This growth heralded yet another change of quarters, and in 1885 the Baker brothers purchased land on Whitesboro Street for construction of a new newspaper building.[20] The proximity of this parcel to the railroad station (several hundred yards) proved prophetic. The Bakers must have foreseen the burgeoning importance of the railroad to their business; as circulation increased, so did the geographic scope of the distribution and thus, reliance on rail transportation for distribution. Railroads linking the populous areas of the country became the first truly effective means of mass transportation, unifying the nation's resources, stimulating production, and encouraging invention. Most importantly, railroads fostered mass markets waiting to be tapped by those who could produce goods with nationwide appeal. One is led to suspect that the Bakers envisioned national, even international, circulation for their fast-growing creation and sought to minimize the time, effort, and expense of transporting thousands of copies to the railroad station by constructing their newspaper's final home in close proximity to the station. The *Saturday Globe*, an omnibus product of light reading matter with content for every taste, was meeting with raging success throughout the region and the forward-thinking Bakers realized that their editorial formula could succeed among a national audience, provided the distribution hurdle could be overcome.[21]

Former newsboy Tom Dodge, who grew up just across the railroad tracks behind the *Saturday Globe* building, often witnessed the weekly railroad ritual. "They used to load the papers up on carts, take them right over to the train station and ship them out in all different directions,'' he recalled.[22]

A more subtle mainfestation of the Bakers' apparent vision of national circulation was the disappearance of the word 'Utica' from the title in the early months of 1885, as the *Utica Saturday Globe* became simply the *Saturday Globe*. Even the cornice on the newspaper's final home bears no mention of Utica, only the name *Saturday Globe*. It would seem that the Bakers believed their newspaper sufficiently established to withstand this slight to the locals in favor of greater regional and national appeal. There is no evidence to suggest that severing the local tie to appear less provincial had an adverse effect on local circulation.

New York City Architect G. Edward Cooper built the final home for the wandering *Saturday Globe*. The brick Whitesboro Street structure was an architectural oddity—it was 190 feet deep, and for the first eighty feet of this depth the building was only twenty feet wide but three-and-a-half stories; for the remainder of the depth it was forty feet wide and one story. The *Saturday Globe*, sporting a circulation of about 45,000, moved in on 1 January 1886.[23]

The *Saturday Globe* made several changes to accompany the relocation. Eight columns per page replaced the previous seven and the double-cylinder press was succeeded by three new Campbell presses in an effort to improve illustration—a sound move, considering the growing importance of illustration to the *Saturday Globe*'s success. This change catalyzed installation of a stereotyping plant so that the pictorial forms could be duplicated for each press, and a photo-engraving plant, eliminating the need to make purchases from picture companies or hire outside engravers. Also that year the Bakers abandoned woodcuts in favor of zinc etchings. This did not effect a significant improvement in the quality of the pictures, but made the production process faster and cheaper. As a result, shortly after the switch the *Saturday Globe*'s weekly pictorial offerings increased.[24]

Another Utica newspaper described the *Saturday Globe*'s illustration department:

> On the third floor a fine photograph gallery is located, containing the finest camera, a complete dark room and an outfit which would do credit to any photographer's gallery. This is under the management of Artist John Ashmore. The pictures after being photographed of any size required pass into the hands of Wm. Carson, the artist-in-chief, who with his assistants prepare the plates for the etchers' hands. Frank F. Baker

> does this work and is continually improving the department under his care. That he is an artist is shown by the beauty and accuracy of the pictures as they come from the press. The entire building is illuminated by Edison incandescent lights, the power being supplied from a 100 light dynamo. The firm employs about 50 persons.[25]

The year 1886 ended with another annual circulation gain of 10,000, pushing the weekly average to 55,000 copies.[26] During that year a particularly gruesome murder occurred in the *Saturday Globe*'s backyard—the kind of story editors dream of, and one that was tailor-made for the Utica weekly's front page.

Roxalana Druse of Warren, a Herkimer County town twenty-five miles east of Utica along the Mohawk River, poisoned her farmer husband because she had fallen in love with the farm's hired hand. She cut her husband's body into pieces and tried to burn them in the family's pot-bellied stove, but was unsuccessful. So, she fed the pieces to the pigs, who greedily devoured their erstwhile master. Mrs. Druse was eventually discovered and sentenced to die. The *Saturday Globe* played this story to the hilt, highlighting the sensational aspects of the murder yet treating Mrs. Druse in a sympathetic manner, doubtless to appeal to the widest audience. The 4 December 1886 issue of the *Saturday Globe* noted:

> There remains only 25 days between Mrs. Druse and the scaffold. She appreciates the terrific character of her situation and entertains no hope of escape from ignominous [sic] death. There still prevails a belief that when the fatal day arrives and there is no longer a possible chance of interference on the part of the Governor, she will break down and make a detailed confession of her crime, which will implicate others and perhaps lead to the trial and punishment of other individuals for complicity in the most horrifying and brutal murder ever recorded in the annals of this county.[27]

When the appointed time arrived, the execution was postponed for two months, kindling hopes for clemency. Throughout this long period of Mrs. Druse's confinement, the *Saturday Globe* continued to massage the sensationalism of the story and elicit sympathy for the murderess, raising the question of whether a woman convict should ever be put to death, no matter how grave her crime. In eighteenth-century England and America, women convicted of capital offenses nearly always committed the crime against their husbands, as Mrs. Druse did. Their fate was usually to burn at the stake. However, the emotional sentiment that women, as the fairer and weaker sex, should be spared capital punishment emerged fully in the Victorian era, clashing with the jurisprudential view that the law recognizes no differentiation between the sexes.[28]

Sixteen days from the execution date, the *Saturday Globe* became more overt in its sympathy for the doomed woman, portraying her as the helpless victim of some insensate evil motivating those who turn the wheels of justice. "Once more the darkening pall of fate is closing around the destiny of Mrs. Roxalana Druse, and none more than she are aware of that dismal fact," according to the newspaper's story. "Mrs. Druse will die with ony the kindest thoughts for those who have been instrumental in working her ruin .... [She] believes in God, and that a brighter day is yet to dawn upon her blighted life. She believes that there is mercy for the merciful and succor for the oppressed in that other world, and that she will gain in that better home what man denied her upon earth—peace."[29]

Hypocritically, the same *Saturday Globe* story takes a swipe at excessive and emotion-stirring newspaper coverage:

> Again and again has an overtaxed public faced the recital and recapitulation of the most horrible crime committed in the annals of Herkimer County, but its gory chapters will never relax an iota of their terrible fascination .... [No area murder in history] can cast a parallel to the intense ferociousness or the dazzling desperation which actuated the perpetration of the Druse butchery .... The press has overdone this matter, and columns upon columns of bosh and hearsay have been put in print without an iota of verification.[30]

The final issue before Mrs. Druse's death discussed her condition ("She has dwindled down to a mere shadow of her former self and would hardly tip the scales at 85 pounds"); the ghoulishness of those clamoring to witness the execution ("Sheriff Cook issued something over 300 passes to his friends and acquaintances to admit them to the horrid spectacle and satisfy their morbid curiosity to see the life of a human being choked from its miserable tenement of clay"); the employment of three professional hangmen to accomplish the task; and the devotedness of Mrs. Druse's spiritual adviser, the Rev. George W. Powell of the Universalist Church in Herkimer, despite his congregation's collective belief that the Reverend's sympathies were misplaced. The story also noted that cranks were crawling out of the woodwork. "This tragedy is developing all sorts of heartless and brainless cranks throughout the State and they hesitate at nothing to accomplish their disgusting ends. Some pitiless wretch made a miniature hangman's noose and inclosing [sic] it in a letter, addressed it to Mrs. Druse.''[31]

Mrs. Druse's execution on 28 February sent circulation soaring to 121,087 for the 6 March issue. Circulation leveled off afterward, but the new weekly average was between 80,000 and 90,000 copies. This dramatic sales boost prompted the need for more equipment and space. Two Campbell presses were added and by November of that year the building had been doubled to a width of forty feet.[32]

The increased demand for the newspaper had created a nationwide market and necessitated an increased number of regional editions. Shortly after the Druse execution, the *Observer* noted in its report on the planned enlargement of the *Saturday Globe* building that, ''This week the editions will reach 80,000, an increase in 15 months of 45,000. Thirty editions are printed each week, the presses being run from Tuesday evening until Saturday noon, with but few stops, night and day. The *Globe* reaches as far south as Florida, west to California and Oregon, east to Maine, and north into Canada.''[33]

The *Saturday Globe* had become the country's first truly national newspaper. By circulating in Canada and to a lesser extent in other nations, it had also become an international newspaper. Other newspapers had wide circulation areas, and a few were even read by denizens of both coasts, but they were tied to a particular geographic region. The fact that a few Californians, Texans, and Michiganders might have read Pulitzer's *New York World* or Hearst's *New York Journal* did not bestow on those publications the status of a national newspaper, just as it did not for Horace Greeley's *New York Tribune* and James Gordon Bennett's New York *Herald*, which attained wide circulation areas a generation before. They were still New York papers that did not make an overt attempt to appeal equally to readers in all parts of the country. Moreover, they did not publish zoned editions for all regions of the nation. The *Saturday Globe* had made journalism history through its revolutionary use of regional editions that provided local and regional news to readers from Portland, Maine, to Portland, Oregon, while supplying national information, much of which was flavored with the spices of sentimentality and surprise.[34]

The Bakers had found an editorial formula with nationwide appeal. Their product was a generalized newspaper, more useful for evoking emotions and stimulating conversation among its readers than for chronicling the weightiest political and economic matters. This fare was accompanied by generous and vivid illustrations, most notably its pictorial centerpiece—a large, striking color drawing centered above the fold on the front page. It was undeniable that the

Saturday Globe's fortunes were inextricably linked to its bold strides in newspaper illustration.

The *Saturday Globe*'s emergence as the first national newspaper did not occur in a vacuum. It was simply another example of the increasing interconnection that characterized the late nineteenth century. The geographic and quantitative growth of all facets of life was initially hailed as progress toward an improved society. As early Americans cleared land, navigated waterways, and moved westward, they were challenged by a nettlesome adversary: Nature. However, with the emergence of trains, telephones, and the telegraph system, and the enormous growth of the postal system and the mass press, Nature seemed overmatched by the late nineteenth century, and Mankind had conquered the impediment of distance. As a result, "social relations are no longer controlled by mere contiguity" and Americans were freed "from the gross and oppressive bonds of time and place," according to sociologist Charles Horton Cooley.[35]

This new freedom exacted a cost, though, for progress meant increased speed, which in turn meant augmented excitability and stress. Technology and social structure were rapidly changing in the late nineteenth century, as electricity, the telephone, mass transportation, and mass production reordered society.[36]

As new developments and products screamed for public attention, people began to rue the increasingly harried pace of daily existence. More demands were made on their time and mental faculties, and waves of printed matter were readily available. In short, life had become more complex, taking its physiological toll. Neurologist George Beard argued that the nervous system, "the center of the nerve-force supplying all the organs of the body," is comparable to an electric generator that supplies power for human functions, symbolized by lamps. Thus, "when new functions are interposed on the circuit, as modern civilization is constantly requiring us to do, there comes a period . . . when the amount of force is insufficient to keep all the lamps actively burning; those that are weakest go out entirely, or as more frequently happens, burn faint and feebly—they do not expire, but give an insufficient and unstable light—this is the philosophy of modern nervousness."[37]

The *Saturday Globe*'s emergence as a national newspaper sheds light on more than its content and distribution. That a newspaper could appeal to readers across the country expressed the national culture that, due to communication, emerged from the interconnection of local and regional cultures. Community, the foundation of American life through the late nineteenth century, was created by communication forms that identified an agglomeration of people living in proximity as a social unit and addressed problems common to the group. Thus, a national means of communication created a national culture. Culture is that which bestows meaning on existence, and is comprised of material evidence and collectively sustained symbolic structure. "The culture of a people is an ensemble of texts," anthropologist Clifford Geertz wrote metaphorically. The national newspaper, as both a symbolic and literary text, is one piece of the cultural puzzle historians must reconstruct in order to understand Mankind in past time.[38]

Texts are cultural forms of evidence, created items constructed of social meanings, that reveal insight into society. The *Saturday Globe* was more than a recorder of social advances and regressions, of depravity and benevolence, of devastation and prosperity; it offered insight into the manner in which people believed and behaved.

The evolution of mass markets, mass production, and mass distribution created a national culture, which in turn encouraged the expansion of the media's geographic reach. Local newspapers, once a reflection of the personality and beliefs of the printer-publisher, had become a mass press. This genre of publications were characterized by four elements: a mass audience, mass production, a mass of centralized population, and a rapid distribution method. The *Saturday Globe*, with its nationwide readership, new facilities, printing technology, and location in the burgeoning city of Utica, had evolved in just seven years from a circulation of 700 copies to an average of more than 100,000. Transportation played a key role in that ascendancy. By the late 1880s, Utica had become a major center of American immigration and industry, but it was particularly notable as a major transportation crossroads, linking New York City and New England with the rapidly-developing upstate region and lands to the west. The Bakers had met the challenge of distributing their mass newspaper to its mass audience.

As circulation climbed, it yielded several benefits. Each increase afforded the *Saturday Globe*'s editorial voice a wider range of influence, thus augmenting its authority. Escalating circulation also translated into growth in advertising revenue, and as the *Saturday Globe* evolved into a national newspaper, it was able to attract more national advertising.[39]

The *Saturday Globe*'s emphasis on geographic diversity was evident as its average circulation in 1888 soared past the 100,000 mark. It printed dramatic page-one stories of events and issues from across the country, such as the grisly slayings of two small children and their grandparents in rural Wisconsin (2 June); George Willson's murder of his wife in their Albion, New York, home by smothering her with a towel while she lay in bed (30 June); the twenty-fifth anniversary-reunion of Union and Confederate soldiers at Gettysburg (7 July) and periodic stories on the illegal immigration of Chinese into San Francisco.[40]

Just as important as the stories to the *Saturday Globe*'s geographic and numerical circulation growth were the newsboys. What had been described as "the greatest risk in journalism" had yielded handsome dividends for the newspaper. To commemorate the efforts of the approximately 7,000 agents in the United States and Canada, the newspaper printed this story on the front page: "The *Saturday Globe*, in its steady advance to the top notch in circulation, finds itself spreading out in all directions and this week we present the features of some of its representatives who are doing excellent work at their respective posts." Mentioned prominently in the story were twelve-year-old Frank Hubbard of Redwood Falls, Minnesota, who regularly sold seventy-five copies per week; M. F. Peterfish of Staunton, Virginia, who peddled 100 copies per week, and Harry Hinman of Westfield, Massachusetts, who sold a remarkable 350 copies weekly on a regular basis.[41]

The *Saturday* Globe's circulation soared again with the March 1889 destruction of the Park Central Hotel in Hartford, Connecticut, after a boiler explosion. The disaster, which claimed dozens of lives and was blamed on the hotel engineers' negligence, boosted the newspaper's sales to 186,347 copies.[42]

Shortly thereafter the *Saturday Globe* printed a letter from a New York City reader that demonstrated the newspaper's growing popularity:

> Wednesday morning in passing over Eleventh Street to take the Sixth Avenue Elevated cars downtown, [I] met "Sam" Hannauer, formerly of Utica, who gave me the last issue of the *Globe*. I took the Elevated at Eighth Street and directly opposite me sat a lady reading the *Saturday Globe*. After finishing my business downtown [I] took the Broadway car for uptown, and three or four seats from me sat a traveling man with sample case reading the *Saturday Globe*. I was quite surprised and wondered if this was the *Globe*'s day in New York City.[43]

The development of mass transportation in the late nineteenth century meant that the middle class could travel in vehicles driven by someone else. This offered thcm ready-made leisure time, which many occupied by reading. However, moving vehicles that made periodic stops were more conducive to light matter, such as the *Saturday Globe*'s weekly offerings. Most of its stories were comparatively short, its illustrations plentiful, and its typeface sharp. Its emphasis on entertainment, rather than ponderous affairs of state, made it ideal fare for commuters and other travelers.[44]

Average circulation in May 1889 hovered around 160,000. Before May gave way to June, an event occurred that shocked the nation, left thousands dead, and tens of thousands homeless—and proved to be the *Saturday Globe*'s greatest story.

4

"The Demon Flood": Tragedy in Johnstown

> The larger part of Johnstown is swept clear from the earth. Where once stood its stores and mansions is now a mud flat. Buildings, sidewalks, street railroads have vanished, and even the streets are obliterated. Four square miles of homes are piled into sixty acres of wreckage. Hundreds of human bodies are lodged in the solid mass with the ruins of their homes, and many were burned while they were yet alive.[1]

This was the scene *Saturday Globe* reporter Hugh P. McCabe surveyed a few days after the devastating Johnstown flood on 31 May 1889. Heavy rains had pelted the Johnstown, Pennsylvania, area since about 4 P.M. Thursday, 30 May, just as Memorial Day activities were concluding. By the next morning, eight inches of rain had fallen on ground that was already saturated from spring thaws and inordinately heavy rains in April and May. Area residents awoke that Friday morning to find that their basements were flooded. Meanwhile, the water levels in Stony Creek and the Little Conemaugh River had risen eighteen inches an hour, until those waterways overflowed their banks.[2]

By noon Johnstown (population about 10,000) was under more than two feet of water, making it already the worst flood in the town's history. Families took refuge in their attics or headed for high ground on Green Hill. The surging Stony Creek water, estimated at six miles an hour, ripped out two bridges. Even worse—the swollen creeks that fed Lake Conemaugh had caused the lake to rise above the crest of the Conemaugh Dam. The lake—three miles long, a mile wide in places, and sixty feet deep at its normal stage—had become a teeming, swirling body of impatient water.[3]

The first break in the dam occurred about 3 P.M., and the entire structure gave way ten minutes later. Witnesses said, "It is an erroneous opinion that the dam burst. It simply moved away," and, "The whole dam seemed to push out all at once. No, not a break, just one big push." Roaring down the mountain, a wall of water as much as seventy feet high smashed through several small villages before it hit Johnstown. Within an hour, the flood had killed 2,209 people in Johnstown and surrounding communities. Johnstown was obliterated; by nightfall, where once had been a thriving mill town stood huge piles of mud, crushed houses, wire, railroad cars, rock and bodies.[4]

The flood had crashed through Johnstown and slammed against Prospect Hill, creating a fierce backwash that rolled over Johnstown again, this time coming from the opposite direction. Much of the debris piled up against the Pennsylvania Railroad's massive stone bridge. When night fell, the debris caught fire, possibly from domestic coal stoves that ignited oil from a derailed tank car. This created a huge and ghoulish funeral pyre for the dozens of people trapped inside the pile. George Swank, editor of the *Johnstown Tribune*, wrote that it burned "with all the fury of hell you read about—cremation alive in your own home, perhaps a mile from its foundation; dear ones slowly consumed before your eyes, and the same fate yours a moment later."[5]

The flood had occurred on Friday afternoon, and the *Saturday Globe* managed to squeeze a nine-inch wire story on page 5, which customarily was reserved for local news. Under the thunderous headline THREE THOUSAND DEAD! (an odd headline to be seen anywhere but the front page), the *Saturday Globe* printed an agitated story—likely drawn from second-hand accounts—laced with the emotional alarm so characteristic of *Saturday Globe* disaster stories:

> The scenes of desolation are appalling, The rushing waters carried away nearly all of Johnstown to the railroad bridge, piling houses on top of each other to a hight [*sic*] of over 60 feet and the accumulated mass took fire, driving many of the people clinging to the buildings into the raging torrent. It is utterly impossible to estimate the loss of life, but it is believed Johnstown alone lost 1,500 people . . . . It is believed that not less than 3,000 people have perished, as several towns are in nearly as bad shape as Johnstown.[6]

The following week's issue was masterful. After working for a week on the tragic story, the *Saturday Globe* printed twenty-eight illustrations in its 8 June edition, which was devoted almost entirely to news of the flood. The front page carried a splendidly chilling illustration of terror-stricken residents clinging to roofs or flotsam while raging waters whisked them away. The artistic depictions of panic and death were accompanied by McCabe's impressionistic, disjointed account, which would seem bizarre to the reader of today accustomed to the torpid but highly organized disaster reports in the modern press. McCabe's piece is not presented in the "inverted pyramid" manner of post-World War II news accounts, but instead uses provocative description of the flood's power to convey the stark devastation it wrought:

> Your correspondent is here in the midst of this terrible scene of desolation and death, but his pen refuses to do the work required of it. Words come readily enough but they are rejected as tame. The English vocabulary is incapable of expressing what everyone here must see and feel . . .
>
> Disaster! Calamity! What shall I call it? The words are feeble, distressingly weak and insipid, when applied to what has happened here. A few days ago? A sweetly romantic valley; towering hills clothed with the varying green of forest and of field; a murmuring, singing stream . . .
>
> A little later? All the furies of devastation let loose; the flood gates of heaven pulled wide open; the valley changed to a hell of horror; the stream transformed into a surging, roaring torrent running mountains high; the demon flood with loosed shackles and drunk with limitless power; falling trees, crashing houses, trembling walls, struggling humanity . . .
>
> Over on the hillside are crouching hundreds, ruined, hungry, hopeless and robbed of all that life holds dear . . .
>
> In these seven days since beauty and order were transformed into ugliness and chaos, young men have grown old, women have died of grief and terror and children have become driveling idiots. Mothers permit themselves to be led to shelter and sit with tearless eyes mumbling the names of their little ones so rudely torn from them . . .[7]

McCabe's sensationalized account was partly intended to sell newspapers, but the agony his story conveyed was not disingenuous. He had left a comfortable newsroom and an orderly life to enter a world of chaos, a kaleidoscope of shattered homes and broken lives which seemed, to an outsider, too fantastic to be real. As a reporter, McCabe observed the full extent of the disaster, interviewed the survivors, and chronicled the toll in life and property, but his ability to witness the scene so soon after the flood stripped him of cool detachment and enabled him to view the desolation differently than had he simply gathered details from telegraph dispatches. This stunned personal awareness provided the narrative excitement of emotions that not only justified the newspaper's expense in sending

McCabe to Johnstown but also reinforced the *Saturday Globe*'s eminency and hallmark.

McCabe and the others quickly adapted to their surroundings, suffering lack of warmth and shelter just like the flood victims about whom they scribbled so many lines. The *New York Times* reported the arrival of a newsman who had apparently misunderstood the extent of the disaster:

> A Philadelphia reporter was sent here to finish up the disaster, but the disaster is likely to finish him. He paralyzed Newspaper Row on alighting from the train today by asking for a restaurant. When he was laughed out of countenance and was told that the newspaper men had to forage on the country, he wanted to know when he could hire a horse and wagon. He was unable to comprehend that a horse could not be procured for love or money, but he capped the climax by asking where he could buy a white shirt. A boiled shirt here is as rare as a mince pie in Africa.[8]

Among the many other flood stories in the 8 June issue, the *Saturday Globe* told readers a possibly fictitious tale of a courageous and martyred "Paul Revere" who rode through Johnstown on horseback minutes before the town was leveled, warning a disbelieving populace to head for the hills (the man was drowned when the flood caught up with him); an account by a survivor who was visiting from Baltimore; a train engineer's story of how his train raced to avoid the looming flood; and an accusation by guard Herbert Webber of the South Fork Fishing and Hunting Club, the organization that owned and maintained the Conemaugh Dam and Lake Conemaugh, that he had repeatedly warned his South Fork employers of the dam's deteriorated condition weeks before the flood, but that his pleas for repair fell on deaf ears.[9]

The excoriation of the South Fork Club was carried on in earnest on the *Saturday Globe*'s editorial page. It was probably editor Tom Baker who wrote, "It was more than criminal to allow this danger, it was murderous, and those who had the power to remove it ought to be conscience-smitten as the ghastly roll is counted up and charged against them."[10]

The 15 June issue contained an incredible forty-four illustrations, including a huge, eerie, front-page picture of a spectral skeleton—Death incarnate—hovering gleefully over beleaguered Johnstown. Beneath it the story began: "It will be two weeks to-morrow since Death rode triumphantly down this valley, then so beautiful, so prosperous and happy, and left his thousands of victims to be mourned by thousands of broken hearts, and what a fortnight it has been!" The story proceeds to tell of the clean-up efforts, the continuing search for the dead and the unceasing agony of the living.[11]

By this time managing editor Albert Dickinson had journeyed to Johnstown to add his personal insight and observations to McCabe's reports. In an interview many years later, Dickinson said that his most vivid recollection of Johnstown was that the only place he found to sleep was in a hotel for blacks, where he was annoyed both by bedbugs and the wild laughter of some boisterous people in the room below. The occupants had found a keg of whiskey washed away by the flood and were chasing their sorrows in the time-honored tradition.[12]

Stirring accounts such as these in the *Saturday Globe*, other major Eastern newspapers, and the Associated Press sounded the nation-wide call for assistance for the flood victims. One New York newspaper noted, "Correspondents for the great papers pictured the scenes in such graphic pen portraiture that almost before the maddened waters had subsided the great heart of the mighty nation had been touched with sympathy, and pocketbooks and check books made quick responses to the cry for help and succor."[13]

For all their apparent altruism, the newspapers made out quite well financially. "For publishers it was one of the headiest weeks ever," according to David G. McCullough, the flood's foremost biographer. "Newspaper circulations broke all records. For days on end, one edition after another was sold out as soon as it hit the streets. The New York *Daily Graphic* was selling an unheard-of 75,000 copies a day. In Pittsburgh there seemed no letup to the clamor for more news. A new weekly picture newspaper called the *Utica Saturday Globe*, published in upstate New York but widely circulated, increased its circulation by better than 63,000 with its special edition on the disaster." Although it is unclear as to which issue of the *Saturday Globe* McCullough referred, the weekly boosted its circulation by more than 70,000 during June.[14]

The *Saturday Globe* was one of the first newspapers to send reporters and artists to the scene of the tragedy. It also was the only newspaper in central New York to keep a reporter in Johnstown during the flood's aftermath. The *Saturday Globe*'s news staff was sufficiently large that productivity did not suffer when reporters were sent away from the newsroom for days or weeks at a time. This press practice began in the mid-nineteenth century, as news staffs expanded in proportion to journalism's growing importance to society. For instance, Pulitzer's *St. Louis Post-Dispatch* quadrupled its six-member reporting corps in just five years. As news staffs grew in the middle and later decades of the nineteenth century, editors gained the wherewithal to make a practice of sending reporters out to cover stories as they unfolded in other cities, states, and nations. This reporting was generally of two types—investigative reporting of ongoing social problems, such as vice and disease, or prolonged coverage of natural disasters, attributable either to human error or divine providence. The former was a high-profile form of sensationalism which later became known as *muckraking*, in which reporters actively track down social ills or improper business dealings with the intention of exposing the findings. The latter was also sensational, although to a somewhat lesser degree, because excited stories came closer to reflections of the disaster's impact and were usually less contrived. In disaster coverage, reporters sought colorful, evocative stories of dramatic sensory impact, augmented by striking illustrations.[15]

The Saturday Globe's Dickinson had learned a valuable lesson during coverage of the Johnstown tragedy. He had seen the importance of sending his own reporters to cover stories and subsequently he dramatically de-emphasized wire service reports on major events, preferring to send someone from his own staff. Dickinson realized that having McCabe in Johnstown, reporting his impressions and allowing readers to see the devastation through his sympathetic eyes, was partially responsible for the June circulation hike. Thus, Dickinson developed a corps of reporters and artists who could, at a moment's notice, depart to the site of any story. Frequently, though, it was Dickinson who took the trip, as the Bakers placed greater trust in him than any other writer and insisted that the biggest stories warranted his personal craftsmanship.[16]

The *Saturday Globe*'s circulation cracked the charmed 200,000 mark with its 8 June issue. More than 205,000 copies were sold to a news-hungry public, nearly twice the sales of precisely a year earlier. The *Saturday Globe*'s principals did not find it premature in the 15 June issue to pat themselves on the back, claiming of the 8 June issue, "In hundreds of places in New England, the Middle States, Ohio, Maryland and the Virginias, a paper was sold to every third member of the population. This is extraordinary and no other paper printed can compare with the showing of the *Saturday Globe*."[17]

Noting that some newsboys sold 100 papers in five minutes, the

Saturday Globe listed some of the major circulation areas for the 8 June issue:[18]

Utica, N.Y.	8,000
Rochester, N.Y.	7,600
Syracuse, N.Y.	3,300
Gloversville, N.Y.	2,700
Johnstown, N.Y.	2,300
Schenectady, N.Y.	2,200
Amsterdam, N.Y.	2,100
Rome, N.Y.	2,000
Binghamton, N.Y.	1,900
Watertown, N.Y.	1,500
Lowell, Mass.	1,200
Hamilton, Ont.	1,050
Pittsburgh, Pa.	1,000

In addition to circulating extensively in Canada, copies went to such distant communities as Nebraska City, Nebraska, to the west; Haw River, North Carolina, to the south; and Eastport, Maine to the east. More than 200 copies of the 15 June issue were mailed to England. The *Saturday Globe* also listed circulation figures for its issues in the second week of June for each year of the newspaper's existence. They illustrate the newspaper's phenomenal growth:[19]

11 June	1881	1,345
3 June	1882	7,835
9 June	1883	15,840
14 June	1884	26,808
13 June	1885	36,780
12 June	1886	47,116
11 June	1887	85,218
9 June	1888	108,850
8 June	1889	205,200

The 15 June issue soared to 268,536, but could have reached 300,000 if not for heavy rains that drenched New England and other Northeastern states, the *Saturday Globe* noted. Pennsylvania readers bought 40,000 copies of the 15 June edition, New Englanders purchased 30,000, and Canadians nearly 20,000. The *Saturday Globe* rightfully credited the vivid news accounts and illustrations of the flood with the leap beyond 268,000 copies. "Our illustrations and description of Johnstown were just what the people wanted and what

they quickly availed themselves of," according to an editorial. "This week the work of restoration in the valley of the Conemaugh is pictured by the editorial writers of the *Globe* who have visited the region. It is an interesting tale and appropriately rounds out the splendid descriptions that have appeared in the *Globe* for June 8 and 15." The self-congratulatory article concluded, "With auspicious skies we will have an enormous sale this week. The reading millions of this continent are bound that the *Saturday Globe* shall lead any and all competitors."[20]

As circulation soared, and as their newspaper attained a wider audience each week, the Bakers and their staff began to believe the *Saturday Globe* was a journalistic juggernaut. In eight years, it had grown from a humble local circulation to national exposure. More than 200,000 copies of the newspaper were being bought each week, and the *Saturday Globe* was becoming a major American newspaper capable of wielding its circulation might to shape public perceptions and tastes. The elevated circulation also demonstrated to the Bakers that their editorial formula of low-level sensationalism combined with entertainment, fashion, literature, and advice was precisely what the public wanted from a newspaper. The triumvirate of Tom and Will Baker and Albert Dickinson found themselves in control of one of the largest newspapers in the United States. They giddily trumpeted their success, anticipating greater accomplishments in the future. In apparent puffery borne of prosperity's sweet taste, the *Saturday Globe* predicted in its 22 June paper that 1,611,261 people would read that issue, assuming six readers per copy. Someone's mathematics must have been amiss, because that constitutes the odd prognostication of 268,543.5 copies, only seven and a half more copies than the previous week. The prediction proved too lofty, though, as "only" 224,462 papers actually were sold, prompting the *Saturday Globe* to save face by explaining away their inaccurate prediction this way: "Though interest in the Johnstown disaster is subsiding the Globe sold remarkably well and patrons were more than pleased with our entertaining letters from the valley of death."[21]

The *Saturday Globe* crew had the last laugh, however, as circulation of the 29 June issue roared to 269,175 copies, its largest press run to that time and the second-highest mark it would ever achieve. In part, this feat was due to optimistic reports of Johnstown's recovery and, in part, to publicity regarding the impending hanging of Sarah Jane Whiteling for poisoning her family. The Bakers could scarcely resist the opportunity to gloat. Noting that more than 967,000 copies were sold in June, the

Saturday Globe boasted, "This wonderful showing rounds out a record without parallel in journalism. The Saturday Globe was founded in 1881 and 700 copies were all that could be disposed of for that first issue. Nobody believed we could survive the infantile stage. And, although we print and circulate 200,000 papers weekly, we believe we are yet in our infancy and that our growth in the eight years ahead of us will be more marvelous than that which has characterized our development in the first eight years of the Saturday Globe."[22]

Just to make sure no one forgot, for several months the *Saturday Globe* carried under the page 4 masthead a picture of a newspaper-waving newsboy superimposed on a globe, similar to the one on the cornice of the *Saturday Globe*'s new home, with a scroll reading, "Our Greatest Circulation: June 29 1889, 269,175."

Although sales declined somewhat after the Johnstown flood excitement quelled and that town began traveling the long road back to normalcy, circulation remained high. The Bakers had seen the awesome power of the unusual and the deadly, and it influenced their newspaper's content. The political coverage which had been a lackluster staple of the *Saturday Globe*'s earliest years gave way to chronicles of grisly crimes, heart-rending executions, and social aberrations. In an effort to retain most of the readers it had lured with Johnstown flood stories and pictures to keep circulation high, the Bakers printed these stories in 1889: the plight of the poor, deformed, and starving in Glasgow, Scotland (10 August); the ongoing bloody feud between the Hatfields and the McCoys in the hills of the West Virginia (7 September); Southern voodoo rituals (23 November); various tales of Johnstown's recovery and the much-publicized hanging of Whiteling. She had poisoned her husband, John, and children, Bertha and Willie, secured inaccurate death certificates and arranged for the bodies to be cremated quickly to destroy the proof of murder, all so that she could claim a $299 insurance policy. The suspicious deaths were later questioned, leading to Whiteling's conviction. The first woman put to death in Philadelphia, Whiteling's hanging "has given a crushing blow to the sentimental theory that capital punishment must not be executed upon a female no matter what her crimes may have been."[23]

As the *Saturday Globe* had become more successful, climbing to the uppermost reaches of newspaper circulation, Dickinson found himself working harder and longer. Besides his editorial duties, he frequently covered the most important *Saturday Globe* stories. The long hours and increased stress seemed to be having an adverse effect on him, and the Bakers noticed. In the closing months of 1889

Dickinson was called into the office of one of the Bakers, who said, "You seem to have been rather dismal the past few days. Pack your grip, Dick, go where you want to go, do what you want to do and we will foot the bill."[24]

"Dick" Dickinson picked up $500 at the cashier's window and walked to the train station. Within a few hours he was in New York City, looking for a story. When a scalper offered Dickinson a one-way boat ticket to Savannah, Georgia, for $10, the Utican traveled south. After docking in Savannah, Dickinson decided to pursue the mysterious system of superstition known as voodooism. Derived from the Ewe-speaking African word *vo* ("to inspire fear"), the practice of voodoo developed in response to the relocation and enslavement of Africans in the eighteenth and nineteenth centuries. In a new land, forced to learn new languages and to submit to a social structure much different from theirs, "slaves were able to find their own sources of power and protection" through voodoo, according to Lawrence W. Levine. He wrote that voodoo practices were more than mere suspicion, and in fact "were legitimate and important modes of comprehending and operating within a universe perceived of in sacred terms."[25]

Writers and gossipers of the day, as Dickinson described, contented that voodoo consisted of:

> negroes holding secret meetings in the hearts of almost inaccessible swamps at the dead of night and there going through scenes and incantations horrible beyond anything that ever occurred in the center of the dark continent [Africa]. They have told how the black men at these gatherings indulge in wild and indescribable dances around pots of boiling water in which were cast live lizards, snakes, toads, etc., and how at the crisis of their excitement the mad creatures plunge forked sticks into the seething mess, draw out the half-cooked bodies of their disgusting offerings and rend them with teeth and nails . . . Grotesque, ridiculous, powerful and disgusting as this negro superstition is, nothing could be farther away from what it has been represented to be.[26]

What voodooism is, Dickinson learned after a journey to the remote interior reaches of rural Georgia, is:

> a belief held by thousands, if not millions, of darkies, that there are certain persons in every community who have the power to bring out terrible evils through a co-operation with evil spirits, that these powers are sometimes delegated to others to be used in revenge, that the most awful results come from thus being "tricked" or "voodooed," and that the only relief lies in securing the aid of a "doctor," more skilled than he who brought about the curse. This statement may seem tame, until the

reader is told that the negroes believe implicitly in this superstition, that they suffer all sorts of agonies and even die lingering deaths through its operation, and that the white men pronounce it the greatest curse of the South . . .[27]

Dickinson supplied accounts of "men being actually conjured to death and of others being cured by charms when the best medical aid was powerless." He even became a "patient" of a prominent voodoo doctor. While in Georgia, Dickinson observed the post-Civil War black of the Deep South through his Northern eyes. He wrote that the Northern mind conceived easy solutions to the racial problems in the South, but his Georgia trip gave him a greater, perhaps less naive, understanding of the relationship between Southern whites and blacks. He concluded that Savannah blacks were too often similar to the negative stereotypes of that race:

Once in a thousand times you will find a negro who is industrious from a knowledge that industry means wealth, or at least comfort, but the other nine hundred and ninety-nine must have a "boss." He is perfectly helpless without the white man, more so than the Southern white man would be without him, which is saying a good deal. Put a gang of blacks at work and stand over them, directing every move and you will get a pretty fair amount of work done, but leave them alone half a day and when you return you will find little or nothing done and they will look at you as much as to say, "You ain't fool enough to think wese goin' to work widout a boss, is you?" One reason for this is that the negro has no idea of self-dependence. He hasn't learned how to go without someone to direct him. Another reason is that he is such a natural thief, he will steal time when he can't steal anything else. But the main reason is that he is indolent, without ambition to excel, and is constitutionally lazy. He knows that the day of the lash has gone by and that the worst his employer can do is discharge him. This doesn't worry him in the slightest. His wants are few and the means of satisfying them is a matter of small consideration to him.[28]

Dickinson also observed that blacks tended to walk barefoot, sing and dance merrily, have little regard for monogamy and morality, and produce staggering numbers of babies—all negative images common to the era. Dickinson's view of blacks was typical of the time as the nineteenth century witnessed the widespread bulwarking of views that blacks were inferior to whites. Craniologists reported that blacks were intellectually deficient, anthropologists debated whether blacks constituted a distinct species, and minstrel shows reinforced stereotypes of blacks as indolent, rhythmic, shuffling, dependent, and deceptive.[29]

Dickinson spent more than a year on the road, writing stories which he wired back to the newspaper. This was an early example of a modern journalistic trend—that of reporters wandering the countryside in search of stories. Extensive coverage of unusual subjects throughout the country by one of the *Saturday Globe*'s own proved instrumental in building the paper's national circulation.[30] (See Appendix for circulation data)

Dickinson graduated from Ontario's Newberg Academy at age 17 with the highest grades reported in that province. At the academy he learned to set type and after a three-year stint as a teacher, journeyed to Utica. Opting to pursue a career in journalism, Dickinson landed a job at the daily *Utica Herald* as a printer and proofreader. He left the *Herald* in the midst of an 1882 strike and helped establish the *Utica Press*. Initially a strike paper, the *Press* (known in later years as the *Daily Press*) thrived until 31 March 1987 as Utica's morning daily. Seeking to shun the printer's case for a newsman's typewriter, Dickinson migrated to the *Saturday Globe* in the fall of 1882. Five years later he became its news editor, allowing Tom Baker to concentrate more on the newspaper's business and managerial affairs.[31]

Dickinson was one of the new breed of professional editor that emerged following the penny-press era. In the eighteenth and early nineteenth centuries, one person filled the roles of proprietor, printer, and editor, enabling him or her to exercise substantial control over all phases of the newspaper's operation and to infuse personal character into its pages. This practice had begun to wane by mid-century, as telegraphic reports, faster presses, and larger newspapers expanded the focus of journalism beyond the active control of one person. Public desires decreed that the gathering and presentation of news become the chief function of a newspaper, and rising circulations catalyzed the division of labor that separated the technical realm of printing a newspaper from the conceptual realm of ideas, facts, and communication.[32]

The labor division created the professional editor in the news business. Traditionally, printers and editors had trained in apprenticeships and later toiled as journeymen, as Tom Baker had, before assuming a position of authority. However, editors like Dickinson, trained in the use of words, not type, were displacing the printers, relegating them to management or production posts. As *Boston Courier* editor J. T. Buckingham wrote proudly in 1840, "I am the only individual now living in Boston, if not in the Commonwealth [of Massachusetts], who unites the printer and the editor in one man."[33]

Paul Williams, a Dickinson contemporary who served as editor of the *Daily Press* from 1923 to 1955, wrote of the man called "Big Dick" behind his back, "He was a tall, rather spare man of impressive mien, who usually carried a cane. He was an excellent speaker, a prolific writer and he had a wonderful eye for pictures. But his best asset was his affinity for people and he knew an enormous number of the great and near-great. His newspaper work took him into every one of the United States, in many of which he was a guest at the governor's mansion."[34]

Dickinson anecdotes abound. Williams recalled that "Big Dick" brought back the first pictures of the tidal-wave destruction of Galveston, Texas, interviewed Kansas's saloon-smashing Carry Nation in her cell and once persuaded a condemned man to have his execution time advanced to meet the *Saturday Globe*'s deadline. Besides studying voodoo in the Georgia swamps, he burned his shoes while working close to the flames of a Michigan forest fire, and covered more than a dozen hangings and electrocutions. The first electrocution of a murderer was performed in 1891 at the state prison in the central New York city of Auburn. Reporters were not permitted at the event, but a change in the law the following year permitted newspapermen to be present as witnesses, and Dickinson attended many. His experience with condemned murderers prompted him to prepare a speech he once gave entitled, "The Good Characteristics in Men I Have Seen Hanged."[35]

One time Dickinson was at New York State's Dannemora Prison to cover an electrocution. The *Saturday Globe* had distributed fliers nationwide promoting its upcoming coverage of the execution, but the event was postponed for thirty days by a gubernatorial stay order. Upset that his paper would be unable to deliver its promised story, Dickinson persuaded the warden to allow him a rare tour of the entire prison. Dickinson contended the resulting story on prison life was nearly as interesting as any execution. "After all," he said later, "an execution is done more neatly and is less sloppy than a man being shaved."[36]

The years immediately following the Johnstown flood were filled with exciting stories and soaring circulations. The *Saturday Globe* had arrived as a major force in the newspaper field, yet it had done so without immersing itself in the yellow-press sensationalism to the extent of other major newspapers of the day, such as Hearst's *Journal* and Joseph Pulitzer's *World*. Its emphasis on the bizarre, the tragic, and the heart-rending was chiefly a smart business move, for it was just such sensational stories readers of the yellow-press era craved. However, the *Saturday Globe* seldom pandered to prurient interests and abstained from promoting exceedingly morbid curiosity in vice and crime. Years after his retirement from the *Saturday Globe*, Dickinson recalled with pride that the newspaper printed nothing that could not be read aloud in the home. It was because of the *Saturday Globe*'s reluctance to plunge too deeply into scandal-sheet journalism that the *Elmira Daily Gazette* in southwestern New York sung the Utica newspaper's praises, noting:

> The Utica Saturday Globe is increasing its circulation in Elmira at a rapid rate. Each week's sales improved over those of the week preceding and the paper, already excellent, is growing better all the time. The Globe is one of the very best weekly newspapers sold in this vicinity and is increasing its hold right along. It is a well-craftied [sic], clean paper that no one hesitates to take in his family and its news is always reliable.[37]

Tirelessly in search of the dramatic and powerful story to maintain the newspaper's high circulation, Dickinson journeyed to New Hampshire the following year to cover a murder. In his articulately rousing style of conveying excitement, Dickinson wrote in the *Saturday Globe*'s 25 July 1891 issue under the headline "Atrocity Unparalleled!":

> Never before did a crime throw the people of New Hampshire into such a state of wild excitement nor excite such a profound and far-reaching desire for vengeance as has the fearful roadside butchery at Hanover, Friday evening last. Among all the many remarkable crimes which figure in New England history, none exceeds in devilishness of design or brutality and boldness of execution the murder of beautiful, rich and cultured Miss Christie Warden by the vindictive, educated and mysterious farmhand, Frank Almy. It is a remarkable story of infatuation, rejected advances and horrible revenge.[38]

The story really began eleven years earlier, when after a youth of petty crimes, twenty-year-old George Abbott went on a burglary spree in his native North Thetford, Vermont, in 1880. He was caught and on 23 June 1881 sentenced to fifteen years in the state penitentiary in Windsor. Abbott became the trusted engineer of the institution and might have earned an early parole for good behavior, but on 30 September 1887 he escaped over the wall by fashioning a rope ladder from bits of string he had gathered. After working at odd jobs throughout much of the country, Abbott, using the name Frank C. Almy, was hired at Andrew Warden's farm in Hanover, New Hampshire, 11 July 1890, and quickly proved himself a valuable worker. It was there that he met and became infatuated with twenty-eight-year-old Christie Warden, the farmer's eldest daughter, who moved in the highest social circles. Although she condescended to grant Almy her friendship, she politely but firmly declined his romantic overtures, citing his temper and refusal to share more than vague statements about his past.[39]

Almy stayed on at the Warden farm through the winter, and in the spring asked Andrew Warden for his daughter's hand in marriage. Warden replied that he believed she did not care for the farmhand's affections. Almy became so persistent and impudent in his argument that the elder Warden should convince his daughter to marry him, and uttered so many veiled threats, that he was fired 1 April 1891. Almy then drifted around New England, pining for the woman who did not return his ardor. Almy returned to Hanover several months later, and on 14 July began hiding in the Warden barn. He hid there for three days, trying to see Christie alone, but the opportunity never presented itself. His passion fueled by liquor and the smart sting of rejection still in his heart, Almy hid along a deserted road near the Warden farm 17 July, and about 9:30 P.M. intercepted Christie, her younger sister Fanny, their mother, and a family friend as they were walking home from a grange meeting. At gunpoint Almy dragged Christie 200 yards into the woods, where he fired bullets into her side and head, mortally wounding her.[40]

Dickinson examined the murder site on Tuesday, 21 July, four days after the shooting. He wrote, "The place bore evidence of the fatal struggle. On the ground beneath the willows were dark stains where the lifeblood of the unfortunate young lady had oozed away and branches of the trees were bent and broken—mute evidence to the struggle that they had witnessed. In one spot was a depression where a pool of blood had collected, the crimson stream having flowed from a wound in the head through which a bullet tore, gouging out the left eye and forcing its way through the skull."[41]

Instead of fleeing the state, Almy inexplicably returned to the Warden property a few days after the murder, where he hid in the barn for a month, foraging around the countryside for food. He repeatedly visited Christie's grave, on which he placed flowers "about a dozen times," he claimed. On 18 August Mrs. Warden noticed some empty cans of food near the barn and called the police. After a ten-hour siege Almy was arrested, but not before two bullets blasted into his leg and one grazed his scalp.[42]

His trial began 16 November 1891 in a cold New England courtroom; the judge wore a fur coat and fur cap throughout most of the proceedings. After initially proclaiming his innocence, Almy changed his plea to guilty in the face of overwhelming evidence. He had hoped to receive a thirty-year jail sentence, but instead was condemned to death. He was hung 6 December. Dickinson recalled that Almy was the only man he was ever glad to see hung. "Frank had the most beautiful eyes I have ever seen," Dickinson later said. "They were overlarge for his face just as his hands were too big. The hands were covered with hair like a gorilla. I did not regret knowing that Frank must die."[43]

Others he did regret, though, for he viewed electrocution as a brutal method of punishment. Only six days after Almy was hung, wife-murderer Martin Loppy was electrocuted at New York's maximum-security jail at Ossining, otherwise known as Sing Sing. Dickinson wrote:

> In all it is said to have been successful so far as the wiping out of the life of a fellow creature is concerned; in many it is said to have been accompanied by scenes horrible, ghastly, thrilling .... As an execution, therefore, the affair went off smoothly enough; but the burning flesh, the struggle for breath, the bursting of an artery in the nose and the breaking of the ball of an eye, the motions of the victim as he sat helpless in the chair of death, all left an impression that while electrocution may be relatively quick it inflicts terrible suffering.[44]

The *Saturday Globe*'s ascension to national prominence in its first eight years demonstrated its facility for handling such influential and important stories as the Johnstown flood, the mysterious death of Jennie Cramer and the assassination of President Garfield. The newspaper's proprietors understood the value of news follow-up as a means of holding an audience. Knowing that new readers would be introduced to the *Saturday Globe* during a major event, such as the Johnstown incident, the Bakers sought to retain them by providing extensive and prolonged coverage of the event for many weeks while introducing them to new and different major stories. This editorial savvy had made the *Saturday Globe* one of the most widely-read newspapers in the United States.

The *Saturday Globe* building, Whitesboro Street, Utica, New York, circa 1891.

The cornice of the *Saturday Globe* building, with the sandstone relief of the street-corner newsboy—the symbol of the newspaper's success.

The *Saturday Globe* building as it appears today.

Will Baker's erstwhile residence on Genesee Street, now home to several small businesses.

Editor Tom Baker in 1891.

Managing Editor Albert M. Dickinson and staff members Hugh McCabe and T. H. Sweeney in 1891.

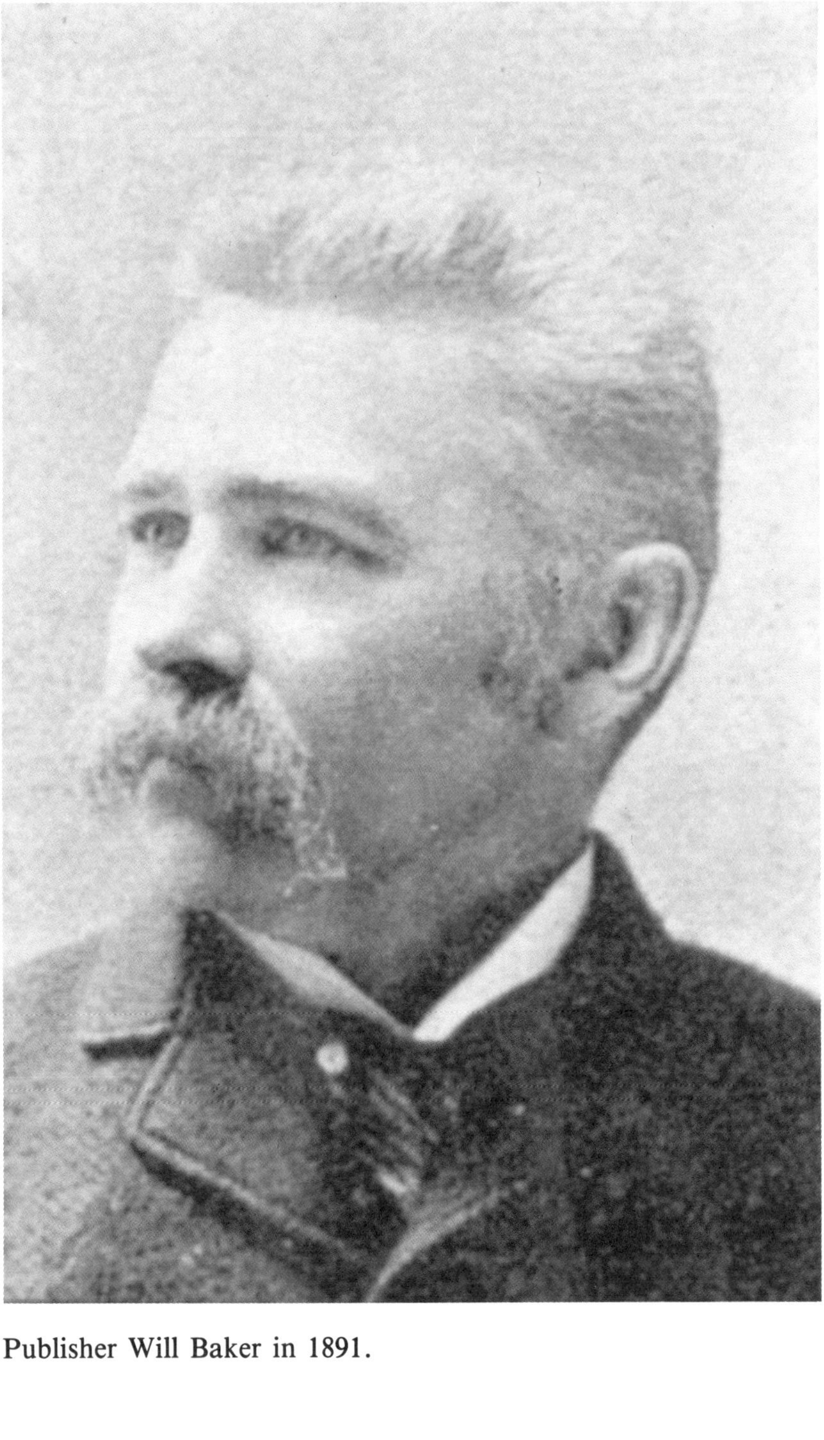

Publisher Will Baker in 1891.

Will Baker as he looked shortly after the *Saturday Globe*'s demise.

Will Baker's grandson Brian Clarke and granddaughter Marietta von Bernuth.

SATURDAY GLOBE.

VOL. IX. UTICA, SATURDAY, JUNE 15, 1889. NO. 6.

...NG JOHNSTOWN'S RUINS.

DEATH'S FROLIC THROUGH THE VALLEY OF THE CONEMAUGH.

The spectral skeleton, Death incarnate, at the Johnstown flood. *Saturday Globe*, 15 June 1889.

SATURDAY GLOBE.

VOL. IX. | UTICA, SATURDAY, JUNE 8, 1889. | NO. 5.

CONEMAUGH'S CALAMITY!

THE BRIDGE OF DEATH OVER THE CONEMAUGH RIVER.

Artist's rendering of Johnstown being destroyed by a wall of water. *Saturday Globe*, 8 June 1889.

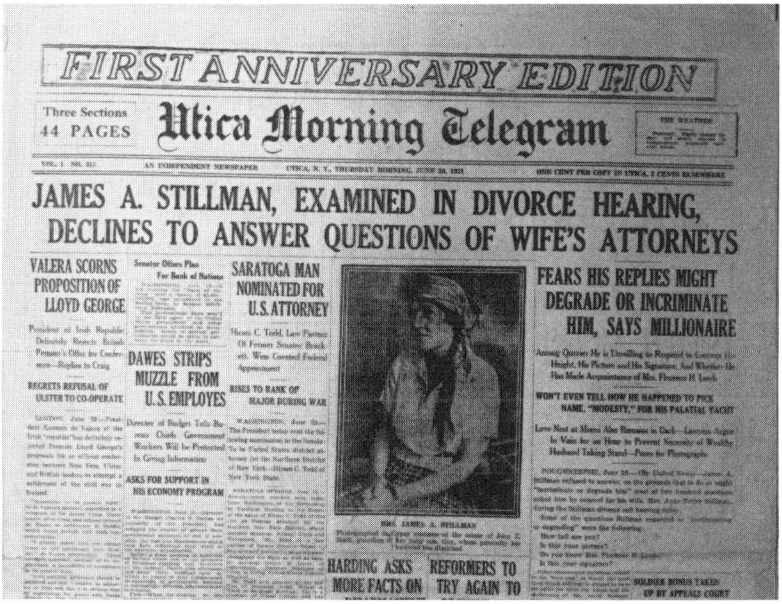
FIRST ANNIVERSARY EDITION

Three Sections 44 PAGES

Utica Morning Telegram

AN INDEPENDENT NEWSPAPER

JAMES A. STILLMAN, EXAMINED IN DIVORCE HEARING, DECLINES TO ANSWER QUESTIONS OF WIFE'S ATTORNEYS

VALERA SCORNS PROPOSITION OF LLOYD GEORGE

President of Irish Republic Definitely Rejects British Premier's Offer for Conference—Replies to Craig

REGRETS REFUSAL OF ULSTER TO CO-OPERATE

Senator Offers Plan For Bank of Nations

SARATOGA MAN NOMINATED FOR U.S. ATTORNEY

Hiram C. Todd, Law Partner Of Former Senator Brackett, Wins Coveted Federal Appointment

RISES TO RANK OF MAJOR DURING WAR

DAWES STRIPS MUZZLE FROM U.S. EMPLOYES

Director of Budget Tells Bureau Chiefs Government Workers Will be Protected In Giving Information

ASKS FOR SUPPORT IN HIS ECONOMY PROGRAM

MRS. JAMES A. STILLMAN

FEARS HIS REPLIES MIGHT DEGRADE OR INCRIMINATE HIM, SAYS MILLIONAIRE

Among Queries He is Unwilling to Respond to Concern His Height, His Picture and His Signature, And Whether He Has Made Acquaintance of Mrs. Florence H. Leeds

WON'T EVEN TELL HOW HE HAPPENED TO PICK NAME, "MODESTY," FOR HIS PALATIAL YACHT

Love Nest at Miami Also Remains in Dark—Lawyers Argue In Vain for an Hour to Prevent Necessity of Wealthy Husband Taking Stand—Poses for Photographs

HARDING ASKS MORE FACTS ON

REFORMERS TO TRY AGAIN TO

SOLDIER BONUS TAKEN UP BY APPEALS COURT

The *Utica Morning Telegram*, the *Saturday Globe*'s short-lived sister newspaper.

--THE UTICA--

SATURDAY GLOBE

THIS WEEK, JUNE 27, WILL CONTAIN FEATURES WHICH WILL MAKE IT WELL WORTH PURCHASING. BE SURE THAT YOU GET A COPY AND READ:

IN THE PUBLIC EYE

ARE MRS WILLIAM MC'KINLEY AND MRS GARRET A. HOBART.

APPLIANCES OF THE TOMB.

FEAR OF BURIAL ALIVE HAS LED TO MANY INVENTIONS.

Sweet the Memories

THAT ARE ASSOCIATED WITH TRINITY CHURCHYARD IN NEW YORK.

A DAY TO BE REMEMBERED.

JUNE 27, WHEN CHARLES XII OF SWEDEN WAS BORN.

PEGGY O'NEIL.

A FAMOUS WASHINGTON BEAUTY OF JACKSON'S DAY.

A FORTUNE FOR HIM

WHO CAN BRING RELIEF TO CALIFORNIA FRUIT GROWERS.

ORDER A COPY OF THE AGENT.

The *Saturday Globe* regularly distributed these leaflets to advertise the contents of the next week's issue.

SATURDAY GLOBE.

VOL. XVI. UTICA, SATURDAY, MARCH 20, 1897. NO. 44.

MYSTERY OF A HEADLESS BODY,

JAMES J. CORBETT AND ROBERT FITZSIMMONS.

FITZSIMMONS!

HOW THE AUSTRALIAN WON THE CHAMPIONSHIP.

The front page from the 20 March 1897 *Saturday Globe* issue which generated its highest-ever circulation of 294,000. It featured extensive coverage of the Corbett-Fitzsimmons heavyweight title fight.

The Saturday Globe.

SATURDAY, MARCH 20, 1897.

FITZSIMMONS!

MYSTERY OF A HEADLESS BODY.

WHEN FITZSIMMONS BECAME THE WORLD'S CHAMPION.

HOW TO FIND OUT.

An inside page of the 20 March 1897 *Saturday Globe* issue, showing the newspaper's multitude of illustrations depicting events during the Corbett-Fitzsimmons fight.

5

The Halcyon Days

Back in Utica, Will and Tom Baker, their newspaper a stirring and lucrative success, began dabbling in other commerical ventures. They bought a sandstone quarry in nearby Higginsville and shipped the stone to purchasers throughout the state via the Erie Canal. The Bakers retained some of it for personal use, though, choosing the reddish-brown sandstone as building material for their new homes, which they commissioned architect G. Edward Cooper to construct. Cooper, who had built the *Saturday Globe*'s Whitesboro Street home, erected adjacent palatial homes on the west side of Genesee Street, just south of Watson Place. Each building was constructed with a large, arching portico and an imposing turret. Tom Baker's house was razed in 1927 in favor of the six-story Roosevelt apartment building, constructed the following year, but Will Baker's home remains, now housing several small insurance firms at 1518 Genesee Street.[1]

This was not the only construction the Bakers ordered. In 1892 the frontage of the *Saturday Globe*'s home was again doubled, this time to eighty-two feet, and a fourth story was added. To meet the growing demand for the newspaper, the Bakers ordered several new presses, bringing the total to eight (six Campbell and two Cottrell). Not long afterward, the *Saturday Globe* acquired some cylinder presses from the Kidder plant in Boston. Steam-powered cylinder presses, which merely rolled back and forth over the typebed, had been in existence since the early nineteenth century, but with the rise of the mass-circulation era, they had proved too slow. The printing process was accelerated in 1846, when Richard Hoe substituted horizontal cylinders for the flat typebeds and employed wedge-shaped rules to hold the type in place while the cylinders revolved at high speed. The type-revolving cylinders presses accelerated the processing of news but also limited the use of multicolumn makeup and were at the mercy of plumbing, to the dismay of Hartford printer Erastus Geer. "A fine Mess we are in now, for our Water pipes are stopped up so we can not draw any water, nor run the press," he complained to his father.[2]

When the *Saturday Globe* acquired the Kidder presses, its production staff devised a method to cast electrotypes into the curved printing plates, thus increasing production. In 1892 three typesetting machines also were acquired, replacing fourteen printers who had set type by hand. That same year the *Saturday Globe* updated its type of illustration from zinc etchings, which had themselves replaced woodcuts six years earlier, to halftone etchings. All these construction and production improvements prompted the newspaper to proudly crow the following year, "The Globe now has a home in which it has room to grow. Nothing less than half a million circulation will find the paper ill-prepared in any way. When that sale comes—well, there's lots of land to build upon."[3]

In the same article, the *Saturday Globe* presented a "walking tour" of the newspaper plant, commenting, "perhaps no better idea can be given our friends of how the Globe is prepared and sent out each week to be read by about a million admiring friends than by accompanying them on an imaginary tour of the present Globe building." The first floor of the building housed the offices of Will and Tom Baker; the twenty-member mailing department; the accounting department, where twenty clerks were supervised by another Baker brother, Joseph; the press room, where 12,000 copies of the *Saturday Globe* were printed each hour; the boiler room and a job-printing office. The fifteen-person circulation department was on the second floor, along with the electrotyping and stereotyping departments. It was here that the type was cast to furnish the presses and the engravings for illustrations were made. The 1893 *Saturday Globe* article reported that the electrotyping department "is the only one in the world turning out electrotype facsimiles of half-tone engravings for use in newspaper work." The third story was home to the artists who drew the sketches, cartoons, and portraits. Sharing the third floor were the store rooms, the carpenter shop, and the machine shop, where a fourth Baker brother, Frank, was a mechanic. The top floor was chiefly the province of the newsroom and offices of editorial personnel. The photography and composing rooms were nearby.[4]

After the enormous circulation boost resulting from coverage of the Johnstown disaster, the *Saturday Globe*'s circulation leveled off in the vicinity of 200,000 for the next few years. The Bakers, Dickinson, and such reporters as McCabe, Fred Reusswig, Byron Merrill, Ward Johnson, John Cogley, and T. H. Sweeney strove to avoid giving too much ground to circulation attrition after they had worked so diligently to boost it in the weeks and months following the Johnstown flood. They wanted to keep as regular subscribers most of the nearly 269,000 people who had bought the paper following the flood, so they tackled one exciting story after another during the early and mid-1890s. Dickinson dispatched his teams of roving reporters and artists to cover unusual stories such as that of a woman, grieving over her husband's death, who hired an embalmer and an electrician to gruesomely preserve the husband's body in a chair and wire the body so that it would stand and bow to the woman. She kept the electrified corpse even after she remarried.[5]

Other stories of the peculiar and offbeat included:

• the arrest of William Woodward, con man and imposter, finally convicted of a crime after thirty-seven arrests. During his infamous career he had swindled more than $1 million.
• a plan to send blacks from the Southern states back to Africa under the auspices of the International Migration Society. Liberia's president offered to make land available to them.
• the outbreak of gold fever in Northern California after gold, ore, and quartz were found in abundance along Coffee Creek in Shasta and Trinity counties.
• the discovery that a Chinese laundryman working in New York City, Chin Hop Sing, had leprosy. This created a controversy over whether he should be confined or allowed to continue to work and fueled the debate in the medical community as to whether leprosy is contagious.
• the tale of how a violin-playing girl regularly charmed a den of about fifty snakes with weird strains from the instrument. The *Saturday Globe* writer observed that as the music grew wilder, "the snakes tumbled over each other in reptilian ecstasy." By changing notes she could make them return to their den.
• the successes of Bishop Samuel Fallows's bar in the basement of Chicago's Reformed Episcopal Church. After only three weeks in business it had 2,400 patrons per day, who ate hash, stew, pork and beans, and drank a non-alcoholic beer.
• the discovery of staggering quantities of pearls found in Miller and Murphy lakes in western Arkansas.[6]

By the mid-1880s, the newspaper's story selection had swung from the conservative coverage of important but bland political stories to spicier subjects such as natural disasters and foreign affairs. These stories were advertised by newsboys and by means of handbills distributed in advance of the newspaper's street sales. These usually bore a few words about major stories—just enough to whet the reader's appetite for news. The handbills unwaveringly guaranteed that the hunger borne of curiosity could be satiated with the forthcoming issue of the *Saturday Globe*. These tales, which combined with the alluring illustrations to form the cornerstone of the weekly's success, were usually handled in a maudlin manner. Although *Saturday Globe* stories of vice and crime were, on the surface, a moral illustration of the ignoble ends criminals meet, these tales exalted the felon's prominence nearly to folk-hero stature in unabashed exploitation. As a circulation-building device, the newspaper staff manipulated readers' emotions by treating selected wrongdoers, particularly women on whom the newspaper took editorial pity, as though they were basically good people who had been cruelly diverted from the straight and narrow by some unseen, amorphous force, a dark evil well beyond control of the unfortunate thief or murderess, or who had perhaps experienced unhappy childhoods.

The newspaper tried to balance tales of the unusual with those of drollery. The editorial staff had a penchant for dark humor, and certain brief news items allowed the writers to promenade their collective wit. Such examples included the sly intimation of bestiality in this news story:

> The body of Christian Seeker, of Williamsburg, Pa., was found in the East river, New York, this week. He disappeared in November and it is now supposed drowned himself for love of a horse. The horse was a great favorite with Seeker, who petted him in all sorts of ways. Finally the animal died and Seeker became greatly depressed. He disappeared from home and no trace was found of him until the other day.

The *Saturday Globe*'s combination of unusual and exciting stories with plentiful pictures succeeded, not only in keeping circulation high but in expanding the newspaper's geographic reach. The article the *Saturday Globe* printed commemorating its twelfth anniversary presents a "review of the career of what is probably the most popular weekly newspaper published on the American continent, one which is sent out to the four quarters of the world." To illustrate the extent of the newspaper's rousing success during its heyday, the story continues:

> And, by the way, "four quarters of the world" is not an exaggerated expression when used in connection with the Saturday Globe's circulation. It is an actual fact that the Globe is read weekly not only by the textile workers of New England, the coal miners and iron workers of

Pennsylvania, the farmers of Ohio and the great West, the tobacco raisers of Virginia, the cotton planters of the South, the conservative citizens of her majesty's provinces to the north; but also by the trapper and fur hunter of Canada's frozen Northwest, the New Mexican smoking his cigarette within the shadow of his adobe hut, the cattle herder on the pampas of Brazil, the missionary and British soldier in the jungles of India, the diamond seeker in South Africa, the trader on the banks of the great Congo, and the American and English merchants in Hong Kong and Tokyo.[7]

About 60,000 of the approximately 200,000 weekly copies were distributed on the East coast during the early 1890s. Canadians were the chief foreign readers among the *Saturday Globe*'s international clientele, buying about 14,000 copies each week. The newspapers distribution network had blossomed to 10,000 agents throughout the United States, Canada, and abroad. The *Saturday Globe* relied heavily on the train to distribute the issues to its agents, and its proximity to Union Station (only several hundred yards east) saved both time and money. During its halcyon days the newspaper published forty to fifty regional editions, containing local news for each geographic region. That the *Saturday Globe* newsboys across the country could cite news of their community or region in their high-volume sales pitches doubtless made the task of selling the newspaper an easier one.[8]

The *Saturday Globe* still sold for a nickel per copy, $2 for a year's subscription, the same rates as those during its infancy. In those early days the *Saturday Globe* relied almost exclusively on circulation income for its revenue. This was a time when a twelve-page newspaper could be sold at a profit for as little as one or two cents, because newsprint cost less than $20 per ton and printers worked for $16 or $18 per week. The *Saturday Globe* was able to maintain the same rates for nearly forty years, in part because of its increased circulation, but perhaps even more importantly, due to the emergency of national advertising.[9]

From the outset, advertising carried a bad reputation. The first advertisement, for a book, was carried in a 1626 British publication. The novelty apparently proved unpopular, as no advertisement appeared until twenty-one years later. After the midpoint of the seventeenth century, advertisements began to appear frequently in the British press. Many of these were placed by bogus doctors peddling nostrums, which they claimed could effect wondrous personal improvements. One 1680 newspaper responded, "Great Abuses have been put upon good People by the Cheats, and Pretences of Quacks and Mountebanks."[10]

In the United States, printers came to realize that advertisements provided more revenue of greater dependability than the erratic nature of subscription fees and political-party support. "It is not our fault that the Patriot is so crowded with Advertisements," the *Orange County Patriot*'s printer asserted in 1810. "A Printer cannot live without money, tho' a farmer may—We can get no pay for our papers (except for a few persons who are punctual), but for advertisements we sometimes get pay." As more printer-editors concluded that reliance on income sources involving social ties or political kinship were unstable, they placed greater dependence on advertising revenue, thus augmenting the growing importance of economic forces in newspaper publishing. Income sources became less promissory and more market-based, as sales and advertising encouraged a cash-up-front mentality which provided proprietors a more steady and predictable financial base.[11]

With the increasing importance of advertising in nineteenth-century journalism, two important changes occurred. First, circulation gradually became more important as a means of delivering potential customers to advertisers than as a source of pride and gauge of editorial power. Second, newspapers yielded much of their moral tone in exchange for profit, becoming less particular about their advertising clientele and more subject to the desires and dictates of advertisers. As Schudson wrote, "Newspapers could no longer judge their advertisers from on high; they were themselves judged by the advertisers." Consequently, some highly suspect advertising matter began to fill the pages of the American press, touting get-rich-quick schemes and potions with preposterous curative powers. Newspapers printed the submissions of an abundance of these charlatans, with many defending the practice from a laissez-faire stance, advancing the view that all advertisers had a right to use the public press provided they paid. The Philadelphia *Public Ledger* declared, "We do not indorse [sic] for the disease-dispelling potency of any of these drugs . . . such things are matters of opinion, about which the community are competent to decide." The *Boston Daily Times* outlined its policy on accepting advertisements, noting that it chose not to make "any inquiry whether the articles advertised are what they purport to be," because, "That is an inquiry for the reader who feels interested in the matter, and not us, to make. It is sufficient for our purpose that the advertisements are paid for, and that . . . we are impartial, and show no respect to persons, or to the various kinds of business that fill up this little world of ours."[12]

In New York, Benjamin Day's *Sun* and James Gordon Bennett's *Herald* were leading carriers of advertising, especially that of the questionable variety. This practice was vigorously opposed by Horace Greeley in his *Tribune*. In 1841 Greeley complained of objectionable advertisements placed by a female patent-medicine peddler:

> The conductors of that paper [the *Sun*] had been publicly and anxiously remonstrated with and shown the iniquity of publishing those advertisements. But what cared they for crime or misery, so long as either could fill their greedy coffers with gold? . . . . And thus, by constant publication and puffing in The Sun, backed by puffing Editorials in the Herald, the dreadful trade of this wretch was made to thrive and gold flowed in streams into her den, and thence to the pockets of her newspaper accomplices.

Many newspaper proprietors found the "iniquity" impossible to resist, though, because ad revenue had proven too vital to a newspaper's economic survival. Thus, when the *New York Daily Times* appeared a decade later, it informed readers of the importance of advertising as a source of newspaper revenue by noting in its inaugural issue, "the amount which we receive [from circulation sales] barely covers the cost of the paper upon which it is printed, the deficiency being made up by advertisements."[13]

Direct revenue was not the only benefit the press derived from the publication of advertisements, for newspapers participated in a symbiotic relationship with businesses and municipalities. As newspapers published more advertisements, they enhanced the prosperity of business, which encouraged community stability and growth. This, in turn, was essential to newspapers' survival. This economic boosterism was an important, if insufficiently acknowledged, social role of the nineteenth-century press, for newspapers created and maintained community in the sociocultural sense.

Advertisements also encouraged the geographic and numerical growth of the American press, providing the income that permitted many newspapers to thrive and encouraging many others to set up wherever there existed the possibility of receiving advertising revenue. "The support of so enormous a number of papers is possible in America, aside from the general interest in politics, through their cheapness, through the mass of advertisements they publish, and the freedom of these advertisements from every sort of tax," a German observer wrote in 1848.[14]

The mass press made advertisements ever more available to a rapidly-expanding populace, characterized by a rising middle class that was beginning to identify more with purchasing goods and services rather than producing them on the farm or in the home. This consumer mentality increased and broadened the potential demand for goods and elevated readers' sense of a marketplace society. National corporations became interested in circulation volumes and coverage areas of the print media to evaluate how to best spend their advertising budget, which accounted for forty-four percent of a newspaper's gross revenue in 1880 and fifty-five percent in 1900. Some advertisers even began seeking demographic information as a means of reaching specific target audiences with their commercial messages. As newspapers and magazines derived more and more revenue from advertisers, they became more dependent. Some publishers and editors even sacrificed press freedom in subtle ways, becoming subservient to mandates from the business community. One former editor at Pulitzer's *World* claimed that the newsaper had become "an appendage of the department store." Another former editor accused advertisers of fostering the kind of scurrilous and irresponsible journalism practiced by Hearst newspapers in pursuit of lofty circulations, noting, "Merchants do not hold long to an attitude of civic virtue when tempted by large circulations."[15]

Although many newspapers barred lewd and indecent advertisements, as well as those which were nothing more than flagrant swindling, *caveat emptor* was the rule. Businesses engaged in such deceptive practices as the "reading notice," an advertisement masquerading as news by its placement and reliance on text, with the product name buried in the copy. This trick took advantage of the public's appetite for news. Advertisers first used reading notices to sell merchandise, knowing people often ignored display ads while perusing newspapers. Frequently this disinterest was borne of suspicion. Advertisers were viewed by the postbellum public as hucksters and shysters, and their advertisements were warily avoided. Reading notices later became more subtle, advancing advertisers' political agendas while challenging newspaper audiences to be ever more vigilant in perusing each edition.[16]

Perhaps the products most responsible for public suspicion of advertisers and their wares were patent medicines, many of which were offered in the *Saturday Globe*. Such advertisements were vague, deceptive, and even fraudulent, but were readily accepted by most newspapers because of the huge sums of money involved. The most consistent *Saturday Globe* advertisement was for Lydia Pinkham's "vegetable compound" for women. Its ads promised the product would cure infertility and prevent miscarriages. Later ads for the same product in the *Saturday Globe* promised it would settle frayed nerves, cure backaches and headaches, and alleviate monthly "pains and irregularity'' as it ''regulates women's peculiar monthly troubles.'' The ads also encouraged suffering women to write to sympathetic Lydia, who would solve all sorts of physical and personal problems for them—most likely with ample doses of vegetable compound.

Other medicinal wonders advertised in the *Saturday Globe* included cures for ''fits,'' ''piles'' and every other conceivable malady. Sarsaparilla was sold as a panacea. Buffalo's Erie Medical Co. brazenly touted a cure for ''lost or fading manhood'' which would ''enlarge and strengthen weak, undeveloped organs.'' Dr. J. H. Dye of Buffalo had the temerity to announce: ''Wives should know how child bearing can be accomplished without pain, danger and annoyance.'' Naturally, ''Dr.'' Dye had the ''cure.'' Probably some sort of vegetable compound! In 1904 Edward Bok exposed the fraudulence in patent medicines for *Ladies' Home Journal*, revealing that the kindly Lydia Pinkham had been dead for years and many of the widely-advertised patent medicines, including some elixirs recommended for children, contained large amounts of cocaine, morphine, and alcohol.[17]

Bok and others exposed the chicanery in turn-of-the-century advertising, casting a pall of suspicion over the entire practice as an outraged public rebelled against deceit and manipulation. Ad brokers had little pride in their craft and the honest practitioners were painted with the same brush as the unscrupulous ones. The negative publicity prompted the advertising industry to improve its image by adorning itself with the trappings of professionalism, such as a discrete body of knowledge and a means of formal education.[18]

The *Saturday Globe* carried few advertisements during the 1880s. Most of these were of the one-column, one-inch variety and were placed by Utica-area businesses. However, as the newspaper's circulation and geographic sphere of distribution grew in the mid-1880s, advertisements from other parts of New York and from bordering states began to appear. The first truly national ads in the *Saturday Globe* both debuted 7 September 1889—for *Ladies' Home Journal* and the Encyclopedia Brittanica.

Daily newspaper advertising enjoyed a period of enormous growth from the 1890s to the advent of World War I. Advertising multiplied three and a half times, at a ratio of more than ten times the increase in the number of daily newspapers. Advertising space rose from twenty-five percent to fifty percent between 1880 and 1910.[19] This meant barrels of money for most newspaper publishers, but the Bakers did not capitalize on this trend. In fact, they seemed to lean the opposite way, relying on greater amounts of advertising revenue (at $2 per line) in the *Saturday Globe*'s first year and using less after the newspaper had become established. The diminished amount of ads may have been in response to public disdain, thus prompting the *Saturday Globe* proprietors to restrict the number of ads, thereby gratifying readers, while charging its advertisers a higher rate for prominent placement, lack of competition with other ads in the newspaper, and large readership. Unfortunately, the newspaper's business records have vanished, making this theory impossible to prove.

Historian Mott claimed the growth of national advertising and newspaper circulation began between 1885 and 1892, prompting thousands of investors to sink millions of dollars into new periodicals. Much of that money was lost during the 1880s and 1890s as thousands of periodicals failed in what Mott termed "the panic of 1893" and the ensuing years. Bok, whose publisher Cyrus Curtis had to borrow $300,000 to supplement his own substantial wealth before the *Ladies' Home Journal* became a success, wrote in 1891, "I should think a man would weigh carefully the chances before putting any money into new magazine schemes. It is not so much a survival of the fittest as the survival of the largest capital." The *Saturday Globe* had proven a survivor by accumulating the needed capital, thanks chiefly to its early successes. It also produced and capitalized on important innovations in its bid to stay ahead of the competition, whose numbers were swelling.[20]

Not far from Utica, Frederic E. Ives had been at work on the problem of reproducing photographs in the printing process since being appointed head of Cornell University's photographic laboratory in 1876 at the age of twenty. He devised a system of separating masses of dark and light by arranging a series of prominences on a plate that would transfer the ink to paper point by point. If the points were closely grouped, the mass would appear dark; the more distance between the points, the lighter the image. Ives perfected this half-tone process in 1886.[21]

The *Saturday Globe* was one of the early papers to capitalize on Ives's work. It was perhaps the first newspaper to print illustrations on a cylinder press and claimed to be the first five-cent newspaper to print a half-tone cut. The *Saturday Globe* was purportedly the first to cast a half-tone cut into a form instead of matrixing it—that is, using a formed, copper plate to mold a typeface—and claimed to be the first newspaper to print cartoons and half-tones in color. The newspaper's first color half-tone appeared 7 March 1896, vividly depicting an apartment-house fire on Genesee Street in Utica that claimed four lives. Cartoons—usually politically oriented—were first produced later that year. The color half-tones were produced by a new multicolor press the *Saturday Globe* had acquired early in 1896. One of the first of its kind in the nation, it stood eleven feet high, nine feet wide and twenty-seven feet long and could print four colors at one impression. It had a printing capacity of 4,000 newspapers per hour and required fifty composition rollers to distribute the different inks, usually red, blue, yellow, and black, or combinations thereof.[22]

Few expenses were spared in making the *Saturday Globe* a journalistic success, not only in its diversity of stories and the literary skill with which they were handled, but also in the newspaper's physical composition. Will DeVine, the newspaper's electrotyper from 1892 to 1914, recalled that Will Baker often spoke of having "the best-printed paper in the United States," and toward that end insisted on using the highest grade of paper stock.[23]

The division of the newspaper's operation that dealt with artwork also received considerable attention. The *Saturday Globe* periodically used pictures to accompany obituaries, as well as its news and feature stories. If a poor photograph was submitted, whether for an obituary or for editorial matter, retoucher Billy Burnett was responsible for fixing it. Obituaries were common fare in the pages of the *Saturday Globe*, and many were written in glowing praise of the deceased. While not all of the obituaries were as glorifying as one written about the father of a *Saturday Globe* cartoonist, his nonetheless demonstrates the style employed when reporting death: "The very many friends of Denis F. Howe, of No. 85 Mary Street, were shocked and grieved by the announcement of his death yesterday .... A better citizen Utica never contained. He was all that makes up the ideal neighbor and genial friend." Born in Tipperary, Ireland, Howe came to Utica in 1852. "Here he has remained, adding to his circle of friends and making happy those around him," the *Saturday Globe* noted in the obituary. With no pretense of objectivity, the newspaper called Howe one of the best tailors in the state, and noted, "So genial and equipose was his temperament that one who worked with him for fifteen years never saw it ruffled." The panegyric concluded, "Mr. Howe's domestic relations were exceptionally happy and no father prized his home or strove more to make it the abode of earthly bliss. He was a great newspaper reader and a man of superior intelligence. In religion he was a devoted Catholic and a worthy son of the church. In every relation he bore himself manfully, conscientiously and as becomes one who squares every action according to the golden rule."[24]

The *Saturday Globe*'s proprietors squared their editorial decisions according to the golden rule for success: If it works, don't change it. Throughout the 1890s, the newspaper's editorial fare remained faithful to the format and style that had catapulted the *Saturday Globe* into fame and fortune. In addition to printing off-beat stories and news briefs, the newspaper's editors exercised their penchant for displaying pictures of attractive women. Virtually any pretty singer or actress who performed at the Utica Opera House or any enchanting belle who appeared at a middling social affair was sure to have her countenance preserved for posterity in the pages of the *Saturday Globe*. Sometimes the newspaper didn't even lean on the pretense of 'news.' Beginning in 1889 and continuing for some years afterward, the weekly featured pictures of attractive young women, sometimes even as the featured page-one illustration, along with brief summaries of their lives and their physical descriptions. The delineation was never racy, although more attributes than the women's physiognomies were described. There was no "news value" in these pictures; they were simply a yellow-press technique for selling newspapers.

The *Saturday Globe*'s success was unmistakably built on a foundation of strange, exciting stories and striking illustrations, but to what extent was it manipulating its audience? Put another way, was the *Saturday Globe* a socially responsible newspaper? Newspapers of the era that pandered to sensationalism placed an "emphasis on emotion for its own sake" in an effort to appeal to people's prurient and base interests, historians Emery and Emery wrote. According to Mott, sensationalized stories "stimulate unwholesome emotional responses in the average reader," and offered as examples "detailed newspaper treatment of crimes, disasters, sex scandals, and monstrosities."[25]

In this sense, *sensationalism* is a pejorative denoting hostility toward a type of journalistic performance. The focus is more properly placed on readers, however. Sensational stories were calculated to arouse powerful curiosity, interest, and reaction by exaggerating the most graphic and lurid details, and readers often reacted with a medley of horror and fascination. Journalism history demonstrates that such editorial fare seems to peak when competition is especially keen. However, the twentieth century has deplored sensationalism in tandem with the development of the concept of social responsibility. This is an important modification on the traditional libertarian theory, because it establishes public right to information, right of access, and expectation that publishers will conduct their presses morally, with the best interests of the public at heart. As John Ferre accurately observed, journalism ethics has a heritage of emphasizing consequences rather than moral propriety. The emerging concept of social responsibility was designed to hold media barons to their fiduciary obligation, advanced by media practitioners during journalism's professionalization process, to serve the public as impartial experts in the commodity of news. As such, they violate their responsibility when they convey news that is libelous, inaccurate, biased or embellished.[26]

However, the *Saturday Globe*'s penchant for sensationalism can be defended as easily as it can be criticized, and allegations of insufficient social responsibility refuted as easily as they can be levied. Although written in an eloquent mode, the *Saturday Globe* was not aimed at the intellectual elite. It would be a difficult chore to establish any substantial circulation by targeting a newspaper to such an unrepresentative segment of nineteenth-century America. The Utica-based weekly instead was designed for the laboring and farming classes, the common-folk majority. These people enjoyed the newspaper not only as a source of news, but as a source of entertainment. They enjoyed reading of the accomplishments, tribulations, and peculiarities of others, not with the conscious desire for accounts that "stimulate unwholesome emotional responses," but because they sought entertainment and provocation for their imaginations. Stories about misery and affliction—like a child without bones or a four-year-old boy who suffered horribly and died after swallowing a huge quantity of strychnine pills—reminded the common people that their troubles, no matter how taxing, were less severe than those of some of their fellows. Stories of success and good fortune, like the Ohio multimillionaire who was a penniless vagrant until his twenties or the brothers who extricated gold worth $106,000 from a Northern California stream bed in less than two weeks, galvanized the average person's adventuresome spirit and showed that others have succeeded through skill, wit, or perseverance. For stories of more practical importance, such as tales of governmental abuses, miscarriages of justice and the more common "sob stories" of suffering individuals, families, and masses, sensationalism was designed to arouse emotions and stimulate action among the readership. But whatever the slant or purpose of the story, the *Saturday Globe* can only be considered sensational in that it mined the human-interest angle and infused breath and pulse into what otherwise would have been dry accounts of newsworthy events and conditions.

In addition to content, two other arguments may be posited to counter the scorn normally reserved for sensationalism. The first is the "Mother Goose" argument of Emery and Emery. "Just as the child ordinarily starts reading Mother Goose and fairy stories before graduating to more serious study," they wrote, the uncultured, rough-hewn public is more likely to prefer sensationalism for its subordination of intellectual challenge for emotional stimulation. Emery and Emery note that this pattern of employing sensationalism to tap a new, neglected public and indoctrinate them to newspaper reading had surfaced in the 1620s, the 1830s, the 1890s, and the 1920s.[27]

The second argument is the "economic determinism" view, which asserts that the social responsibility of the press, as a business, is to make money. Despite the highly public nature of journalism, a newspaper is a private enterprise, and a distinct one at that, for it is the only one to receive specific Constitutional protection—the First Amendment guarantees but does not define freedom of the press. As a private industry, free from public control, journalism technically has no public interest, and is in fact whatever its proprietors want it to be. According to a *Wall Street Journal* writer,

> A newspaper is a private enterprise owing nothing whatever to the public, which grants it no franchise. It is therefore affected with no public interest. It is emphatically the property of the owner, who is selling a manufactured product at his own risk ...

Thus, media power-wielders are at liberty to do whatever will yield them the greatest return on the product they submit for public consumption, provided they break no laws. Under the economic determinism theory, market forces, not self-censorship, should govern media content and regulate the degree to which newspapers engage in sensationalism.[28]

The *Saturday Globe*'s editorial course appears to have been charted according to the latter argument, as it experimented in its earliest years with a large cargo of staid political and economic news before seeking stories conducive to a level of emotional excitedness that would appeal to the widest and largest audience. The Bakers stopped short of the yellow journalism of Hearst and Pulitzer, but nonetheless qualified their brainchild as a member in good standing on the roster of sensationalistic newspapers.

Although the *Saturday Globe* filled its pages with respiring, sanguine stories throughout the 1890s, circulation slipped, slowly but inexorably. By 1896 it was down to 150,000, a decrease of 50,000 in about six years.[29]

In an effort to boost sagging circulation, the *Saturday Globe* ballyhooed the 16 March 1897 heavyweight title fight between James

J. Corbett and Robert Fitzsimmons in Carson City, Nevada. The purse was $15,000 and the stake $10,000. This was not the first major fight, nor would it be the last. Everyone knew there would be many more prizefights—boxing had become an American social institution. However, the 1897 Corbett-Fitzsimmons match was probably the biggest contest up to that time, and the press treated it accordingly. Legions of reporters descended on the small mountain capital of Carson City to give the highly-touted event a ride. Hearst, in the throes of a newspaper war with Pulitzer and his *New York World*, arranged with the respective fight managers to secure exclusive rights to all interviews, photographs, and signed statements for his *New York Journal* and *San Francisco Examiner*.[30]

The reigning champion was Corbett, a Californian who had held the heavyweight title since 1892, when he won it from the legendary John L. Sullivan in a twenty-one-round affair and defended it two years later with a three-round knockout of Charley Mitchell. Fitzsimmons, a balding Australian, was no neophyte to boxing titles either. He had been the world middleweight champion since 1891, but forfeited that crown, bypassed the light-heavyweight division, and added the requisite number of pounds for a crack at Corbett.[31]

The match was to be fought outdoors, which prompted concern about the weather, the *Saturday Globe* writer—although there are no telltale initials at the end of any of the boxing stories, it was almost surely Dickinson—noted in setting the scene for the pugilistic Armageddon:

> Probably every man in Carson City cast an anxious eye westward as the sun went down Tuesday evening. Every man was his own self-interested weather prophet, for on the condition of the skies next morning rested the fate of the greatest pugilistic contest ever fought. Should the day break bright and clear from 5,000 to 7,000 spectators would witness a fight to a finish between two men who were perhaps the two most magnificent specimens of physical manhood the world had ever seen. Larger men, men of greater stature, men of more muscular strength there had been, but probably no two men have ever yet combined the muscular strength, the nervous force, the agility, the endurance, the perfect physical culture which distinguished James J. Corbett and Robert Fitzsimmons. Either man was capable of running from six to ten miles without weariness; for either man it was pastime to tire out in wrestling or boxing bouts half a dozen burly trainers. Weariness for them was almost an impossibility. Each knew the fight of the morrow was to be the struggle of his life.[32]

Betting leaned toward Corbett at about ten to seven odds. Many bets were made but the total amount of money handled was paltry, as numerous bettors suspected the underdog Australian might upset the reigning heavyweight champ. Shortly before the fight, Sullivan himself appeared in the ring, "grown grey and fat since his last appearance in the ring," the writer noted. Although he had not had a title fight since Corbett swiped his crown five years earlier, Sullivan told the assembled throng, "I think there is one more fight left in me."[33]

Restricted merely to description of the event because of Hearst's monopoly on interviews, the *Saturday Globe* writer chronicled the fourteen bloody rounds in detail, providing a summary of the blows thrown and damage done in each stanza. Finally, the winner emerged:

> As the fourteenth began no man who had witnessed the fight so far could guess the winner. Bob was the worse punished but Corbett seemed the more tired. Corbett opened the round with a right and left lead which Fitz blocked. The Californian got in a left jab on Fitzsimmons' head but Bob returned it with a right swing which reached Corbett's neck. The Californian felt the blow and it probably dazed or rattled him, for when Fitz drew his right back and sent it out again for Jim's face the latter, instead of dodging sideways, threw his head and shoulders back to escape the blow, thus protruding his stomach and leaving it unguarded. Fitz saw the opportunity and seized it instantly. He sent his left glove forward and upward, reaching Corbett in the stomach just under the heart. The Californian went into the air and as he pitched forward Fitz plugged him on the jaw. Corbett dropped to his knees, toppled sideways and clutched the ropes to save himself from falling prone on the boards. His face was contorted with agony and the referee slowly counted him out.[34]

Fitzsimmons was not the only winner that week. It was coverage of this fight—not the more important stories (although some boxing fans may beg to differ) such as those about the Johnstown flood or later tales of the Spanish-American War, the devastation of Galveston, Texas, or the assassination of President William McKinley—that resulted in the *Saturday Globe*'s highest circulation in its history. The boxing match proved no more spectacular than the coverage the *Saturday Globe* afforded the event. The front page of its 20 March, 1897 issue bore a beautiful, half-page color illustration of the two pugilists, with insets of fight scenes from the boxing and gladiatorial worlds. A Maiden of Victory stood between the head-and-shoulder color photographs of the combatants, all with a background of a pink-and-purple hue. A total of twenty-four other fight-related illustrations graced the newspaper, interspersed throughout twenty-eight sidebar stories on such topics as injury reports; prospective challengers to Fitzsimmons' reign; hindsight analysis; the rigors and expense of training for a boxing match; brief sketches about the cornermen, referee, timekeepers, and others; and an account of how the beaten Corbett rushed into the ring several minutes after the fight ended, seeking to continue the battle. In all, the *Saturday Globe* devoted nearly three pages of the eight-page issue to the bout.

Providing additional incentive for readers to buy the 20 March issue was a major murder story sharing the front page with the fight. The headless body of what proved to be a Greencastle, Indiana, woman, Pearl Bryan, was found in tangled undergrowth near Fort Thomas, Kentucky, on 1 February 1896. Through canny detective work it was determined that the murderers were Bryan's boyfriend Scott Jackson and his college friend Alonzo Walling. Written by McCabe, who authored the Johnstown flood chronicles, the story recapped the murder, trial, and appeals and noted that the duo would hang the following day. That story warranted five pictures, four on the front page, for a page-one total of eight. The entire issue brimmed with fifty-five photographs and drawings, not counting those found in advertisements. Fueled by the nationwide interest in the Corbett-Fitzsimmons match, with the "headless body" story serving to further stimulate interest, circulation of the 20 March 1897 issue exceeded 294,000 and established itself as the zenith in the *Saturday Globe*'s forty-three-year history.[35]

Fitzsimmons declined Corbett's challenge to a rematch, claiming that he planned, according to his wife's wishes, to retire to a quiet family life. He apparently was unable to resist the lure of the prizefight ring, though, and at age thirty-seven attempted to defend his title against young James J. Jeffries in 1899 on New York's Coney Island. Fitzsimmons lost in eleven rounds, and also succumbed in the rematch three years later. He then retreated to the seemingly greener pastures of the light-heavyweight division, where he held the title from 1903 until 1905, when he was forty-three years old. Corbett never won another crown, losing heavyweight title fights to Jeffries in 1900 and 1903.[36]

Like Corbett, the *Saturday Globe* descended from its pinnacle. Despite several major turn-of-the-century stories, the newspaper was never again able to capture nearly so large an audience, and it began its slow, inexorable slide into the valley of mediocre circulations.

6
Adherence to the Formula

The 1897 Corbett-Fitzsimmons fight was the chief impetus for the *Saturday Globe*'s attainment of its circulation zenith, and its principals eagerly looked forward to the new century and the bright future it held for the newspaper. The Bakers' immediate goal was to eclipse the 300,000 mark in single-copy sales, but the prosperity the *Saturday Globe* had enjoyed since its inception inspired visions of a half-million circulation and beyond. In the years following the Corbett-Fitzsimmons fight, the editorial staff eagerly tackled major national stories and presented them by consistently applying the formulaic emotional excitement and low-wattage sensationalism that had catapulted the *Saturday Globe* to international prominence.

The first big story following the boxing match was the outbreak of war with Spain. The war's roots lie in Cuban soil. Beginning in February 1895, the island colony rose up against Spain in its struggle for independence. Fighting on the island was damaging United States investments in Cuba, estimated at $50 million, but it was more than the economic investments that caught Uncle Sam's sympathetic eye. Stories of Spanish butchery and cruelty were disseminated by Hearst's *Journal*, Pulitzer's *World*, and many other American newspapers. The humanitarian sentiment evoked by the mass press, and the inherent sympathy for underdog colonies battling for independence thoroughly ingrained in American culture and fostered by the press, prompted the executive and legislative branches in Washington to unite in support of Cuba. However, escalating tensions in the island nation meant increasing danger to U. S. citizens and property there. When riots broke out in Havana in December 1897, President McKinley sent the battleship *Maine* to Cuba.[1]

One of the tales calculated to demonstrate Spain's brutality that the *Saturday Globe* and many other newspapers printed in the prelude to war was the sad story of Evangelina Cisneros. The niece of Cuba's revolutionary president, she was sentenced to twenty years' imprisonment for attempting to liberate her uncle from an island penal colony with the aid of insurrectionist sympathizers. Reflecting the pervading antagonism toward Spain, the *Saturday Globe*'s account described the awful conditions at the Ceuta prison, where supporters of Cuban independence were incarcerated:

> The barbarity of Spanish methods in Cuba finds another exemplification in the case of Evangelina Betancourt Cisneros, a young and beautiful woman, and niece of President Cisneros y Betancourt, who heads the civil government of the insurgents in the jungles of Camaguay. Simply because she was in the Isle of Pines, where the outbreak of Cuban prisoners occurred, she was arrested and had now been tried in a military court . . .
>
> Doctors, lawyers and literary men of Havana break stone and shovel in the trenches shoulder to shoulder with murderers and robbers from the peninsula.
>
> They work in chains, keeping entire silence. A single word brings the lash of the guard down on the offender, and when the day's work on the stone pile is done he is triced up in the prison yard and flogged till he faints. They are fed on food that has become foul under the fearful heat of the African sun, and they are tortured, with all the ingenuity and ferocity imaginable, at the pleasure of their guards and governors . . .
>
> Fancy this young girl being subjected to such treatment as this and the worse fate which can only be hinted at for sympathizing with her own harried land and the cause for which every near male relative she had in the world was fighting.
>
> This girl is no Amazon to take the chances of war like a soldier; she is little more than a child in years, delicate and educated. She is not even a conspirator. She is as powerless to harm Spain as a babe in its mother's arms. If Spain must have her as a victim it would be better for the girl to be stood against a stone wall and shot to death than to be condemned to twenty years of such hideous shame and slavery.[2]

By the time the fifty-fifth United States Congress convened 6 December 1897, the press had developed a fascination for the ready-made sensationalism of the Spanish chronicles and generated enormous public support with its daily stories of atrocity. Competition for news of the Cubans' plight had become fierce, and teams of correspondents were sent to the region. Characteristic of the yellow press, many of the stories they filed were exaggerated, and purportedly eyewitness accounts were written by reporters who never set foot in Cuba. One observer noted of Hearst's New York *Journal*, "It soon became the fixed policy of the paper to exaggerate and misconstrue every military act of the Spanish commander in Cuba." Richard Harding Davis, one of Hearst's star employees who embraced sensationalism to the point that he regarded himself not a reporter but a "descriptive writer," resigned because of a fraudulent story.[3]

While stopping short of the flagrant fabrications appearing in Hearst and Pulitzer newspapers on a daily basis, the *Saturday Globe* joined other newspapers in magnifying anti-Spain public opinion. Announcing the commencement of the fifty-fifth Congress, the newspaper noted, "The Cuban horror still continues and the blood of murdered patriots cries to us for aid. This pitiful appeal rings in the ears of the national lawmakers and some there are who want to extend a friendly hand. Others object, not that they deem the cause unworthy, but on the selfish ground of personal safety."[4]

The newspaper war on Spain reached a climax in the wake of the *Maine* incident. While moored in her Havana anchorage 15 February, the ship exploded, killing 266 people. Culpability for the blast was never determined, although a U. S. naval board located convincing evidence that an explosion outside the hull, perhaps from a torpedo or mine, detonated in the ship's forward magazine. The Spanish government offered to submit the issue of its responsibility to arbitration, but the American public, whipped into a war frenzy by sensational press accounts of the blast and its antecedent events, lusted for a fight. "Remember the *Maine*, to hell with Spain!" became a popular slogan. Spain declared a truce 9 April, but Congress issued resolutions recognizing Cuba's right to independence, demanding Spain's withdrawal, authorizing President McKinley to use military force and refuting Spanish allegations that the motive behind American involvement was annexation of Cuba. Once Congress authorized intervention in Cuba, Spain broke diplomatic relations. This prompted the U. S. Navy to blockade Cuba 22 April and in retaliation Spain declared war two days later. The United States followed suit the next day.[5]

The fighting began in Manila Bay 1 May 1898, and from the outset it was pathetically one-sided. Commodore George Dewey led his squadron into the bay before dawn and sank the anchored Spanish ships. Remarkably, no Americans died, and only seven were slightly wounded. Headlines in the 7 May issue of the *Saturday Globe* resounded with unbridled excitement, "Dewey A Hero, A Marvel of the Century, The Most Glorious News America Ever Heard." The story, beneath a striking color illustration of the raging naval battle, continued, "GLORIOUS! Marvelous! The most magnificent naval triumph of all ages! A Spanish fleet destroyed, a city captured, from 300 to 400 Spaniards killed and yet not an American life is lost! Surely the God of hosts is protecting the men who fight under the

Stars and Stripes and who to-day, as in all times, battle in the cause of freedom, honor and justice."[6]

The balance of the front page was composed of official reports from Washington, several communications from an unnamed New York *World* correspondent (doubtless Edward W. Harden),[7] a story about the joyous reactions of Uticans and a glowing front-page editorial:

> The roar of Dewey's guns has been heard in every quarter of the globe and the echoes ring with praise of American valor and prowess. Spain's crushing defeat in Manila bay Sunday morning has sent a thrill of joy through the American people, foreshadows the inevitable result whenever Spaniard and American meet and increases the nations' respect for American sovereignty and greatness.
>
> It was a glorious achievement and Americans are proud of the victors—from the commodore to the coal heavers. It will fill a bright page in the history of sea warfare and will put Dewey's name on the roll of honor with heroes like Jones, Perry, Decatur and Farragut. His coaling station was a collier. His base of supplies was a transport. Neutrality proclamations were closing the ports all about him. His fleet was half way around the world from home. He must either capture Manila, suffer defeat or ignominiously turn his back on the foe and seek American waters for safety. American seamen have never shown the white feather and Dewey had no thought of doing so. Straight as an arrow from its bow, his fleet cut the waters between Hong Kong and Manila and then, in the darkness of midnight, boldly entered the enemy's harbor. Mines and torpedoes and shore batteries were ignored. At dawn he charged upon the Spanish fleet and in a storm of shot and shell from ships and forts pounded away until the death blow had been given.[8]

Inside pages presented a cornucopia of war-related stories, including a feature on Dewey's lieutenants, an anecdote about a "Dewey defeat" at the hands of a schoolteacher with whom a teenage Dewey picked a fight, and several stories about the 44th Separate Company, consisting of Utica men, situated at Camp Black, Hempstead, Long Island, New York. These men were impatient to fight, *Saturday Globe* staff writer George P. Reuter related. Longtime staff scribe McCabe penned a poem to honor "The Gallant Fourty-Fourth," and the *Saturday Globe* printed a story about Spanish ignorance, citing various stories in Spanish newspapers that make laughable assertions. *El Diario* contends that McKinley, an Ohioan, "is a naturalized Chinaman, having been born at Canton." Another Spanish newspaper referred to the U. S. Navy as consisting of a "few old vessels left over from the civil war of 1876 and clumsily plated with rusty boiler iron."[9]

By the end of July, 11,000 troops had arrived in the Philippines, and on 13 August they occupied Manila. After the Manila Bay victory, American attention turned to the Spanish fleet of four armored cruisers and three destroyers commanded by Admiral Pasqual Cervera. This fleet was located in Santiago Harbor, on Cuba's south coast. American naval forces blockaded the harbor entrance, while the Army closed in behind Cervera on land. On 3 July, Cervera led his squadron out of the harbor and tried to escape along the western coast, provoking the last significant battle of the Spanish-American War. The fight resulted in the beaching of all of Cervera's ships as they were burning or sinking. American casualties were few. Two weeks later the city of Santiago surrendered. For all intents and purposes, the war was over.[10]

MacKinley, however, was in no hurry to discharge the soldiers and sailors. Under a page-one color illustration of a mother, a wife, a sweetheart, and an employer all beseeching MacKinley to "Give Us Back Our Soldier Boys!" the *Saturday Globe* wrote with uncharacteristic terseness:

> They enlisted to fight for the United States flag in a war which was declared in the interest of humanity. The war is over. They have done their whole duty. Let them come home. For garrison and police duty men are needed. They are to be had by tens of thousands for the mere asking. Then why not muster out the wearied lads who have already sacrificed so much, and fill their places with others who are ready and anxious to go?

Treaty negotiations resulted in an agreement 12 August 1898 in which Spain pledged to allow Cuba its independence. It was all over four months later when Spain signed the 10 December 1898 Treaty of Paris, ceding Guam and Puerto Rico to the United States and transferring sovereignty over the Philippines to the United States for $20 million.[11]

The Gulf of Mexico was the scene of the next major American conflict, two years later. This time the enemy was not a foreign nation, it was Nature, and the attack launched on domestic shores was almost a complete surprise. On 8 September 1900, the Texas coastline was pounded by a vicious hurricane, which caused massive flooding. The storm leveled the island city of Galveston, causing about 6,000 deaths and more than $100 million in property damage. The 15 September *Saturday Globe* described the tragedy:

> This city to-day is a hospital and a morgue. Death is on every side. Suffering is on every hand. Grief, agony and despair are the feelings that

> torture human hearts, searing them as with tongues of flame .... The city you once knew is no longer familiar. It appears like some buried town that the sea through some mighty convulsion spat up from its depths. Its streets reek with mud and mire. Its buildings are washed away, or wrecked. Its people—many of them—are gone, killed in Saturday's awful visitation of combined hurricane and flood, or are being nursed back in temporary hospitals to better health, but never to forgetfulness of the scenes of elemental horror that almost wiped Galveston from the map of Texas.[12]

Dickinson and an artist named Townsend journeyed to the beleaguered city, as did reporters from a few other large newspapers. Other newspapers, such as the *Chicago American*, the *San Francisco Examiner*, and Hearst's *New York Journal*, made a spectacle of the disaster, sending relief trains that allowed them to engage in substantial self-promotion in their news columns.[13] It took Dickinson and Townsend days to make the 4,000-mile train trip, and as a consequence, Dickinson's account was not available until the 29 September issue. However, for *Saturday Globe* readers it was surely worth the wait. Dickinson used personification to convey the hurricane's destructive power:

> Our nostrils were repeatedly assailed by an overpowering and nauseating stench which could only emanate from putrefying carcasses and human bodies. The landscape was as level as a table, the flat prairie stretching as far as the eye could reach with scarcely an undulation. Here and there were ruined houses and outbuildings; many of them demolished; some of them still occupied by their suffering and impoverished owners. Trees were broken short off or were uprooted and lying prostrate. The hurricane which had ravaged Galveston and reveled in death in that ruined city had refused to be satisfied with its murderous orgy there, but had swept inland and like a malicious demon had not spared the homes of the poor farmers or the negro cabins. For mile after mile, for hundreds of miles, it had swept on, a devouring, destroying monster, slaying and wrecking to the last vestige of its Titanic strength.[14]

Galveston was under martial law, which gave military personnel extraordinary discretionary powers, including shooting on sight those who endeavored to rob the dead and destroying private property to prevent anyone from photographing the city's devastation. Nonetheless, Dickinson brought his camera and was busy snapping pictures of the ruined city when he ran afoul of a soldier, who fired a bullet through Dickinson's camera plates. Dickinson's cunning prevailed, though—the shattered plates were decoys. He had hidden the real negatives in another pocket. These yielded forty-five photographs in the 29 September issue of the *Saturday Globe*.[15]

The same issue carried Dickinson's account of his and Townsend's arrival in Galveston, an experience that caused the longtime newsman to suffer a brief crisis of religious faith:

> We step upon the wretched dock and stand appalled for a few minutes at the sight which meets our gaze. To the right, wreckage; in front, ruin; to the left, devastation! Our hearts sink within us and there arises a rebellious thought against a Providence which permits such things. How does the merciful God permit the elements which He holds in the hollow of His hand to thus torture and slay poor humanity and render as worse than nothing the harvest of our weary toil?
>
> Then the answer comes.
>
> We look about us. We see a great ship discharging her cargo amid the wreckage on the dock. We see hundreds of men with carts and drays loading their vehicles with this cargo. We go nearer and we see that the cargo is made up of canned meats, vegetables, bread, biscuits, coffee, fruits, clothing, medicines—nourishment and raiment for the afflicted. We realize that this vast store of supplies comes from the pitying people of the world; from people whose hard, commercial, money-grasping hearts have been softened and made to pulsate with love and sympathy and charity. We see Sisters of Charity, Salvation Army lassies, Red Cross nurses—women with the Christ-look in their faces. We see men hurrying hither and thither on errands of mercy. On hundreds of breasts we see pinned badges bearing the legends "I.O.O.F. Relief," "Red Men's Relief," "Royal Arcanium Relief" and many others of this noble kindred.
>
> The answer has come. The rebellious spirit in our hearts melts and gives place to reverence for the Divine Being who thus through tragedy to the few makes God-like the many.[16]

This spiritual reconciliation with "a Providence which permits such things" as the Galveston disaster underscores the press emphasis on moralism inherited from the colonial press. Early-American journalists like Benjamin Franklin and William Goddard viewed the purveyance of moral instruction as essential to the social utility of printing. This view survived in different forms through most of the nineteenth century, but by the onset of the twentieth century had been replaced by notions of objectivity, that reporters should gather and transmit facts with scientific precision and detachment. Famed muckraker Lincoln Steffens advocated that reporters should "start out with blank minds and search like detectives for the keys to the mystery, the clews to the truth," an absolute, objective reality that would thus be achieved "scientifically." This repudiation of subjectivity and pursuit of truth as a commodity to be ferreted out and presented to the public in its pristine purity was revolutionizing journalism in the early twentieth century, but in no way was this reflected in Dickinson's Galveston coverage, or more generally, the *Saturday Globe*'s journalism. Its dogged reliance on the tried-and-true was as firm as it was imprudent.[17]

A Kansas woman wielded her moralism like an ax, chopping her way into history by raiding saloons from San Francisco to New York armed with a hatchet and a zealous determination to combat the evils of alcohol. Carry Amelia Moore was born in Garrard County, Kentucky, 25 November 1846, and married Dr. Charles Gloyd in 1867. He proved to be an alcoholic, a condition that made married life intolerable for her. Pregnant and frightened, she left him after several months, permanently embittered against liquor. Gloyd died six months later of delirium tremens. Carry's sister experienced similar misfortune, as that woman's husband was "ruined by drink," causing him to squander a $150,000 fortune in several years. Carry remarried in 1877, this time to David Nation, a lawyer, minister, and editor of the *Warrensburg Journal*. However, her seething disdain for alcohol never waned, but seemed to increase in intensity, culminating in her vow of "saving men from a drunkard's grave."[18]

In 1891, while living in Medicine Lodge, Kansas, she began her campaign against saloons in Kansas, a state in which alcohol consumption had been banned since 1880. She construed the illegality of saloons flourishing there to mean that anyone could destroy them without penalty. A formidable woman of 175 pounds on a six-foot frame, she entered saloons dressed in black and white garb, sang hymns, prayed, preached, knocked men's drinks from their hands, and smashed bar fixtures and liquor supplies. Arrested and fined repeatedly, she relinquished her vow for a few years, but revived it in 1901, extending the geographic scope of her surprise attacks on bars to cover the entire state. It was in a Wichita watering hole that she first wielded her trademark hatchet. The *Saturday Globe* reported the resurrection of her crusade, noting, "Kansas has a new form of cyclone. It is the fury of a woman whose opposition to the liquor traffic amounts to hatred for all who are engaged in it and who, impelled, as she declares, by a divine command, is sweeping through the State, leaving wrecked saloons in her path." The cyclone also left a wrecked marriage in its wake, as Carry's husband divorced her on the grounds of desertion the same year.[19]

Jailed for breaking and entering, she agreed to meet with

Dickinson in her prison cell. He wrote in the first-person style with which he was so comfortable, relating the details of his trip to Kansas and the broad spectrum of comments made to him about Carry Nation by those he met on the way. Dickinson wrote bemusedly of Nation's prating and fierce, if overzealous, conviction, and lamented his powerlessness to control the pace and direction of the interview. "I'm merely an instrument in His hand," Nation told Dickinson, calling saloons "murder shops." Dickinson observed, "had she been willing, she could have had her liberty, but she refused to furnish bail and promise to keep the peace." She eventually did post bail and made many return trips to prisons across the country, each time paying her fines from lecture-tour fees and souvenir-hatchet sales, at times earning as much as $300 per week.[20]

Nation damaged saloons on both coasts, and at many places in between, building up a small but loyal army of followers. Her oft-told tale about the woes of life married to an alcoholic made many young women suspicious of their beaus and drove a few to paranoia. The *Saturday Globe* told the tale of one such female at the height of Nation's crusade:

> Allentown, Pa., June 22—Because her fiance treated his prospective father-in-law to a glass of beer, Rose Shoemaker, of this city, jilted Charles E. Clewell an hour before the time set for the wedding.
>
> When Clewell went to the Court House with Miss Shoemaker's father to get a marriage license he invited his companion to have a drink. The two had a glass of beer apiece and then separated.
>
> A few nights later when Clewell called at the house for his bride she said she had changed her mind. When pressed for the reason she told Clewell that she would not marry a young man who would buy beer for his father-in-law, and that it was useless for him to try to persuade her, as the wedding had been declared off.[21]

Within a few years Nation was old news, and slowly faded from the limelight. Perhaps the best summary of the reasons for her failure to effect measurable social change during her day is found in a brief 1908 *Saturday Globe* item. "Redoubtable Carrie [sic] Nation, of hatchet fame, called on Judge William H. Taft Thursday at his home in Cincinnati. She wished to talk temperance and began one of her harangues but Mr. Taft very courteously declined to enter into any argument. Carrie breaks into public notice ever [sic] so often, but her extreme methods have robbed her of whatever influence for good she ever possessed." However, she is credited with creating the climate for public opinion leading to enactment of the Eighteenth Amendment, which established Prohibition in 1920, nine years after her death.[22]

Another person in the same decade armed with a cause was Leon Czolgosz, but he carried out his mission in a more destructive manner than Nation and, as a result, enjoyed a considerably shorter lifespan. William McKinley had earned his second presidential term by soundly defeating William Jennings Bryan for the second time. Shortly after his reelection, McKinley made a public appearance at the Pan-American Exposition in Buffalo, New York, on September 6, 1901. Much to the crowd's delight McKinley agreed to shake hands with all who wished to greet him. At the rear of the line was Czolgosz, a swarthy, diminutive man of twenty-eight, his right hand hidden by a bandage. He was a resident of West Seneca, a Buffalo suburb, and was known to area police as a dangerous anarchist.

Born in Detroit, Czolgosz eventually landed a job in a Cleveland wire mill, where he was attracted to radical doctrine. Anarchism began as an outgrowth of the same Utopian theory of socio-economic parity and free love that had produced the Oneida Community and other communal societies. Anarchists envisioned perfect economic equality for all, but eventually came to view governmental leaders as enemies of the working class by perpetuating the separation of rich and poor. Anarchists rationalized the removal of powerful personages by violent means, leading to the assassination of Empress Elizabeth of Austria in September 1898 and King Humbert of Italy in July 1900. As he neared the President, Czolgosz kept his head lowered so that no police standing near McKinley would recognize him. As the chief executive smiled mechanically and extended his hand to Czolgosz, the anarchist removed a pistol from beneath his phony bandage and fired. The first shot ricocheted off a button, but the second found its mark—McKinley's abdomen. John Parker, who was next in line to meet McKinley, leveled the assassin with a blow to the head before Czolgosz could fire a third shot, and police immediately seized and pummeled him. McKinley, who had remained conscious, said feebly, "Be easy with him, boys,"[23]

The lead story of the 14 September *Saturday Globe* contained few facts about the incident, for everyone in the country already knew the grim details. Instead, it passionately conveyed the sorrow precipitated by the blasts and adopted the same hopeful tone for McKinley's full recovery it had employed after the shooting of Garfield nearly twenty years before:

> Buffalo, Spt, 13—To the Milburn residence in this city, where the President of the United States is triumphing over death, the eyes of a sympathetic world are to-day directed.
>
> Not so long since the people of the universe bent their gaze toward the McGregor cottage at Saratoga, where the magnanimous Grant met his

only conqueror; and to Elberon-by-the-Sea, where the martyr Garfield breathed his last; and now civilization pauses in its work of development to catch the sounds that flow from the Nation's sick chamber in this city. Within the walls of this now historic mansion, a national wound, as deadly as sin and treachery and betrayal can make it, hangs in the balance of incompleted tragedy. Here the distinguished victim of a Judas deed is slowly recovering from the assassin's murderous assault; here with calm, sweet face, but with a heart bleeding at every pore and a soul steeped in the bitter sorrow of wounded affection, is the tender, sympathetic, delicate wife pouring forth her grief and hope in tears and prayers; here are gathered in sympathetic sorrow the members of the President's official family, their hearts torn with grief and anxiety, their minds stupified by the revolting and devilish atrocity; here are assembled in the inner and sacred circle of affection the victim's closest friends, whose every remembrance of the kind acts and words of the sufferer through years of unvarying consideration places an additional burden on their hearts; here are centered the thoughts, the sympathy, the hopes of a people, who mourn with a personal sense of loss and mingle with their feelings of respect and reverence for the President their admiration and regard for the citizen and man. Here, too, patriotism bows its head in shame and indignation; manhood shudders at the depth of infamy to which a creature can descend; religion mourns over the violation of Heaven's divine injunction and justice weeps over the hell-inspired crime that can lend even to blackness a darker hue.[24]

But newspaper readers spent their nickel on more than a verbose front-page encomium. The page was dominated by a thrilling color illustration of the scene of the crime at the instant Czolgosz fired the second shot. The picture is drawn from a description of the incident provided by an eyewitness. Other stories include a call to oust George Wellington of Maryland from the U. S. Senate because of uncomplimentary remarks he made about his longtime enemy McKinley after the assassination (p. 4); a review of the fallen President's life and political career (p. 8), an amusing story of how visitors to the Pan-American Exposition located Parker several days after the shooting and bought swatches of his clothing as souvenirs, netting Parker a tidy profit (p. 4); a recapitulation of the stories of the Lincoln and Garfield assassinations (p. 6); the revelation that Czolgosz carried a newspaper clipping in his wallet about the methods used by the anarchist who assassinated King Humbert (p. 4); and an attempt at explanation of Czolgosz's motives for shooting the President (p. 1). The latter story perceptively notes:

The assassination of the President was a blow aimed not at the man, but at the magistrate. It was not the individual, but the authority vested in him that gave offense, and thus the bullets of the assassin were directed at our system of government and at every citizen of the United States.

The unreasoning fury of the assassin blinded him to the fact that even if the President fell, the republic would endure, unchanged. Theoretically, it would not affect the perpetuity of the republic if the President, Vice President and members of the cabinet ceased to be. Reorganization, peaceful and orderly, would be effected and a new executive head, clothed in full constitutional power, would be given to the nation ...

One vision only filled his brain, one passion ruled his heart, one impulse possessed his mind, one idea swayed his intellect, one vitiated determination consumed his soul. That was to strike a blow that history would commemorate. It mattered not how innocent the victim; it mattered not how infamous the act, provided it were immortal.[25]

Eight days after he was shot, McKinley died of gangrene of the pancreas, although some believed that inferior medical care was as much to blame for the President's death as the gunshot wound. A surgeon who operated on McKinley recalled that lighting in the operating room was poor, that no one in surgery wore caps or gauze, and that the wound was not drained, thereby creating a medium for infection.[26]

Czolgosz had apparently found inspiration in the yellow-press attacks on McKinley, for they confirmed in the anarchist's mind that the President was the enemy of workers and must be removed by any means necessary. According to the *Saturday Globe* and many other anti-Hearst newspapers, Czolgosz had been particularly influenced by Hearst's seething editorials that excoriated McKinley. The most vicious, printed on 10 April 1901, declared, "If bad institutions and bad men can be got rid of only by killing, then the killing must be done." and this startling quatrain, printed in the wake of Kentucky Governor-elect William Goebel's assassination:

The bullet that pierced Goebel's breast
Can not be found in all the West;
Good reason, it is speeding here
To stretch McKinley on his bier.[27]

The *Saturday Globe* and other journalistic enemies of Hearst published reports that when Czolgosz shot McKinley, he carried in his pocket a copy of the *Journal* in which the quatrain was published. This was a fabrication, but once created it was reproduced throughout the country, prompting patriotic and business organizations to boycott Hearst newspapers in New York, Chicago, and San Francisco. Previous calls to reject the scurrility of the yellow press, such as this one in the *New York Times*, were unsuccessful: "If every reputable citizen would refuse to purchase sheets that thrive on the assassination of character and the degradation of taste, they would soon cease to be profitable to their owners, and their business of debauching public morals and making criminals would come to an end." The boycott had not been the first time public censure was threatened for Hearst's journalism in particular, but it became the most effective with the encouragement of many of the largest newspapers and the unspoken blessings of the new President, Theodore Roosevelt. In his first speech to Congress, he reviled "the reckless utterances of those who, on the stump and in the public press, appeal to the dark and evil spirits of malice and greed, envy and sullen hatred. The wind is sowed by the men who preach such doctrines, and they cannot escape their share of responsibility for the whirlwind that is reaped."[28]

Hearst defended himself and his "reckless utterances," writing, "From coast to coast this newspaper has been attacked and is being attacked with savage ferocity by the incompetent, the failures of journalism, by the kept organs of plutocracy heading the mob .... One of the Hearst paper's offenses is that they have fought for the people, and against privilege and class pride and class greed and class stupidity and class heartlessness with more daring weapons, with more force and talent and enthusiasm than any other newspapers in the country." To publicly assert his patriotism, Hearst changed the name of his *Morning Journal* to the *American*, but his prolonged assaults on McKinley cost him not only substantial circulation after the shooting, but also the political backing of conservative Democrats, who supported the Republican McKinley's approach to enforcing the Sherman Antitrust Act and did not believe Hearst's editorial vituperation was justified. This dampened Hearst's own political prospects, including his aspiration for the Democratic nomination for President.[29]

Nine days after McKinley's death, Czolgosz, whom the *Saturday Globe* called a "reptile in human form" upon presenting his photograph to its readers, was tried and convicted. He said nothing in his own defense, not even to his court-appointed lawyers, and refused to take the stand. His only comments were that he was not sorry for the deed, which he perpetrated for the working classes. On 29 October he died in the electric chair at Auburn Prison in Auburn, New York. After the electrocution, sulfuric acid was poured on the assassin's corpse, causing it to decompose within hours. McKinley's successor, Vice President Theodore Roosevelt, thereafter ordered the Secret Service to assume complete responsibility for guarding himself and all future presidents.[30]

In the *Saturday Globe* issue following the anarchist's execution, the newspaper vented all of its editorial wrath upon the disdained Czolgosz. In doing so, it gave editorial form to the public outrage that had marked the assassination. "Unrepentant, unforgiving and unforgiven, the miserable wretch died. He spurned the offices of a clergyman and declared that he wanted no church services over his body and no one to pray for his soul. He died as he had trained himself to live—hating law, defying God and scorning society." The weekly described how Czolgosz "slothfully" dragged his feet while being led to the electric chair. When he tripped, it was because "he was apparently too lazy and indifferent to raise his feet in stepping. His whole demeanor conveyed the impression that he was either in reality or in simulation, a listless, lolling, shambling fool." The article, written by Thomas H. Curry, noted, "Now that he is dead, and every vestige of his remains obliterated, he will no doubt be considered as one of the most remarkable, as well as one of the most despicable criminals in the history of the world."[31]

Two years later, one of the most famous boxers in the history of pugilism captured headlines. James J. Jeffries, who wrested the heavyweight crown from Bob Fitzsimmons, prepared for his fifth title defense. This time Jeffries' opponent was James J. Corbett, the man Fitzsimmons had beaten six years earlier in the bout that was instrumental in yielding the *Saturday Globe*'s loftiest circulation ever. The unprecedented fifth defense in four years caused the *Saturday Globe* to comment, "The wheels that grind out heavyweight championship fights have moved faster since Jim Jeffries in 1899 became champion of the big fellows than during the reign of any other champion since the Marquis of Queensberry rules were adopted by American heavy-weights." Jeffries knocked out Corbett in the tenth round with two lefts to the stomach and a right to the jaw. The *Saturday Globe* reporter in San Francisco covering the fight opened his story, "James J. Jeffries demonstrated last night his invincibility as the heavy-weight champion pugilist of the world."[32]

In 1906 another heavyweight came to San Francisco, but was not nearly as welcome as a pugilistic battle. San Francisco had suffered damage from severe earthquakes in 1836, 1838, 1865, and 1868, but they were nothing compared with what occurred at 5:13 A.M. 18 April 1906, when the rocky masses of the San Andreas Fault, the largest fracture in the Earth's crust, heaved violently with a force of six million tons of TNT, ravaging San Francisco. The cataclysmic earthquake was followed by a fire that ravaged the city's center and burned until 21 April, when the ashes were dampened by rain. Four square miles in the center of town—about 500 city blocks—disappeared. Approximately 500 people and 28,000 buildings were incinerated or crushed. As many as 250,000 people were left homeless, and the city sustained about $500 million in property damage. Hyman Levy was one of the survivors of that disaster. "I was only four," he said. "It was about 5 in the morning and it was dark outside," then "the whole Earth shook. I was thrown out of bed and across the room. My father and I ran outside and the whole city was burning."[33]

The disaster had crippled postal service in the San Francisco area, causing newspaper editors to become frantic for pictures, Hearst's New York *American* use a retouched photograph of a 1904 Baltimore fire, which other newspapers gleefully proclaimed fraudulent. As the story of the calamity was being transmitted over the wire, the *Saturday Globe* editors knew their newspaper also would have to rely on guile if pictures were to accompany the story, because the news-service photographs sent by mail would not arrive in time for the next issue. With increasing importance placed on illustrating the news as a means of helping to tell the story and attracting readers, a news event as important as the San Francisco earthquake required a picture. Heroics were needed in a hurry, and Denis Howe was up to the task. The veteran *Saturday Globe* artist requested to see the wire story about the ravaged city he had loved so much but had only visited several times. After reading details of the damage, he created a color illustration based on his recollections of San Francisco, which the much-relieved editors displayed as the principal front-page artwork. It was not until after the issue was printed that the *Saturday Globe* brain trust received a pleasant surprise. The photographs of the damage arrived and bore a striking resemblance to Howe's conception.[34]

Howe was born in Utica 9 November 1869 and attended the same Assumption Academy that had produced the Bakers a generation earlier. After graduation Howe was hired by the *Saturday Globe* about 1888 and, except for a military hitch during the Spanish-American War, remained with the newspaper until about 1911. He later served as secretary of the Utica and Jamestown, New York, chambers of commerce, a social worker for the United States Ordinance Department, director of Americanization for the United States Department of the Interior, and managing editor of a weekly newspaper in Jamestown. Howe's daughter Sally Luther recalled him as "a remarkable man, as near perfect as any I've ever known." Upon Howe's death on 6 January 1947, he was eulogized by his old friend Paul Williams, editor of the *Utica Daily Press*, as a "simple, unassuming man, who started 30 years ago on the hard job of trying to promote his community. He had a mind which looked forward to include all kinds of people, so he was eventually made secretary of the Chamber of Commerce. He was professionally a good newsman of his generation—that of 40 years ago. He did well for his town when he knew it, in much harder days."[35]

During Howe's years with the *Saturday Globe*, the newspaper reported some peculiar stories, especially around the turn of the century. The following are some of the *Saturday Globe*'s many interesting tales of the era:

- Mrs. Lena M. Lillie sent a list of 13,000 reasons to the U. S. Supreme Court explaining why she should not be sentenced to life in prison. The David City, Nebraska, woman was convicted of murdering husband Harvey Lillie by shooting him while he slept, despite her claim that a mysterious intruder perpetrated the deed. Her list embraced four large volumes. The *Saturday Globe* reported that her list consisted of insignificant glances and inflections she observed during the trial. "Every minor happening, every look, word and gesture that occurred in the court-room where the famous trial took place is declared by Mrs. Lillie to have worked to her disadvantage and finally brought about the verdict which resulted in her conviction."[36]
- An elderly judge and his wife traveled to frozen Alaska in search of a son who had left home in 1875, twenty-eight years earlier, and from whom nothing had been heard since. After exhausting all possibilities to find the son, the parents consulted a spiritualist, who correctly identified the particular region of Alaska, and the son was located.[37]
- Although most traces of the Victorian era had faded by the twentieth century's eighth birthday, a few relics remained, notably in Providence, Rhode Island, where the mayor sought to levy a tax on bachelors who were more than twenty-five years old in an effort to induce them to matrimony.[38]

The newspaper also printed a front-page photo that would be considered shocking even today. In 1898, the *Saturday Globe* printed a photograph of a severed head to accompany its story on the solution of the mystery surrounding the identity of the decapitated victim. The head, which belonged in life to Emma Gill of Southington, Connecticut, was found by several boys playing on the bridge over the Yellow Mill pond in East Bridgeport, Connecticut. The spied several wrapped packages in the water, which contained the head and various parts of the mutilated body. The gruesome head, resting on a white pillow, appeared on the front page, merely as illustration for the story. The newspaper offered no explanation or apology for printing the startling photograph, but if this represented a policy change at the *Saturday Globe* it was a short-lived one, as succeeding issues never again rose (or sunk) to such a level of ghastliness.[39]

Such macabre matter was uncharacteristic for the *Saturday Globe*, which built an international following through its superb artwork, its expressions of irrepressible excitement, its presumption to claim detailed knowledge of people's emotions and its embellishment of facts. Despite these attributes of sensationalism, the newspaper had stubbornly resisted pandering to the prurient and gratifying the public's dark fascination with horror and gore. It forswore the shocking and scandalous for the merely eccentric and intriguing. The *Saturday Globe*'s human-interest stories were fashioned to provide innocent entertainment and produce dignified yet passionate responses. The *Saturday Globe* applied this editorial philosophy to the nation's events for decades.

It was this adherence to formula, however, both in the presentation and selection of stories, which caused the *Saturday Globe* to founder. The new century brought substantial social changes: the progress of science and technology, along with the democratization of politics and the influence of the diverse cultural forms introduced by immigration, weakened the hold of Puritanism on the American mind. The public broke away from Victorian delicacy and experimented with new social conventions and personal beliefs, as the doctrine of tolerance for difference began to supplant expectations of conformity to established norms and values. As national and international events became more complex, and as advertising exceeded its role of simply providing commercial information and entered the realm of persuasion (thus giving rise to the field of public relations), American readers sought more news, presented with an emphasis on fact. While the reading public changed, the *Saturday Globe* remained stagnant in the years preceding World War I, applying its omnibus, sensational formula to a series of major stories as circulation fell.

7

Increasing Competition and Declining Fortunes

The prewar years of the twentieth century brought about a continuation of the social changes inspired by science and wrought by technology. These, in turn, had a dramatic effect on journalism. As media historian Willard Bleyer observed of that period:

> The rapid pace and high nervous tension everywhere manifested in American urban life affected the character of newspapers. The average person spent only from twenty minutes to half an hour in reading a newspaper. Hundreds of thousands of men and women in large cities read papers in the midst of the distracting conditions of subway and surface cars and suburban trains. Newspapers, therefore, found it advantageous to present news so that it could be read at a glance. Display headlines, condensed news reports, illustrations, and other devices to aid the rapid reader were accordingly adopted.[1]

Technology had not changed people, but it did alter their reading habits and needs. In the midst of a fast-paced and increasingly urban society, Americans had grown accustomed to frenzied action and apparently wanted this reflected in their newspapers. The organizational and technical structure of business and industry were in constant flux, vigorously upgrading production methods to satiate a burgeoning consumer culture, while transportation and communication modes were becoming more rapid and more diverse. People had less time to read the newspaper and thus sought more concision, larger type, and simpler writing than had ever been asked or expected of the press. This was a clientele the *Saturday Globe* was not designed to serve. Throughout its nineteenth-century existence the paper was intended for leisurely reading by the worker enjoying a weekend respite, perusing the *Saturday Globe* chiefly for entertainment and possible conversation topics. As such, reading the *Saturday Globe* was designed to be a form of entertainment in itself, whereas market forces were demanding that newspapers serve as a tool, a means to some other purpose. Faced with more choices of how to spend their leisure hours, readers began turning to newspapers more to provide them information about those choices rather than to serve as one.

Reporters and editors encouraged this concept of "using" the newspaper. They developed a rebirth of the public-service ideology that had lain comparatively dormant for more than half a century. Members of news staffs began to find a higher purpose to their work, envisioning themselves more as guardians of the public interest than puppets in the industry-wide grasp for escalating readership that was the underpinning of sensationalism. As more journalists became college-educated and developed an admiration for the clarity of the physical and social sciences, they, along with their readers, began to pine for the pristine precision of facts and realism. Lincoln Steffens was a graduate student in a German psychological laboratory, where he learned "the discipline, the caution, and the method of the experimental procedure of modern science," which he later applied to his reporting. Newspaper writers since the penny-press era were more akin to literary figures than journalists, more crafters of prose than recorders of reality. Since the development of the modern concept of the reporter in the 1830s, these journalistic foot-soldiers had spent more than half a century serving the political and economic purposes of their employers, from party bosses to profit-driven publishers. However, as a new century unfolded, journalists experienced a renaissance of the public-service ideology that had first surfaced in the American press during the mid-eighteenth century. By donning the mantle of public service, reporters reconceptualized their social role, transforming it from that of entertainer to information agent. Facts changed from being incidental to stories, present merely as a literary device to advance the narrative, to a position of supreme importance. The collection and transmission of facts to convey reality to readers and to help them make political, environmental, social and lifestyle choices came to justify the entire existence of the press.[2]

These changes had several manifestations. First, for reporters to be recognized and legitimized as fact-brokers, they needed special training. Vocational education in journalism and printing is a centuries-old tradition in both Europe and America, as prospective mass communicators received on-the-job training through the apprenticeship system. In colonial America, the training of youths through the apprenticeship system was essential to the stability and continuity of the early-American printing trade. Beginning at a young age, apprentices commonly spent up to seven years as unpaid laborers bound by contract. They usually had to promise not to gamble, marry, fornicate, frequent taverns, buy and sell, or divulge secrets of the business. They worked long hours, often performed menial tasks and were subjected to beatings—all without pay. Benjamin Franklin recalled that when he was apprenticed to his older brother James, "my Brother was passionate & had often beaten me." Yet apprentices endured the arduous existence because it held for them the promise of eventual self-employment. Their goal was to learn a craft that they could practice when their apprenticeship expired. The apprenticeship system was essential to the growth of the early-American press, for this means of vocational education replenished and augmented the craft's practitioners and enabled the "art" (special skill) and "mystery" (special knowledge) of printing to be passed on from one generation to the next.[3]

However, journalists in the late nineteenth and early twentieth centuries required a more formal, systematic mode of instruction than the centuries-old apprenticeship system, which by the late nineteenth century was virtually obsolete. To be transmitters of facts, which had become treasured commodities in a society weary of sensationalism and fakery, reporters like Steffens required scientific precision. The process by which scientific logic and measurements became interwoven in popular culture closely paralleled the rise of the modern university in the late nineteenth century. Thus, for reporters to convey reality to their audiences, they had to observe, select, test, measure, and describe facts with scientific objectivity, a skill that could best be developed through the academic discipline of a university education. Just as society sought impartiality and truth from the press, it sought authority from universities. These became sources of "nonpartisan expertise and technical know-how," as well as the origin "to which practitioners trace the theoretical basis of knowledge upon which they establish authority," according to Burton Bledstein. Universities found substantial social legitimacy by gradually assuming the responsibility, previously held by professional organizations, for providing and testing vocational training. In addition, they also offered the catholic education no professional group could supply. Part of that education involved the application of rigorous scientific standards of method and procedure, which universities espoused to students and successfully rendered credible to the American public. Neither proved to be difficult tasks in the increasingly complicated and diverse society of the late nineteenth and early twentieth centuries, for "science established a rational and orderly process of development beneath the fragmented experiences of American life," Bledstein wrote. "It revealed hard, documentable realities within the fluid American environment; it bolstered the self-certainty of the specialist which only the foolhardy would dare contest; it separated the professional expert who defined the limits of the possible in a given social instance from the amateur reformer who wished to make the entire world over by moralizing every issue."[4]

Reporters became the "specialists" and "professional experts" in the science of facts. They clothed themselves in the raiment of objectivity, a concept that emphasizes reportorial detachment and neutrality while constructing a formidable barrier between tangible facts and fickle opinions. In tracing the origins of the concept to the beginning of the twentieth century, British press critic Anthony Smith wrote that objectivity "was the remnant of reality left behind when the reader had been protected from the one-sided truths of the press agent and the double-edged truths of the politician." Sociologist Gaye Tuchman concluded that journalists use the concept as a bulwark against critics. "Attacked for a controversial presentation of 'facts,' newspapermen invoke their objectivity almost the way a Mediterranean peasant might wear a clove of garlic around his neck to ward off evil spirits." Schudson claimed that objectivity came to mean that "a person's statements about the world can be trusted if they are submitted to established rules deemed legitimate by a professional community." As such, facts are not components of reality, but rather statements which are deemed factual, and thus "truthful," by consensus.[5]

The chief method by which twentieth-century journalists appealed to this haven of consensus is by following established codes of conduct that are supported within the profession. These formal rules, which emerged around the beginning of the twentieth century and endure as newsroom norms a century later, usually serve as exoneration from criticism. They include:

1. The presentation of conflicting assertions of the truth;
2. The use of attribution and quotation marks to indicate that opinions expressed in the story belong to others than the reporters;
3. The presentation of supplementary evidence to support what is presented as fact;
4. The presentation of the most important material at the beginning of the story.

Although recent scholarship has indicated that these codes of conduct are riddled with inherent problems and inconsistencies,[7] these practices were integral to public reconceptualization of journalism as an important force for social good and journalists as impartial experts in the brokerage of facts. These journalistic mores, coupled with the development of display headlines, bylines, modular layout, and shorter stories designed to be read more quickly, constituted sweeping changes in journalism. The industry-wide changes to accommodate the new breed of newspaper reader were foreign to the *Saturday Globe* until its last, gasping years, when a new editor under new ownership tried to infuse the weekly with big-city display methods in a futile effort to save it from the newspaper graveyard.

The *Saturday Globe* under Dickinson and the Bakers was slow to adapt to the changing needs of readers and the changing role and appearance of the American newspaper. As early as the late nineteenth century, other newspapers altered their headline style from the single-column format of layered decks to larger, darker headlines spanning several columns, and even the entire page for major stories, in the escalating efforts to attract readers' roving eyes. The *Saturday Globe* did not make this change until the 1910s, preferring to retain the practice of separating headlines for major stories into three or more vertical sections, or tiers, with smaller yet slightly bolder typeface and more lines per tier as the layers descend. Headlines are the expressions of the editor's emotional excitement, and the *Saturday Globe* played them like the beating of a drum. Whereas modern newspapers use larger headlines for more important stories, such stories were signaled in the *Saturday Globe* by an increased number of tiers. Its headlines were often written in a highly subjective manner guaranteed to provoke excitement and curiosity, thus retaining its link to sensationalism in an era when that mode of journalism had fallen out of fashion.

Bylines were uncommon until well into the twentieth century because "the by-line gave the reporter greater authority in relation to the copy desk," according to Schudson.[8] A more plausible notion is that the byline afforded reporters greater public recognition. Ultimately this recognition proved beneficial, as it promoted familiarity and thus a decreased interpersonal distance between the reporter as communicator and the reader as receiver. Dropping the cloak of anonymity also became both a method of encouraging news tips and feedback from the public and a fringe benefit for reporters, whose reliance then and now on the pseudocelebrity status has served as a compensation for paltry wages. Yet another advantage is that bylines encouraged public trust. According to Walter Lippman, bylines and documentation are useful "in fixing personal responsibility for the truthfulness of news," toward which end he exhorted that, "We ought to know the names of the whole staff of every periodical."[9]

Bylines in the *Saturday Globe* were virtually unseen, rarely appearing prior to about 1915. Before then their only manifestation was at the bottom of a story, and almost always as initials. Because Dickinson covered the plurality of major stories, he occasionally rated an "A. M. D." at the end of such key reports. Throughout the *Saturday Globe*'s history, bylines were reserved for first-person, opinion-laden stories, although countless stories of this genre carried no byline.

Throughout its history, the modular layout customary in modern newspapers was as foreign to the *Saturday Globe* as swordplay to hemophiliacs. The weekly used the strictly vertical style common in the eighteenth and nineteenth centuries but employed by only a few newspapers today, most notably the *Wall Street Journal*. Most issues carried a large picture, at least two columns wide and four inches high, centered just beneath the nameplate yet not extending beneath the fold. In the *Saturday Globe*'s early years these were normally head-and-shoulder woodcut portraits, but by the late 1880s many of these illustrations were of action scenes, such as a fire or a shooting. In the early 1900s these front-page portraits and action etchings gradually gave way to still photographs and political cartoons, usually of national interest. The latter is probably due to the country's coincidental move toward nationalism and the concomitant slow but steady growth of national political power. Front-page political news coverage, which had dropped off during the *Saturday Globe*'s heyday, increased as the vitality of national politics increased.

That staple of modern newswriting, the inverted pyramid, in which the most important news is summarized in the first paragraph or two and then amplified later in the story, debuted briefly during the Civil War, when telegraphic reports of battlefield action and troop movements had to be quick and concise. Part of this concision included the development of the lead paragraph, in which the "five Ws and the H"—Who, What, When, Where, Why, and How—were summarized. However, this story structure did not emerge as a journalistic custom until the late nineteenth and early twentieth centuries. Mott proposed the 1890s as a transitional period for the format of news stories. He found many instances of the inverted-pyramid structure and the five-Ws-and-H lead, but also "many of the older-fashioned, tantalizing kind which seem never to get to the point."[10] By the early twentieth century, the inverted-pyramid structure was rapidly gaining acceptance in American newspapers, but it was a seemingly unknown entity in the *Saturday Globe*'s pages. For nearly its entire history, the *Saturday Globe*'s articles were written in a highly literate yet storytelling manner, in which the facts of the story gradually unfolded. Both the striking horrors of nature and mankind as well as breezy features were treated in this fashion. The first few paragraphs often set the scene and mood and provided the reader antecedent events before revealing that a black man in his nineties had sired eight children, all deformed and retarded, by his forty-five-year-old daughter; a Columbus, Indiana boy fell asleep for a week or more at a time and upon waking described occurrences that took place elsewhere while he slept, supposedly watching them from heaven; or that a person's facial expression was determined by his or her occupation, according to a physiognomist's study. The articles were often written chronologically by a journalist equipped with an ornate writing style who played out the story much as a skilled spinner of tales. This mode is far more pleasurable to read than today's lackluster and uniform news reports, although it is sometimes sparse in such details as places, dates, ages, and first names.

The erstwhile style also was not conducive to a quick read of the lead to understand the crux of a story. The fact that *Saturday Globe* stories were crafted with the implicit understanding that readers would leisurely peruse the entire story became problematic due to the accelerating pace of the early twentieth century. Newspaper readers appreciated the inverted-pyramid style because it freed them from the responsibility of having to read the entire story in order to understand the news, and it enabled them to fit newspaper reading into such forced periods of inactivity as traveling via mass transportation. This signaled the development of dual identities in journalism. For some, newspapers were designed primarily for entertainment. This was the legacy handed down from the colonial forebears that justified the existence of the press throughout most of the nineteenth century, including its recurring romance with sensationalism. However, other newspapers preferred an emphasis on facts. Schudson called these two models of journalism the ideal of the "story" and the ideal of "information."[11] Without doubt the latter model was becoming dominant in journalism of the early twentieth century. More and more, readers found they lacked the time, patience, and surroundings conducive to concentrating on *Saturday Globe* tales and began to turn elsewhere for their information.

This was just one of the many reasons for the *Saturday Globe*'s decline. Three discrete factors external to the *Saturday Globe* and two internal spelled its doom. The external forces were competition from other newspapers, wider circulation of newspapers and growth of magazines.

Competition from other newspapers took two forms—changes made by existing newspapers that cut into the *Saturday Globe*'s audience and the growing number of newspapers competing for readership. A crucial blow to the *Saturday Globe*'s huge circulation involved the component which was perhaps the newspaper's greatest strength—its illustrations. The newspaper demonstrated its leadership in the field of illustration by being one of the first to print color halftones. Paradoxically, it was the development of the screen that allowed newspapers to print halftones on their presses that catalyzed the *Saturday Globe*'s decline, according to Will DeVine, the newspaper's electrotyper from 1892 to 1914. DeVine produced much of the artwork for the presses by forming the plates for the editorial cartoons and other illustrations. He speculated that the screen, used in the photoengraving process so that newspapers could stereotype halftones for printing, allowed newspapers to print more pictures at less expense. This effectively nullified the *Saturday Globe*'s chief advantage over other newspapers, particularly the dailies—its huge budget for artwork and its resultant cornucopia of pictures. By the 1910s, other newspapers were following the *Saturday Globe*'s lead, adding liberal portions of pictures and cartoons, as many of both in color as budgets would allow.[12]

Compounding the problem was the burgeoning number of newspapers and their success. The two decades preceding World War I constituted a period of enormous press growth. Mott noted that in this era the press had become a major American industry. "In circulations, in the number of pages per issue, and in volume of advertising, the great newspapers grew to sizes scarcely dreamed of before, while figures representing investments, costs, and revenues reached astonishing totals," he wrote. Mott added that while only ten newspapers concentrated in four cities could boast in 1892 of more than 100,000 circulation (one of which was the *Saturday Globe*), by 1914 more than thirty of that size existed in twelve cities, Between 1892 and 1914 the average circulation of American daily newspapers doubled. This growth of existing newspapers encouraged scores of new publications to commence during the same span, attaining the largest number of newspapers in American journalism history before or since. Dailies increased from 1,650 in 1892 to 2,250 in 1914; weeklies grew from 11,000 to 12,500; and semiweeklies mushroomed from 200 to 600. However, newspaper growth as measured by number of newspapers is limited by the number of readers and their economic ability to support newspapers by paying the price of the newspaper and to support advertisers by purchasing their goods. This socioeconomic force was articulated by Simon N. D. North, special agent of the Census Office of the Department of the Interior, whose report on newspapers was included in the 1880 census and reprinted separately several years later. In the report, North advanced his theory of newspaper growth, which held that, "There is a well-defined limit, having due relations to population and the character and pursuits of that population, where too many newspapers become an impediment to prosperity, and therefore to the usefulness of each other. There is a law of supply and demand in the matter of newspaper publication which asserts itself in due process of time, to the control of the natural tendency to overdo newspaper printing." In the years just before World War I, there were more newspapers than the American public could support, and some, like the *Saturday Globe*, collapsed under the weight of the competition.[13]

The second contributor to the *Saturday Globe*'s demise was the fact that other newspapers were enjoying wider geographic circulation, thus competing for the patronage of the rural families that formed the backbone of the *Saturday Globe*'s readership. Not only were increasing numbers of newspapers employing the *Saturday Globe*'s distribution methods, thus increasing their circulation area and amount, they were also taking advantage of postal regulations designed to make it less expensive for newspapers to reach wider areas. In the last two decades of the nineteenth century, the federal postal system extended its free delivery service within cities, and in 1885 instituted a one-cent-per-pound rate for newspapers and magazines, making low-cost mail delivery of publications a reality. The advent of rural free delivery in 1897 also was damaging, as it brought metropolitan daily newspapers to rural America. The low postal rates plus the advent of free rural service enabled newspapers to widely extend their circulation areas into the heart of the *Saturday Globe*'s national readership.[14]

Although the *Saturday Globe* was a newspaper, its editorial fare of the bizarre, the amusing, and the peculiar, coupled with its literary miscellany and lack of geographic focus, made it more similar to a magazine. Thus, the *Saturday Globe*'s third external problem was that it faced more competition from magazines than newspapers. The late nineteenth and early twentieth centuries witnessed the rise of the illustrated magazine tailored to a general, national audience. The leading monthlies in the late nineteenth century were *Harper's*, *Century*, and *Scribner's*, and in the early twentieth century

McClure's, *Munsey's*, and *Cosmopolitan*. Among weekly magazines, the *Saturday Evening Post*, *Collier's*, and *Leslie's Weekly* enjoyed the largest circulations. Magazines attained mass circulation the same way daily newspapers had in the 1830s—they slashed prices from the norm of thirty-five cents to fifteen, and then to ten. Magazines enjoyed wide appeal because of the salubrious postal regulations, their ability to recruit stellar writing and editing talent, and their reliance on illustration, which Mott noted "was by means of woodcuts executed with an immense amount of fine detail and well printed." Thus, magazines offered serious competition for newspapers, particularly those of the general-interest variety like the *Saturday Globe*, by the early twentieth century. The competition for advertising was especially keen. "These new popularly circulated magazines made the biggest inroads on available advertising revenue, arising as they did to public notice at the moment when national advertising was expanding," according to Emery and Emery. Local and regional magazines also enjoyed vast popularity during this period.[15]

In an unprecedented journalistic development, magazines began to compete for newspaper readership. In this era, general-interest magazines embraced fact in much the same way as their newspaper brethren. Magazines paid greater attention to social, political, and economic problems, at the expense of their erstwhile emphasis on history, biography, travel, and literature. Thus, by placing greater importance on ponderous news and less on light entertainment, magazines became more similar in content to newspapers. This journalistic trend gave rise to muckraking. Theodore Roosevelt coined the term, comparing the expose writers to the man with the muckrake in *Pilgrim's Progress* who did not see the celestial crown offered to him because he doggedly continued to rake the mire.

This reform journalism in the first decade of the twentieth century was a fact-based variation on the dubious and sensationalized reports of the 1880s and 1890s, and supported the axiom that truth can be just as astonishing as fiction. Muckraking found a home in weekly and monthly magazines. Prominent examples included *Cosmopolitan*'s "The Treason of the Senate," identifying numerous senators as tools of special interest; *Collier's*' "The Great American Fraud," an indictment of the patent-medicine trade; and Ida M. Tarbell's "The History of the Standard Oil Company," which *McClure's* published serially from 1902 to 1904. Lincoln Steffens also contributed a series exposing corruption in city and state governments for that magazine. As the editor of *McClure's*, Steffens was one of the foremost muckrakers of the era. He came from a newspaper background, and his editorial practices reflected that experience. When he was interviewed for the *McClure's* job, he announced that his policy would be to make news an integral part of the magazine. He recalled, "It had occurred to me that there were some news stories which ran so long and meant so much that the newspapers readers lost track of them." In his view, a monthly magazine "could come along, tell the whole, completed story . . . and bring out the meaning of it all with comment." Steffens's crusading liberalism was tempered in print by the magazine's proprietor, S. S. "Sam" McClure, who "was interested in facts, startling facts, not in philosophical generalizations." This ideological rift prompted Steffens and other *McClure's* staff members to resign and purchase the *American Magazine* in 1906, but not before *McClure's* had surpassed the half-million circulation mark and catalyzed journalistic muckraking. These crusades, based on carefully-constructed interviews and documentary evidence, thrust magazines into the arena of facts and news, thereby siphoning off some newspaper readers.[16]

These three external forces were inextricably linked to social changes of the times. The growing national desire for neoteric news was a child of the times. The character of the American reader had become more excitable than that of the English-colonial forefathers, and a fast-paced, urban age had replaced the erstwhile days of leisurely small-town life. Suburbia was reaching fruition and the wide patches of terrain that had separated communities were being developed at a feverish pace. The automobile was converting long journeys of ten or fifteen miles into a matter of minutes, and telephones were conquering the communication obstacle presented by geographic distance. People sought more to entertain them, quicker ways of doing things, and improved, faster communications.[17]

It was just such a period that molded the definition of daily newspapers, weekly newspapers, and magazines that has endured through the twentieth century. Daily newspapers became the primary sources of news. Articles gradually became shorter, and some dailies even imposed strict length requirements on reporters' stories. Writing became more concise and structured and less florid. Inverted pyramids began taking shape. Headlines became vital tools not only to attract but to inform. Photographs became almost exclusively story supplements and shed their aesthetic qualities. Modular layout—formulated for quicker, easier reading—developed and newspaper design became more regimented. The romance and adventure serials, poetry, and corn-pone jokes had all but disappeared. The evolution of the daily newspaper was directed toward a faster, more focused presentation of news. Even the function and direction of daily newspapers has changed in the past three decades due to the rapidity with which radio and television can deliver news. Newspapers, epitomized in recent years by *USA Today*, have become more visually appealing through color photos, charts, and design. The stories are now shorter than ever, leaving minimal room for description, scene-setting, or instances of fine writing. The modern newspaper's design has been altered to permit a quick read that is appealing to the eye while the newspaper is scanned on the subway or during a meal.

Sensing cultural change, magazines of the early twentieth century began to focus more on the presentation of the longer, analytical articles Steffens and other magazine editors decided should be part of the regular literary fare. Such stories did not have to be presented immediately in order to be interesting and worthwhile. Thus magazines turned their weakness—a lack of timeliness—into an asset, as it allowed them to develop the more polished and comprehensive articles that newspapers had neither the time nor the staff to produce. At the same time, magazines retained fiction, essays, serials, artistic illustrations, and poetry—the components of pleasure reading that dailies had summarily dismissed—to retain its wide appeal. This increased emphasis on developing depth stories by using the additional time further impinged upon the niche the *Saturday Globe* had carved for itself, because the weekly took pride in making use of the time dailies could not afford in order to present related stories, known as sidebars.

Where did this leave weekly newspapers? Dailies and magazines had gobbled up substantial pieces of the mass communication pie. Weekly newspapers had only one recourse—emphasize their close community ties. "The spread of mail circulation of the city dailies into the villages had gradually forced the country weeklies to become more local in point of view," Mott wrote. He added that the insertion of more and smaller items, using as many names of residents as possible, was an effective circulation-builder. More than ever, weeklies became the repository of printed items their daily brethren did not have the space or inclination to print and for which magazines were not designed due to their regional or national scope: wedding and birth announcements, awards ceremonies, graduation and promotion notices, and local social gatherings. The news became strictly local, as weeklies sought to cover their own community or cluster of towns more thoroughly than the city daily, but not venture past the borders of safe provinciality. Journalism history suggests that the primary reasons popular newspapers die are competitors copying innovations, excessive competition for advertising dollars, a greater number of papers than the reading public can support, and lack of initial capital. Particularly appropriate to the *Saturday Globe* is Donald Abramoske's description of the death knell for many turn-of-the-century weekly newspapers. "Steadily increasing competition was gradually constricting their field," he wrote. "Country weeklies were improving all the time. Small dailies were springing up in the growing towns. Metropolitan dailies were reducing their prices and, as a result of improved postal service, were being delivered to distant rural sections early on the day of publication."[18]

These were problems chiefly external to the *Saturday Globe*'s operation. However, it faced two internal problems: a lack of purpose and direction, and the stagnation and aging of the editorial staff. The first of these two internal factors is the most complex and had the most serious consequences for the *Saturday Globe*, for it began to lose its heterogenous audience and did not seek a more defined one.

Journalism and all other forms of communication were changing dramatically as a result of social and cultural alterations taking place around the turn of the century. Newspapers, especially the nondailies, were being forced into specialization. The partitioning of the print media placed the omnibus *Saturday Globe* in a precarious position. It could not compete with the rapidity of the dailies in presenting news, and it had lost its own competitive edge because photographs and color illustrations were featured by most dailies and even some small weeklies. After the first decade of the twentieth century the use of serials and other fiction, poetry, and biographies of prominent statesmen began to seem archaic for newspapers and were generally identified as magazine fare. As a publication with broad geographic scope, the *Saturday Globe* was becoming a relic of bygone days.

The *Saturday Globe* tried to fight the tide by expanding, by becoming even more of an omnibus product. Instead of conforming to one of the evolving niches and recognizing the changing needs of readers, the newspaper increased to twelve pages in the spring of 1905. It featured more national, color, and display advertisements; initiated "Religious" and "Sporting" pages; offered more news from Canada, presumably to counter the circulation slide by increasing sales there; began using color illustrations on inside pages; and initiated two weekly features, "Anecdotes by Well-Known Men" and "Globules," a list of one-sentence notes and comments from across the country. About a decade later, the *Saturday Globe* expanded again and established two sections, one for news and one termed the "magazine" section. This became the depot for women's fashion information, sports, and religion news, advice and gossip columns, and articles on such general topics as what has become of Shakespeare's ashes and the present status of various foreign governments. Serial romances and articles providing household hints increased as women were recognized as a growing readership force.

Nonetheless, the *Saturday Globe*'s circulation dropped steadily. An increasingly literate public, earning better wages and becoming more interested in news, was able to afford a newspaper every day. The financial ease of buying a daily newspaper was exacerbated by the dailies themselves, many of which were able to reduce prices because of the rise of national advertising. National advertising gradually became the chief source of a newspaper's revenue, so that by the early 1900s newspaper buyers were seen in an economic sense as attractive lures for advertisers. With the growing importance of advertisers the consumers paid for little more than the newspaper company's cost of getting the newspaper to them. It was a convenient trade—reduced prices in exchange for increased advertising. In their newspapers, consumers demanded a presentation of facts that was free from value judgments. Thus, the journalistic trend toward fact and objectivity was impelled by a public weary of more than half a century of sensationalism and an entire century of overt political partisanship. These were factors that stood in the way of the pristine truth people came to demand from the press. At the same time, this new, serious, public-service ideology elevated the social status of journalists, just as it had in the mid-eighteenth century.

Fewer people were turning to weeklies such as the *Saturday Globe* as their primary source of news, which cost the weekly some readers. Its refusal to change as the times had changed, to present news with concision and clearly-defined structure, cost more readers. With daily newspapers pressing their advantage—the ability to deliver news faster than a weekly—and with all print media spending princely sums to improve and increase their artwork and photography, the *Saturday Globe*'s days were numbered.

Compounding the problem were the Bakers and Dickinson, whose time was sapped by civic activities and vigor drained by the ravages of age. Dickinson was no longer the robust young man who had traveled across the nation for weeks at a time, covering murders, disasters, elections and electrocutions, and the Baker brothers were busy with outside endeavors. By the late 1890s the Baker brothers, wealthy men in their fifties, lapsed into patriarchal philanthropy. As people in the higher social spheres are wont to do, they became involved with outside business interests and civic affairs, leaving more of the responsibilities of running the newspaper to Dickinson and others.

In 1893, Will Baker was chosen a director of Utica's Second National Bank. He continued as director when it was succeeded by the Oneida County Trust Co., and remained in the same capacity when that establishment merged with the First Bank and Trust Co. in 1926. In 1898 he became a director, and later president and chairman of the board, of the Utica Knitting Co. This company became the largest knitting concern in the world, producing between 35,000 and 40,000 garments per day. When a sister organization, the Clayville Knitting Co., was spawned, Baker became its president too. In 1901 he became a partner in the Roberts, Parry and Co. hardware dealership and remained until 1929. In 1902 Baker was tabbed a director of the Utica Gas and Electric Co., becoming its president in 1925. He was also a member of the Oneida County Historical Society, the Fort Schuyler Club, and the Yah-nun-dah-sis Golf Club, and was a member of St. John's Roman Catholic Church.

Tom Baker's activities were equally voluminous, if not more so. He was a director of the Utica, Clayville, and Olympian knitting companies; the Syracuse Stove Works; the Utica City National Bank and the Utica Trust and Deposit Co. He was a member of the Utica Chamber of Commerce, the Oneida County Historical Society, the Utica Soldiers and Sailors' Monument Association, the American Publishers' Association of New York, the Board of Managers of the Utica State Hospital, the Sadaquada and Yah-nun-dah-sis golf clubs, and St. John's Roman Catholic Church.

It was not long before Dickinson, himself possessing an enviable measure of social standing, got into the act. He served as alderman of Utica's 15th Ward for six years, president of the Utica Common Council (the city's legislative body) for six years, Oneida County treasurer for six years and was active in various political affairs of the Republican Party.[19]

These responsibilities sapped the three men of much of their time and energy and forced thoughts of the newspaper business farther back in their minds. Wealth and a string of business ventures caused the trio to drift away from the *Saturday Globe* just when they should have been marshalling their resources and honing their journalistic acumen to combat the stiffening competition. All of the *Saturday Globe*'s problems coalesced in circulation figures. From a euphoric high of more than 294,000 in 1897, circulation plummeted to 122,368 by 1912. By 1915 the newspaper had slipped to 100,000 and the following year sank to 80,589.[20]

The *Saturday Globe* staff was then visited with a tragic occurrence that made its circulation woes seem small by comparison. On 15 May 1916, Tom Baker died. The 20 May *Saturday Globe* devoted several columns, both in the form of an obituary and an editorial, to honor its fallen founder and praise his virtue and decency. As the encomium affords a better glimpse of the man than anything that has been attempted in these pages, it is reproduced here almost in its entirety. It says as much about his editorial philosophy as his character:

> Thomas F. Baker, one of the founders of the Saturday Globe and since its foundation its editor, passed beyond this life Monday morning of this week.
>
> We grieve that his task is completed, we who worked for and with him, some of us for more than three decades, and our hearts are heavy, for he was not only employer and fellow-worker but friend . . .
>
> From the beginning, Mr. Baker was an inspiration to those who labored with him. His heart was in the Globe, and no fellow worker could be comfortable whose heart was not so placed. Indefatigable, cheerful, optimistic, his was the vision which always pictured a better and constantly better Globe.
>
> Himself fair toward all and generous, the paper of which he was the editorial head reflected his characteristics. Decent in his own mind and having respect for the decency of others, he never put pen to paper nor permitted a subordinate to do so, except for words which could bring no blush to the cheek of the most innocent. It might on occasion be necessary as a purveyor of the world's happenings to recount the deeds of crime and the acts of vice, but such recounting must be in language which could be interpreted only by the sophisticated and which suggested nothing to the unformed intellect. Expressions common to many of the best papers he forbade. Write nothing, was his order, which cannot be read aloud at the breakfast table. So tender was he of the feelings of others that nothing but the sternest necessity excused the appearance in his paper of the word "suicide" and the unfortunates of the Police Court were never the object of either amusement or curiosity on the part of those who perused the columns he governed.
>
> His pride was in his paper, and he insisted that it must be a paper of which he might be justly proud.
>
> Year after year he labored with us assiduously, encouragingly, cheerfully. And then illness laid its heavy hand upon him and forced his willing grasp from the directorate, but never, to the very last, did he lose his interest either in the paper or in those who tried to make of it the

paper which his ambition idealized. So long as he was able he visited the plant, disseminating his words of cheer and hopefulness through all departments and buoyantly picturing his hoped-for return to active participation in the work he so loved.

We of the Saturday Globe have lost a loved and loving chieftain. You of the Globe's international parish have lost a friend and well-wisher, one whose mind and hand were devoted to making the world better and happier.

Both you and we have reasons to regret that he might not have remained with us for a longer season.[21]

The editorial suggests that Baker suffered a debilitating illness of some duration, but in the genteel manner of the day the ailment was not mentioned in the obituary or editorial. He was interred in St. Agnes Cemetery. The obituary is equally panegyrizing, and describes the funeral at St. John's Roman Catholic Church and recapped the editor's life and career. It concludes with this ode:

Peace! for the day is over
And night envelops the scene;
The vineyard's work is ended;
The Master beckons, unseen.
Peace! for the dawn has broken
In rays of unending light;
Peace and rest and joy and love
In the Palace of Delight![22]

Without Baker, the *Saturday Globe*'s faltering accelerated. Will Baker and trusty employee Dickinson remained of the vital triumvirate that had piloted the *Saturday Globe* through waters both stormy and placid, but the men were well advanced in years, and the Bakers had no sons to whom they could pass the mantle of responsibility. Tom Baker had two daughters and Will Baker four, most of whom had married and moved away, several to foreign countries. Dickinson had a child in the business, his daughter Reba, who started with the *Saturday Globe* as a reporter, but her talents lay in writing, not managing. She later joined the *Observer*, remained when that Utica daily merged with the *Herald-Dispatch*, and became a society editor for the resulting *Observer-Dispatch*, writing interviews, features, and a widely-read "People Worth Knowing" column.[23]

Will Baker held on to the newspaper until 1920, when at age seventy-five he sold it. Will's granddaughter Marietta von Bernuth believes that the newspaper was vended because neither Baker had a male heir to take over. The purchasers were numerous Utica businessmen organized under the corporate name of the Utica Investment Co. They were some of the most prominent capitalists in the city. Julius Rothstein was president, Frederick B. Smith was secretary and treasurer, W. C. J. Doolittle was the vice president, and Brian Clarke was the general manager, overseeing business affairs. Major stockholders included Walter Jerome Greene, Robert D. Fraser, Charles W. Cushman, Nathan Robbins, Jenner Lowery, Samuel J. Wolfe, who owned a periodical and newspaper distributorship, and Francis X. Matt, founder and president of Matt's Brewery, then as now producing various beers sold in upstate New York.[24]

None of these men had any experience in newspaper work or newspaper management, which often showed, but they had plenty of capital, thanks to the economic boom following World War I. Searching for a profitable investment that needed only ample capital, they bought the *Saturday Globe*, but also decided that there was room for a fourth daily newspaper in Utica.

8

The *Morning Telegram*: A Short-Lived Sister

Calling themselves the Globe-Telegram Co., the Utica businessmen published the first issue of the *Utica Morning Telegram* on 1 July 1920. Attempting to overcome the ravages of wartime on the average household, the newspaper entered the market inexpensively, selling for one cent in Utica, two cents outside of the city. This represented a financial gamble, for daily newspapers had long since been claiming single-copy prices of three and five cents. The penny-paper's heyday had been in the 1830s, but experienced a revival later in the decade, as Chicago's *Daily News*, New York's *Morning Journal*, Kansas City's *Star* and others slashed prices from three, four, and five cents in an effort to increase circulation, and thus to attract advertising dollars. Most of the penny-papers initiated in the late nineteenth century met with early demises, though, because ad revenue was insufficient to offset the losses concomitant with the price reduction. However, this did not faze the *Morning Telegram* proprietors, who could invest substantial postwar capital to find a niche for their creation in the teeming Utica newspaper market.[1]

Since they had a fully functional production facility, and thus would have comparatively low start-up costs, the Globe-Telegram Co. envisioned that the still-thriving Utica could support a new daily, despite the fact that the city already had two afternoon newspapers, the *Observer* and the *Herald-Dispatch*, and one morning paper, the *Daily Press*. The fledgling newspaper, intended as a sister publication to the established but fading *Saturday Globe*, would be in direct competition with the *Daily Press*.

One serious managerial handicap for the *Morning Telegram* was that none of the founders had any newspaper experience. Business manager Brian Clarke was able to import William P. Hamilton from New York to take over the reins as managing editor. Hamilton came to the *Morning Telegram* from the Navy, but had previously worked for the *New York Tribune* and the *Wall Street Journal*. He was at somewhat of a disadvantage, though, as his newspaper experience was limited to financial news and his familiarity with other phases of a newspaper's operation was questionable. Although his newspaper experience was specialized, he was given the additional title of general manager upon Clarke's early departure from the *Morning Telegram*. Hamilton's ideosyncrasies allowed him to fit right in with a staff of peculiar characters. According to Williams, drawing from the recollections of *Morning Telegram* day city editor Gerrit Hyde, Hamilton wore a regal, flowing cape during the winter, was addicted to eating bananas and, in a rare occurrence of the day, banned smoking in the newsroom.[2]

However, the real power in the newsroom for the first year of the newspaper's existence was wielded by George M. Grady. A native of Quincy, Massachusetts, and a graduate of Harvard University, Grady was a humorless man who had worked for the *Boston Post*, as well as dailies in Syracuse and Auburn, New York. He arrived in Utica a month before the *Morning Telegram* commenced publication to familiarize himself with the city and construct a news staff. The owners had assumed much of the news staff could be recruited from existing Utica newspapers, probably thinking that local talent would provide instant credibility to the *Morning Telegram* due to public recognition of their names and would not require the indoctrination to Utica politics and society that imports would need. However, Grady's local recruiting efforts were virtually unsuccessful, yielding only a few area newsmen, and he was forced to hurriedly assemble a staff of journeyman imports.[3]

One post Grady was especially interested in filling with a local man was assistant city editor. Renowned area athlete Bartle Gorman had graduated from nearby Hamilton College in June and was working in New York City. Several of Gorman's friends knew he was unhappy with his job there and told Grady he would be the ideal candidate. Gorman accepted Grady's offer but was not on the job long before his lack of newspaper experience became evident. Consequently, Grady converted Gorman to a reporter, replacing him with former Chicago newsman Joseph Kelly, but not cutting Gorman's pay correspondingly. Thus, Gorman's $35 weekly salary made him the second-highest-paid reporter on the staff. Besides Gorman, the only noteworthy Utica recruit was the assistant sports editor, Harold Semple.[4]

The highest-paid reporter on the *Morning Telegram* was its star, Stuart McGuire, who had come from the *Boston Globe*. He was a stocky man with boundless self-confidence who introduced himself by announcing, "I am McGuire of the *Telegram*." His Utica contemporaries recalled that he was always prepared to assist another staff member, whether or not that staffer required assistance. McGuire quickly gained the reputation of milking a story for all it was worth, but occasionally he went too far. One time a rookie reporter had written a story about an injury that occurred on an open-air trolley on Bleecker Street in Utica. A man who was facing the rear while riding on the trolley's running board had been knocked unconscious when his head struck the body of a parked truck protruding into the street. When McGuire saw the typed account he could not resist the temptation to sensationalize it with concocted facts designed to make the injury seem more tragic. The accident had taken place shortly past noon, and in McGuire's version the man was returning to work from lunch. He stood on the trolley waving farewell to his wife, who held their baby in her arms, when the accident occurred. After McGuire's story was published the injured man demanded a retraction. He was unmarried and his fiancee did not appreciate reading about his wife and baby.[5]

Walter Schied, Harry Johnston, Stan Clarke, and Frank Wood all worked part-time on the city desk, with the latter two sharing night responsibilities. This quartet is remarkable by modern journalistic standards in that all four were employed by other newspapers, a practice today's editors would not permit. Clarke worked days for the *Utica Herald-Dispatch* and Wood for the *Utica Observer*. Another man who split time between two newspapers was William Carson, on loan from the *Saturday Globe*. The aged Carson was a brilliant artist who had created many of that weekly's spectacular illustrations. Still another was William Pope, employed by day as a linotype operator at the nationally-circulated, Welsh-language weekly *Y Drych*, which was published in Utica. At night he performed the same function for the *Morning Telegram*, and spent his few free hours tending to his second-hand bookstore on Utica's Charlotte Street. Pope was a regular at the Saturday-morning poker games held by printers, pressmen, and newsmen after the paper had been put to bed and the pay envelopes distributed. Pope was there when the game started until it ended at noon Sunday, when work began on the Monday newspaper. He is remembered as having slept little and shaved less, using his omnipresent derby hat indoors and outdoors to cover his long, wispy gray hairs. According to Williams, he looked decades older than his approximately fifty years, and no one ever reported seeing him in a clean shirt, but he was very knowledgeable about books and their authors, grammar, and spelling.[6]

Other key staffers included police reporter George O'Neil, who had no previous newspaper experience yet was a student of literature and often shared his thoughts on Fyodor Dostoyevsky, Alphonse Daudet, Leo Tolstoy, and other authors whose work he admired; reporters Leon Woodworth, Gerrit S. Hyde, Howard Maywalt, and Ralph Spinning; and Sports Editor Walter Ross, imported from Elmira. As Hyde recalled, Ross was not the first choice for the job. The original nominee celebrated his selection so enthusiastically that he did not show up for ten days. By that time the post had been handed to Ross. Amsterdam, New York, refugee John Donnelly began as the courthouse reporter, but quit after an office dispute over a taxi fare and took a job with the *Ilion Citizen*, a weekly several towns east of Utica. He was replaced by former *New York Times* reporter Joseph Keating. Edward Moore and Leo Taylor, respectively the theatre reviewer and obituary writer, were both poets who occasionally composed verse for use in their writing chores.[7]

The business operations were under the direction of Fred B. Stuart, who supervised Advertising Manager Harry Benner and his assistants Elmer Pierce and Ivan L. "Dinty" Moore, National Advertising Manager Charles Buddle, Classified Advertising Manager Herman Batty, Bookkeeper Pierce Condon, Circulation Manager Sidney L. O'Connor and his assistants John Dowd and William Barton. Secretaries included Marie Batty, wife of Batty and sister of Benner; Agnes Craves; and Dora Mittleman.[8]

Malachi "Mal" Doyle was a strapping, hoary man who operated the telegraph wire. He had managed boxers and owned horse stables, but the risky finances concomitant with both pursuits periodically prompted him to return to the telegraph key. Because of his contacts with jockeys, the *Morning Telegram* staff often hounded him for racing tips. He reluctantly agreed once but the horse finished out of the money and Doyle vowed not to give another tip until he was absolutely confident of the prognostication. He eventually returned to racing, and one Thursday contacted the *Morning Telegram* staff from New Orleans. He tabbed a horse racing at the New Orleans Fair Grounds as a sure thing and advised them to bet all they could. Because it was one day before payday, everyone on the staff was broke and business manager Stuart refused to give advances. The staff ignored news reporting for a while as the members went in search of loans. About $50 was given to Ross, who hurried to a bookmaker but arrived too late. The horse won and paid forty-to-one.[9]

It was with this motley crew that the *Morning Telegram* was unveiled 1 July 1920, sporting eight columns per page on sixteen pages. The layout and design was different from the *Saturday Globe*'s format, reflecting the increasing importance of catching the public eye in an era of escalating newspaper competition. The *Saturday Globe*'s strictly vertical design was modified to weave some boxes and stories of two columns' width into the fabric of the *Morning Telegram*. Large, sprightly banner headlines, a modern classified-ad format in which ads were sold not by space (as in the *Saturday Globe*) but at the rate of one cent per word, the presence of comic strips, and the increasing appearance of bylines were new wrinkles not usually found in the *Saturday Globe*. In fact, the new owners left the *Saturday Globe*'s layout and design virtually unaltered after Will Baker yielded the helm.

One similarity to its sister weekly was that the *Morning Telegram* carried no political affiliation, proudly proclaiming in a box on the nameplate, "An Independent Newspaper." This was part of a journalistic trend. In a dilatory but inexorable process still taking place in the American press, a growing number of newspapers were forswearing partisanship and trumpeting their political independence as a means of self-advertisement.

The first issue's inaugural statement carried the obligatory statement of purpose—the editorial philosophy by which the newspaper's directors planned to conduct the paper. Such statements became common for debuting newspapers in the eighteenth century, when printers typically advanced their conceptions of press freedom, promising to publish such "useful and entertaining" matter as foreign news, ship arrivals, agricultural prices, political screeds, household hints, and moral instruction. Nineteenth-century inaugural essays also asserted press liberty, regardless of whether they were under political control, but as the decades passed, they reflected the evolution from personal to institutional journalism with the rise of the mass press and the division of labor. The colorful but predictable partisanship that had characterized the antebellum press eroded by the end of the century, replaced by a greater concern with facts and objectivity. This resulted in an unprecedented physical and conceptual division in newspaper pages between editorials and news. First-issue essays in the late nineteenth and early twentieth centuries reflected this emerging conception of news as a commodity to be funneled from gatherer/distributor to consumer, promising that the new paper would purvey impartial, truthful statements of fact in an accurate and responsible manner.

The *Morning Telegram* commenced publication declaiming its independence, freedom, and honesty, and seeking to appeal to the widest possible readership through its series of promises of how it proposed to serve Utica-area readers, under the headline "What the Telegram Stands For":

> It will tell the truth as it sees the truth, without fear and without partisanship.
>
> It will fight hard for what it believes to be right, but it will fight openly, honestly and fairly.
>
> It will stand for integrity and sincerity of purpose and against all sham and pretense.
>
> It believes in the sacredness of contract and in the fairest, squarest dealing between man and man, employer and employed, labor and capital, the political leaders and the people.
>
> It will stand for a real Americanism and a practical patriotism.
>
> It will strive to be alive to all that is best and of most vital interest in American life and to reproduce it in its columns.
>
> It will advocate for the individual the fullest liberty of action that is consistent with safeguarding the rights of others.
>
> It will do its best to be a force for good in the life of the city.
>
> And it will be for Utica first, last and all the time.[10]

Accompanying the inaugural statement on the editorial page was an attack on other Utica newspapers, which the *Morning Telegram* accused of unfair business practices. It accused the other three local dailies, the evening *Herald-Dispatch* and *Observer* and the morning *Daily Press*, of trying to undermine the new competitor. Because all three refused its paid advertising designed to announce its appearance, the *Morning Telegram* suggested these papers were motivated by a "sinister influence at work in the city of Utica." The *Morning Telegram* dismissed the *Daily Press*'s refusal "as distinctly a compliment," for "If the Press had not esteemed the Telegram as a dangerous competitor it would of course have been glad to have run the announcement and thereby added to its advertising revenue." That the two evening papers should decline seemed sinister to the editorial braintrust of the new journal, though, as they contended their morning paper would present no competition. The *Morning Telegram* complained that many Uticans "hesitate to give out information of even the most ordinary kind, to express publicly an opinion or to identify themselves with any enterprise without first assuring themselves, before they do so, that they have the sanction of some entity in the background." Motivated by "a curious sort of fear," such people "intimate that, if they act otherwise, they believe consequences will ensue inimical to themselves." This led the *Morning Telegram* to wonder, in bold capital letters, "IS THERE A

REIGN OF TERROR IN UTICA?'' and to plead for ''A FAIR FIGHT ON A FAIR FIELD.''[11]

As any current or former reporter will testify, it is an exasperatingly common phenomenon for even the most assertive person to become timid and reticent when confronted with the prospect of speaking to a reporter, even for the most trivial of stories. Employees in businesses, government agencies, and other institutions are chronically afraid that they lack authority to speak to the press, or fear infuriating some superior. This is one of the most irritating parts of a reporter's job, but it has been an unflagging dimension of the journalist-source relationship for centuries. People also have a natural fear of what the reporter might write or observe, poet Robert Burns noted. He warned eighteenth-century Scots about newsmen, or ''chiels,'' writing:

> If there's a hole in 'yer coat, you'd better ten't it;
> There's a chiel amang us takin' notes, and faith, he'll prent it!

In an effort to stir up controversy and cast a pall of suspicion over the three incumbent Utica newspapers in revenge for their refusal of the ads, the *Morning Telegram* exploited this social phenomenon to siphon public support from its competitors and portray itself as the underdog. Suspicion of insidious plots against individual newspapers has ample precedent in history. ''Many newspaper proprietors magnified trivial incidents into widespread conspiracies,'' according to historian Milton W. Hamilton. ''Some of the most bitter controversies in the press could be traced to this feeling on the part of newspaper publishers that they were suffering from unfair competition. Their resentment found frequent expression in scurrilous attacks upon those whom they regarded as their oppressors.'' One early proprietor considered an upstart rival as ''an obtruder'' and vowed to do all possible to discourage his success. Another considered the economic implications of competition, noting his adversary's intention of ''forcing an extensive circulation'' of the newspaper to ''make it an object for merchants and others to give . . . their advertising support.'' A third cautioned the public that a competing newspaper meant ''that one or both must fall.''[12]

While the three existing Utica newspapers went to no such lengths to publicly express their contempt for increased competition, surely they resented the *Morning Telegram*'s encroachment and declined its advertising with the intention of dealing it a financial blow. There is substantial basis for their animosity, for as the number of newspapers in a community increases, and as new entries gain a place in the market, public loyalty and support are further divided. An area's population increase sometimes justifies the multiplication of papers, but Utica's nineteenth-century growth had nearly ground to a halt due to the diminishing importance of waterway travel in twentieth-century America, the prosperity of other central New York cities such as Syracuse and Albany, and the westward population migration as living conditions in Midwestern states rapidly improved. Additionally, the post-war inflation meant Uticans were less likely to purchase more than one daily newspaper, and the fact that the *Morning Telegram* could be had for just a penny in town was sure to cut into the other's circulation, including the evening papers, despite the inaugural statement's contention. This augmented competition meant both reduced sales revenue and, more important, reduced advertising patronage.

After the inaugural editorial on newspaper competition, the name of the *Daily Press* and its editor, George E. Dunham, did not appear in the pages of the *Morning Telegram*, doubtless as a means of reprisal for its refusal to publicize the *Morning Telegram* via the advertisements. When mentioning its morning competitor became necessary, *Morning Telegram* reporters were instructed to refer to it as "a certain morning publication." Nine months after the *Morning Telegram*'s inception, Hamilton College held a ceremony to honor Dunham. When the newspaper ran a story about the ceremony and omitted any mention of the event's purpose—to stellify Dunham—a member of the *Morning Telegram* staff (probably Hyde) complained to some of the owners, who relented and permitted a revised story to appear. One of Dunham's aides, perhaps Paul Williams, later revealed that Dunham repeatedly read the item, searching for some hidden meaning.[13]

Yet a third editorial invited readers to be the *Morning Telegram*'s friends. Simply titled, "The *Telegram* and its Readers," the entreaty anticipated the inevitable problem faced by all newspapers—that editorial matter would not always prove acceptable to all its readers—and submitted its dilemma for public consideration:

> This newspaper wants its readers to be its friends. Even friends—the best of friends—cannot agree on all things. Friendship would be a dull thing, if that were so. It is difference of opinion and individuality of viewpoint that impart interest to human intercourse. The Telegram, although a newspaper, will be human, with an individuality of its own. It is probable that some of its readers will disagree with it at all times, and all of them sometimes. But in spite of this—no, rather because of it—The Telegram hopes that it and its readers will always remain friends.

It hopes, too, that those of its readers who cannot accept its opinions will nevertheless credit those opinions with being honest ones honestly held, and not adopted from motives of expediency or self-interest.

Always The Telegram will welcome from its readers expression of their own personal opinions. The Editor will be glad to have the paper's constituents write to him. Effort will be made to give space to such letters from subscribers as merit, because of their general interest, publication.

The Telegram repeats that it wants its readers to be its friends.[14]

This policy statement is remarkable, for it combines the issues of controversy, press freedom, public access, community support, and public service in one statement calculated to ingratiate itself, address a chronic problem of journalism, and appear human, rather than corporate and impersonal.

After asking readers to be pals and on the same day, the same page, paranoically finger-pointing at Utica's other dailies as though they were a cabal responsible for some heinous, eerie evil creeping through Utica's streets and possessing ordinary citizens to engage in a shocking conspiracy of silence, the *Morning Telegram* settled in to the task of carving a niche, building circulation and luring advertisers. Its editorials, some of which were written by Rabbi Reuben Kaufman of Temple Beth-El, supported business and Republicanism, although it supported Ohio Governor James M. Cox, a Democrat, for the presidency in 1920. Cox, a veteran newspaper reporter and publisher, was thrashed by another newspaper publisher, Warren G. Harding. The *Morning Telegram* also proclaimed skepticism about the government's success in enforcing Prohibition, which had just become law the previous year. Some editorials were serious political or social criticism, such as the one in which the *Morning Telegram* deplored the practice of parents withdrawing their children from grade school and forcing them to get jobs, while others were humorous, such as the editorial that asked "Is Love-Making an Acquired Art?" This peculiar bit of prose, which used humor to daintily disguise its thesis that men are insensitive to the sexual desires of women, concluded, "Testimony seems conclusive that the average American husband is a hopeless blunderer in the art of making love."[15]

The news pages were exuberant, filled with stories that continued the *Saturday Globe*'s tradition of middle-range sensationalism. For instance, before its first month had elapsed, the *Morning Telegram* scooped all other newspapers with a front-page story about a "murder farm" in the nearby village of Oriskany, where the bones of several babies were unearthed. The story was accorded banner headlines for days, until it was discovered that the bones were merely calf bones. The newspaper did not learn its lesson easily though, for shortly afterward it encountered a similar story. Relying on an anonymous tip, *Morning Telegram* reporters found what appeared to be human bones in a Utica cellar and gleefully presumed homicide. After trumpeting its exclusive, the *Morning Telegram* staff was mortified to discover that the evidence had been planted by the *Herald-Dispatch*'s police reporter George Bradley and actually consisted of dog bones.[16]

The *Morning Telegram* was the first daily in Utica's long newspaper history to use color, a contribution from the *Saturday Globe*, which shared its engraving plant with its youthful sibling. The *Morning Telegram* also offered the first funnies page in the city. The cartoon fare featured "Toots and Casper," "Tillie the Toiler," and "Joker Poker." Regular advice columns included "The Home Kitchen," "Your Health" and "Revelations of a Wife," an "Erma Bombeck" predecessor.[17]

Tragedy struck the *Morning Telegram* on 12 August 1921, when Grady died suddenly of a brain hemorrhage, leaving the newspaper without a daytime city editor. Grady had befriended cub reporter Hyde and taught him some aspects of desk work, including how to assign stories and write headlines, so the young reporter was tabbed as a temporary replacement. Thomas Maloney of Norfolk, Virginia, was hired and arrived a week later, but because Hyde had made a smooth transition to city editor he was kept on days, with Maloney assuming the post at night. The following month Hamilton was replaced as managing editor by Harry Stearns, who had been procured from the *Syracuse Journal*.[18]

The *Morning Telegram* exuberantly feuded with local government officials during its brief but tempestuous existence. After several *Morning Telegram* stockholders were cited for automobile violations on Genesee Street in what was then part of New Hartford, a community adjacent to Utica, the newspaper lambasted Oneida County Sheriff Arthur Pickard's speed trap and New Hartford Justice William Williams's complicity. The stories prompted an Automobile Club representative to visit Williams's court, which was held in a barn. The speed trap was finally discontinued at the request of the New Hartford Town Board. The simmering feud with Pickard erupted again when the newspaper alleged that the county jail was a breeding ground for disease and the prisoners it held were underfed. The articles instigated an insult-laden dispute in the county Board of Supervisors, which the newspaper duly reported. The squabble snowballed into a state investigation, which found no such health problems. Mayor James Keegan O'Connor also incurred the *Morning Telegram*'s editorial ire, and the two parties locked horns throughout the waning months of the 1921 mayoral campaign. The *Morning Telegram*'s editorial opposition to O'Connor doubtless contributed to his defeat at the hands of Dr. Fred J. Douglas in the Republican primaries.[19]

Anyone who earned the support or scorn of the prominent *Morning Telegram* owners was likely to receive corresponding news coverage, for the principals fostered a with-us-or-against-us attitude that profoundly influenced editorial content. For example, Edward L. Wells of the J.B. Wells Department Store irritated the owners with his refusal to advertise in the *Morning Telegram*, so when a Wells employee sustained a minor injury while working in the store, one of the *Morning Telegram* owners called City Editor Hyde and demanded that a reporter be sent at once to cover the catastrophe. When Hyde retorted that no reporter was available, the investor ordered Hyde to drop everything, cover the story himself, and print it the following day.

Another instance of the subjectivity of management directives involved Samuel J. Wolfe, one of the *Morning Telegram*'s ten key stockholders. Numerous arrests were made for freight-car robberies on the New York Central railroad, which resulted in a series of grand jury indictments. Playing a hunch, Hyde instructed his court reporter to remain at the courthouse after the other reporters had left. As a result, the *Morning Telegram* learned of an additional indictment—Wolfe's—and scooped its morning competition, the *Daily Press*. The next day Hyde was chastised by the owners for placing Wolfe in an unflattering light and was ordered not to print additional stories on the matter. Thus, when the trial began, the *Morning Telegram* was forced to ignore it. However, Hyde was permitted to print the news that Wolfe was eventually acquitted.[20]

It was not until its waning days that the *Morning Telegram* followed the *Saturday Globe*'s lead and printed a front-page color cartoon, but the *Morning Telegram* was the first of any Utica daily newspaper to do so. The illustration was the figure of a World War I soldier outlined in red, with a red banner line reading "Forget-Me-Not Edition." Color cartoons also adorned the front page of the Christmas and New Year's issues.[21]

Despite its innovations and muckraking, the *Morning Telegram*'s days were numbered. It was not blessed with the auspicious beginning its weekly sibling enjoyed nearly forty years earlier and quickly began to sputter. The proprietors' gamble of making the *Morning Telegram* a penny paper was an utter failure. Having assumed that the low price would garner the newspaper a large circulation, and thus deliver a large number of potential customers to area businesses in exchange for substantial and lucrative advertising patronage, the owners sacrificed the surety of sales revenue for the prospect of reaping a fortune in advertising. Although its news coverage had improved the last few months, the *Morning Telegram*'s circulation never exceeded 12,000, an unimpressive figure to area advertisers, whose dollars were not adequately filling the coffers. Globe-Telegram Co. President Julius Rothstein complained that every time the paper was delivered to his door it cost him $33. The lack of advertising became such a serious problem that a full-page advertisement from one of the *Morning Telegram*'s stockholders, Matt's West End Brewery, was inserted periodically, usually without charge, just to keep up appearances. The same was true for ads touting the Utica Investment Co., composed of all the *Morning Telegram* owners, as it was all in the family. The dearth of advertising revenue was exacerbated by the evaporation of the postwar boom (which is what led to the *Morning Telegram*'s inception and the *Saturday Globe*'s change of ownership), the rise of unemployment, and the fall of the national market.[22]

Another grave problem was the declining popularity of morning newspapers. Reader and advertiser preference for afternoon papers, plus their advantage of getting same-day news, particularly European war accounts, into their pages, helped slice the number of morning dailies from 500 in 1910 to 388 in 1930.[23]

The third strike against the *Morning Telegram* was the most serious—excessive competition. The introduction of a fourth daily proved to be the saturation point for a city whose growth had slowed dramatically. Once forecast to become a major metropolitan area, Utica was clearly destined for no more prominence than that of a county seat. Competing against three well-established newspapers, the *Morning Telegram* never really secured a foothold in Utica. Its morning competitor, the forty-year-old *Daily Press*, had built up a 27,000 circulation by 1922 and the evening dailies also boasted of large followings. Utica's journalism experience was part of a nationwide decline in newspaper competition. In 1910, the number of general-circulation daily newspapers in the English language peaked at 2,200, along with the number of U.S. cities with competing dailies, which crested at 689. However, just ten years later, when the *Morning Telegram* commenced publication, the number of cities hosting press competition fell to 552 and the total number of dailies dropped to 2,042, most of the deaths attributable to excessive competition. The trend continued in 1930, as the number of dailies dwindled to 1,942 and the number of cities with daily competition shrank by nearly half, to 288. These statistics indicate the inception of the twentieth-century phenomenon of one-newspaper cities. This net loss of 258 newspapers and the loss of daily-newspaper competition in the staggering number of 401 cities over the twenty-year period is all the more astonishing in view of the fact that the population of the United States increased from 92 million to 122 million persons from 1910 to 1930. The rampant growth of American journalism, which had continued unabated since the Revolutionary War, had finally reached its limits. Confronted with the growing popularity of radio and magazines, and later television, daily newspapers began engaging in the social Darwinism which would result in the net loss of about 200 more newspapers and the virtual obsolescence of competing dailies. The *Morning Telegram* was simply one of the many newspapers that fell by the wayside, a victim of cutthroat competition.[24]

Another result was often a merger, a different form of demise for a newspaper. The upstart Gannett Co., based in Rochester, New York, bought and merged the *Observer* and the *Herald-Dispatch* in 1922, shortly after the *Morning Telegram* folded, thereby reducing the number of Utica daily newspapers from four to two within a few months. The hybrid *Observer-Dispatch* had a 33,660 circulation by 1923. The merger allowed the evening newspaper to surge ahead of Utica circulation leader the *Daily Press*, which nonetheless managed a 27,823 circulation in the same year. The *Daily Press* was acquired by Gannett in 1935 and survived for more than fifty years until the media conglomerate killed it in 1987, leaving Utica with just one daily today.[25]

The *Morning Telegram* staff had little knowledge of their newspaper's impending doom until 10 January 1922, when Business Manager Stuart informed the staff that the 11 January issue they were busily assembling would be the last. When Stuart informed the newsmen that the paper had folded, one of the staff composed a whimsical obituary notice for the newspaper that died in infancy, but it was quashed by a stuffy editor.[26] The only announcement appeared in a front-page box:

> With today's issue of the Utica Morning Telegram this newspaper has discontinued publication, having disposed of its interest.
>
> During the year and one half that the Morning Telegram has been in existence it has steadily grown in influence and it has made many staunch friends. The publishers of this paper take this occasion to thank the public for its loyal support and in leaving the daily field it allows of

> greater efforts to further the success of the Utica Saturday Globe, which will continue publication as heretofore, upon a greater scope than in the past. All unexpired subscriptions to the Morning Telegram will be refunded in accordance with the time for which the term of each still has to run.[27]

The final chapter explains just how successful the Globe-Telegram Co. was in publishing the *Saturday Globe* "upon a greater scope than in the past" after the *Morning Telegram*'s demise.

Editor and Publisher also noted the short-lived daily's passing. Under the title "Utica Telegram Suspends," it revealed to its national audience of media practitioners that "The *Morning Telegram*, started here a year and a half ago, announced its suspension today. The publishers, a dozen or more of Utica's leading business men and capitalists, say they discontinue the daily to devote their efforts to the *Utica Saturday Globe*, a weekly with national circulation." The translation of both notices is that the *Morning Telegram* was losing money hand over fist—reportedly more than $300,000 in its brief, tempestuous history, although it had an excellent plant to start with.[28]

Nearly everyone on the *Morning Telegram* who wanted a newspaper job was offered one immediately. Managing Editor Stearns, who had attempted to infuse the *Morning Telegram* with the big-city display methods he had learned in Syracuse, was made editor of the *Saturday Globe* when the *Morning Telegram* folded. Sports Editor Ross was offered a job with the Albany *Knickerbocker Press* the same night as Stuart's somber announcement, and he accepted. His assistant, Semple, remained in town with the *Utica Observer*. Police reporter O'Neil moved on to the Bronx *Home News* and later the *New York Journal*, while courthouse reporter Keating landed a job with the *Syracuse Post-Standard*. Theater reviewer Moore was hired at the *New York Journal*, Hearst's flagship newspaper, and obit man Taylor became a clerk in a Manhattan bookstore. Reporters Maywalt and Spinning also went on to other newspapers, the latter latching on at the *Herkimer Evening Telegram*, twenty-five miles east of Utica, and later at the Springfield, Massachusetts, *Republican*. City Editor Hyde took a post with the *Syracuse Journal* and later became editor of the weeklies in Waterville, New York, and Washington, New Jersey; as editor, he converted Oneida, New York's weekly, the *Dispatch*, into a daily and covered northern New Jersey for *The New York Times*. Business-office employees Benner and Pierce took similar jobs at the *Utica Observer-Dispatch*, and Buddle became an executive with J. P. McKinney and Sons, representative for the Gannett newspaper chain. Assistant city editors Gorman and Kelly had both left the *Morning Telegram* during summer 1921, the former pursuing a law career and the latter returning to the Chicago newspaper scene.[29]

After its demise, the *Morning Telegram* faded rapidly into obscurity. Except for the Williams report, only a few sentences mentioning the *Morning Telegram* exist in public documents, and those are mostly in connection with the *Saturday Globe*. Even fewer people remember the short-lived daily, but former newsboy Tom Dodge is one. In addition to his sales of the *Saturday Globe*, Dodge sold the *Morning Telegram*. ''It was a good paper, but people didn't seem to buy it,'' he recalled. ''It started out good, but people stopped buying it after a while.''

9
A Demise and a Legacy

In the wake of the *Morning Telegram*'s failure, the Globe-Telegram Co. principals were forced to confront the *Saturday Globe*'s dwindling circulation and vanishing profits. The newspaper was a generation removed from its heyday, and its editorial offerings had not changed considerably, although society—and its readers—had. The venerable *Saturday Globe* was foundering, and the newspaper's survival required decisive action. However, the investors were less concerned about revamping the outmoded newspaper than their profit and loss columns. Thus, in an effort to recoup the losses it incurred as a result of the *Morning Telegram's* failure, the Globe-Telegram Co. boosted the *Saturday Globe*'s single-copy price from five cents to seven cents and its yearly subscription price from two dollars to two dollars and fifty cents.[1]

This was a serious error. By concentrating on short-range finances, the investors asked more money for a product that was steadily losing value. This alienated some of the farmers and laborers who comprised much of the *Saturday Globe*'s readership, and whom the Baker brothers had worked so hard to cultivate. The same collapse of the postwar boom which had contributed to the capitalists' decision to disband the *Morning Telegram* had hit ordinary workers much harder, and many couldn't afford the newspaper's price hike. This caused a further circulation erosion, as newspaper sales fell well below the 100,000 mark.

Another grave problem was a lack of leadership. To the absentee owners, the *Saturday Globe* was merely another property, one of many investments bearing a value measured only by the bottom line. It had been the Bakers' primary source of income, and they devoted a corresponding amount of effort to its development, although outside interests whittled away at their time in later years. The new owners simply left the *Saturday Globe*'s operation in others' hands and concerned themselves with profit margins.

Compounding the leadership problem was Dickinson's departure. The veteran editor jumped ship in 1921 after thirty-ninc years with the *Saturday Globe*, all but five of them spent as managing editor. Instead of seeking employment with another newspaper, Dickinson devoted himself to politics on a full-time basis, winning election as Oneida County treasurer and serving three terms. When the *Saturday Globe* ceased publication, the *Utica Observer-Dispatch* praised Dickinson in glowing terms, noting, "Dickinson was editor of the Saturday Globe in its palmiest days and his service was a large factor in presenting the greatest news stories of the time in the manner which won thousands of admiring subscribers to the publication."[2]

After the *Morning Telegram* folded, Stearns took over as editor of the *Saturday Globe* in February 1922, but he was not happy. He preferred working on daily newspapers, and when Hearst started the *Syracuse Telegram* later that year, one of seven papers Hearst initiated or purchased in 1922, Stearns took a job at that daily. The newspaper fared little better than its Utica namesake, folding within a few years, although its *Syracuse American* Sunday edition lives on along with the old *Syracuse Herald*'s Sunday edition as the hybrid Sunday *Herald-American*, now owned by the Newhouse chain, along with the morning *Post-Standard* and the afternoon *Herald Journal*.

Stearns was replaced at the *Saturday Globe*'s helm by twenty-nine-year-old John J. O'Connor, a graduate of Holy Cross College and a World War I veteran. The Troy, New York, native had little previous newspaper experience, "but he was very literate. All his life he wrote stories and essays," said Florentine Slyer, O'Connor's daughter. O'Connor had planned to become a Catholic priest and was in a seminary for several years. Ten days before his ordination, he decided to resign. "He told them [at the seminary] 'if I became a priest and broke my vow of chastity I'd kill myself,'" Slyer said. "Throughout his life he was very religious. He was like a little saint." O'Connor relied on his religious beliefs during his stint as the *Saturday Globe*'s editor. "He used to say, 'If you tell people the truth, they won't like it. If you don't tell them the truth, God won't like it,'" she added. After the *Saturday Globe* folded, O'Connor taught at Siena College in Loudonville, New York, and St. John's Law School in Brooklyn (now Jamaica, Queens), New York.[3]

With circulation dropping steadily, in May 1922 the *Saturday Globe* published the third of its three self-histories, less than two-and-a-half years after the second autobiography, although it was the first published under the new owners. Largely a rehash of the 1920 history that traced the newspaper's genesis and early years of struggle, the 1922 annals noted in a self-congratulatory manner that writers and artists of the *Saturday Globe* covered "cyclones, forest fires, floods, coal mine disasters, electrocutions, railroad wrecks, labor troubles such as those at Homestead [Florida], inaugurations of Governors and Presidents, conflagrations in cities, lynchings, night riders, white cappers [Ku Klux Klan members] and such bizarre incidents as Carrie [*sic*] Nation's crusade and Coxey's Army march on Washington."[4]

The account also reminded readers of its brilliant color cartoons. "The cartoons in colors of the *Saturday Globe*, dealing with current events of national and international interest, are famous and called forth many compliments from people of distinction the country over. It was one of the *Globe*'s cartoons that attracted the attention of Count von Bismarck, one of the three great architects of the former German empire, and brought the appreciative letter from his secretary."[5]

Probably mindful of the plummeting circulation and migration of national advertisers to magazines, the *Saturday Globe* neatly deflected the pressing question of what the newspaper's future would be, preferring instead to rest on its laurels. "What will the future be? We know not, but if the past is a criterion of the future we are sanguine that the *Saturday Globe*, still growing and improving with the years, will be brighter, better, more entertaining and more interesting with each recurring anniversary."[6]

Despite this flagrantly obvious attempt at self-promotion, the *Saturday Globe*'s fortunes only deteriorated, eclipsing all hopes for its recovery. Finally the businessmen had all they could endure. Circulation had plunged below 50,000 and showed no signs of rising. The paper had been losing money like water through a sieve. After a 14 February meeting between the Globe-Telegram Co. principals and a committee from the local Typographical Union, the group reached a decision to cease publication with the 16 February issue. This move put hundreds of employees out of work, including three who had been with the newspaper since its inception forty-three years earlier—chief artist William Carson and printers Thomas Jones and Edward Dillon.[7]

The investors had made the mistake of running the newspaper like a retail establishment, letting others look after the business while the proprietors kept a wary eye on the balance sheet. Reporting on the demise of the once-mighty *Saturday Globe*, the *Utica Daily Press* identified this problem. It noted that the group of investors "was made up of prominent businessmen who were and are unfamiliar with the newspaper game and its workings. The business and management was left to outside interests, while the stockholders devoted their time to their own personal connections. The arrangement did not prove a financial success, and suspension follows." The reference to a lack of financial success was an understatement. The Globe-Telegram Co. filed for bankruptcy 7 June 1924, claiming debts of $326,265 while possessing assets of only $188,805.[8]

The *Utica Daily Press* halfheartedly eulogized its fallen fellow Bagg's Square denizen, writing on its editorial page:

> The suspension of the Saturday Globe, which has been published in this city for forty-three years, calls for a word of comment and possibly an expression of regret. This paper was an innovation when it started. It represented a new idea, that of publishing pictures for the purpose of more vividly presenting the news. Like every new idea it had its struggles at the beginning, but perseverance and faith in the enterprise triumphed and the paper became one of the most widely circulated weeklies in the country. Its success was primarily due to the illustrations it carried, which were a new thing in journalism at that time. When new and cheaper processes for making cuts came, daily newspapers began the publication of pictures and thus the field which the Globe had made peculiarly its own became open to competition, making it difficult for the weekly to compete against the daily. It is possible that the Globe might have survived if it had adapted itself to changing conditions, but that can be only speculation, although since its advent, successful weeklies along the same line have been launched. The Globe was a distinctly Utica institution, conceived by Uticans, who for many years made it a great success. There are doubtless homes in this and other counties to which it has been a weekly visitor throughout its existence and in them it will be missed. There have been men employed on its staff who will contemplate with regret the fact that it is no more. It has run its course, but in the annals of Utica newspapers it will be recorded as a venture which shone with unusual brilliance for a time and then flickered out.[9]

Editor and Publisher also noted the *Saturday Globe*'s passing, reporting that "The Utica Saturday Globe has ceased publication, and '30' has been written on the career of an illustrated weekly newspaper that was famous as well as prosperous in its best days .... It was a 5-cent paper containing features, news and pictures; editions being printed nearly every day of the week for various sections of the country. It was founded in 1881 by two brothers, Thomas F. and William T. Baker, residents of Utica, one a printer, the other a marble cutter."[10]

The mightly presses that once cranked out the newspapers read by farmers, merchants, and heads of state were sold to the newly-formed *Newark Press*, a New Jersey daily, for $9,100. It is anyone's guess what became of all the other equipment and the newspaper morgue. The fate of the business records and correspondence has never been conclusively determined, although von Bernuth, Will Baker's granddaughter, suspects they were destroyed in a fire years after the *Saturday Globe* folded.[11]

William Baker remained at the helm of the Utica and Clayville knitting companies until his death 9 April 1934 at age eighty-nine. He was also president of the Utica Gas and Electric Co. at the time of his death. Baker's obituary in *Editor and Publisher* seems to imply that these activities, as well as those of his brother, diverted their attention from the *Saturday Globe*, perhaps at a time when it was needed most. The trade publication reported "the brothers enjoyed great success as publishers and amassed great personal fortunes which, more or less directly, brought them into other businesses." It cited Will Baker's aforementioned positions outside the publishing world and added, "He also was much interested in many other business enterprises in his section." Calling the elder Baker "one of the nation's leading journalists," *Editor and Publisher* noted that the *Saturday Globe* was an "early picture newspaper [which] gained nationwide prominence and influence, and at its height reached a circulation of more than 250,000 copies." The obituary cited the newspaper's early "precarious existence until the assassination of President Garfield. Then it took a new lease on life and was much enlarged and improved."[12]

Neither Tom nor Will sired sons, probably a major factor in the latter's decision to sell the *Saturday Globe* to the investors in 1920, von Bernuth observed. She remembered growing up in Baker's opulent home. "My mother had seven children and we lived in the old house on Genesee Street. Although we all ran around the house that he owned, he never said 'boo.' He was very moderate in everything," she recalled. Much of the fortune Baker amassed from the *Saturday Globe* and the knitting mills was lost on failed business ventures, and he was not affluent in his twilight years. "He invested lots of money in Utica businesses which didn't succeed," von Bernuth said. "He was a real Utica booster, you see." Will and Tom were also ardent supporters of laborers, which is why the *Saturday Globe* never joined the many other newspapers in excoriating unions. "The whole family had been raised Irish poor, so they were very pro-union and prolaborer," von Bernuth said. Will Baker was also in favor of walking. He daily walks to and from work constituted his chief form of exercise. "My grandfather never learned to drive," she said. "I sometimes used to go on walks with him. He was shaky walking in his later years, and he used to hold on to my wrist. He had an iron grip which I'll never forget. It really used to hurt sometimes."[13]

Shortly after the *Saturday Globe* folded, the building was occupied by the Horrocks-Ibbotson Co., a manufacturer of fishing equipment, until its bankruptcy in summer 1978. The building still stands, vacant since then, although the ravages of time have exacted a stiff price. The building was purchased in 1982 by the Bagg's Square Association, a historical preservation society, which sought to safeguard the *Saturday Globe*'s home from the wrecker's ball. The organization had planned to convert the structure into a national news media hall of fame and museum, but funding presented problem, and the plan never reached fruition. The *Saturday Globe* building was condemned in 1988 and now faces the possibility no one wants to think about but everyone knows looms on the horizon—the building, in the state and national Registers of Historic Places, may have to be razed, lest it collapse. Granddaughter von Bernuth said she hopes to save the most important part of the structure before then, though—the striking sandstone relief of the newsboy superimposed on a globe that adorns the building's cornice. "We, my siblings and I, hope to obtain the relief before the building falls down," she wrote.[14]

Besides the crumbling building, few legacies remain from the weekly newspaper. In Utica, an assortment of *Saturday Globe* back issues may be found at the Oneida Historical Society and the Utica Public Library. Utica's Howe and Dickinson streets are named for the veteran *Saturday Globe* artist and managing editor, respectively. Denis Howe died in 1944 and Albert Dickinson followed two years later. Outside of Utica, back issues may be found scattered throughout a few historical repositories, particularly the New-York Historical Society. Books, journals, and magazines pertaining to mass-communication history have been strangely silent on the internationally-circulated weekly with the enormous circulation.[15]

The Baker brothers' formula for success was to illustrate the news articles, featuring not only head-and-shoulders pictures of those prominent in the news but also the events themselves. The paper printed some beautiful, vivid illustrations throughout its history, thanks in large measure to Dickinson's consistent pairing of reporters with artists on major story assignments. Dickinson's insistence on vivid writing and exhaustive accounts of news events, regardless of the location and expense involved in sending a news team to the scene, paid handsome dividends in circulation revenue and geographic scope of circulation.

On the managerial side, the Bakers had their share of successes. Possessing some prior newspaper experience and profound business acumen, Will and Tom lived by the time-honored maxim, "You have to spend money to make money." They expended enormous sums to produce a multitude of quality illustrations, which they displayed conspicuously. The newspaper was targeted to the farm, the family, and the comon laborer, and there was no presumption of women's ineligibility to read the *Saturday Globe*. In fact, Dickinson remarked at a public speech thirteen years after his retirement from the newspaper that he was especially proud that the *Saturday Globe* published nothing which could not be read aloud in the home.[16]

That the Bakers courted such salt-of-the-earth types as farmers and blue-collar workers to be chief constituents of the newspaper's readership was a stroke of genius. It was just such common folk who would most appreciate illustrated stories, yet who might be the least likely to buy a daily newspaper. To maximize the possibility that laborers and farmers would buy their newspaper, the Bakers decided to sell it on Saturday. This was payday for laborers of the era and a convenient day for farmers, who welcomed the paper for reading on Sunday, traditionally a day of rest among Christians.

The *Saturday Globe* was born in an era of profound growth, both in Utica and across the nation, but it was still very much an agrarian, community-oriented period, a far cry from today's "global village" syndrome and instantaneous delivery of news worldwide. The *Saturday Globe* was often a reader's first source of information about remarkable occurrences in other towns, states, and nations. Its competitive edge fizzled, however, when rival newspapers and magazines began to crowd the field and use the *Saturday Globe*'s own innovations. As a pair of business writers observed recently, "Competition makes it next to impossible to earn high rates of profits for very many years running. However secure the possessor of the business may feel, others will find a way to get a piece of the action, and the competitors will drive down . . . profit margins. As theory, this is as old as Adam Smith . . ."[17] Concurrently, the public became more sophisticated in its reading habits and grew less enamored of newspapers such as the *Saturday Globe*, which played up the tragedies and aberrations. The lure of the sensational press had waned substantially by the early twentieth century, giving place within the first decade to greater degrees of journalistic objectivity, balance, factuality, and restraint, which both encouraged, and was encouraged by, a growing public sense of informed and critical consumption of news.

Although the *Saturday Globe* did not customarily match the sensationalism of Hearst's *San Francisco Examiner* and New York *Journal* and Pulitzer's New York *World*, it was a newspaper that was born and raised to national circulation during the height of yellow journalism, and thus adopted some characteristics of the method in vogue. But as public needs and interests changed, the *Saturday Globe* remained static. In response to a larger and more intricate society, people demanded that their news be fresh and delivered promptly—the most obvious advantage a daily newspaper can have over a weekly. So much of what the journalistic trade defined as news was taking place in ever-growing communities that average citizens could no longer keep abreast of developments even in their own towns and cities, and thus turned to the press to supplant their direct experience with a mediated one, governed by factuality. Media critic Walter Lippman took a jaundiced view of this greater reliance on the surveillance function of the press. "The world about which each man is supposed to have opinions has become so complicated as to defy his powers of understanding. What he knows of events that matter enormously to him, the purposes of governments, the aspirations of peoples, the struggle of classes, he knows at second, third or fourth hand. He cannot go and see for himself," Lippman wrote. As a result, people trust in journalism for their information, even though "News comes from a distance; it comes helter-skelter, in inconceivable confusion; it deals with matters that are not easily understood; it arrives and is assimilated by busy and tired people."[18]

The *Saturday Globe* could not provide the timeliness of a daily, and it never tried to be an objective and comprehensive factual journal—that would have been too stark a transmogrification of its identity. Its format did not change until its final seasons, and by then the atrophy had gone too far. In the decade before and after the turn of the century, newspapers and journalists throughout the nation were severing their ties with sensationalist journalism—not so much for the sake of morality as for the economic prudence of posturing themselves as dignified public servants, newly scrubbed clean of sensationalism's taint. In 1904, the *Toledo Blade* claimed that its interest in public matters "IS AND WILL BE PURELY THE INTEREST OF THE PEOPLE .... The Blade feels itself to be a PART of Toledo—it feels the PEOPLE'S interests to be ITS interests." Beginning in 1908, the *Minneapolis Tribune* claimed in its masthead to be "a paper which any father or mother may welcome into the home circle as they would a friend—an interesting, intensely entertaining, well-intentioned family friend whose presence is cheerful as the sunlight." Even *Utica Observer* editor W. W. Canfield launched an assault on sensationalism, claiming that newspapers should be regarded as "a companion," and thus "surely the intelligent would not accept as a companion the vicious and the depraved." By not changing as its audience changed, the *Saturday*

Globe fell victim to the developments and reader preferences which had elevated it to national prominence in the first place.[19]

It was also doomed economically. As a general newspaper, the *Saturday Globe* could not offer a specialized market to advertisers, and it could not offer the circulation guarantee its magazine competitors could. In an era of specialization, the *Saturday Globe* found itself lacking in quantity of readership and breadth of content to compete with national magazines, but not quite parochial enough to deliver a select and geographically discrete body of readers to advertisers. According to the axiom from the advertising field, specialized publications offer specialized readers to specialized advertisers. Despite its relatively high circulation (approximately 50,000 in its final year), the *Saturday Globe* folded, proving large circulation does not necessarily translate into financial solvency.

Perhaps no better eulogy can be written for the *Saturday Globe* than the one it crafted for itself, four years before its actual demise. Just before it was sold to the Globe-Telegram Co., the newspaper reviewed its long and illustrious life. In an article probably written by Dickinson, the paper presented "A Glance Back to the Babyhood of the Globe":

> Along the highway leading from then to the present there are many milestones, and among these are many monuments to which we who have long been with the Globe look back with quickened pulses. We flush with pardonable pride when we recall that the Globe was the first five-cent paper in the world to print a half-tone cut; that we were the first to print on a cylinder press a paper illustrated with halftones; that it was in our office that the first half-tone cut was cast into a form instead of being "matrixed;" that ours was the first newspaper to print cartoons and half-tones in colors; that ours was the only paper in central New York to send a man to Johnstown and keep him there during those awful weeks succeeding the great disaster; that ours was the only paper in the state outside the metropolis to send a writer and photographer to Galveston when that beautiful city was destroyed by wind and wave; that in order to get the exact facts and legitimate pictures we have sent our representatives direct from the home office into more than three-quarters of the States making up the union; that our subscribers have come from the wilds of Alaska and the teeming cities of China; that we have received personal letters of approval from Supreme Court judges, Presidents of the United States, and even from Queen Victoria herself.[20]

The "Glance" hearkens to the newspaper's former greatness. Now all that remains is the building, some copies of the paper, and the memories of a few elderly Uticans.

The building remains at the west end of Bagg's Square, which is no longer the heart of town. Despite signs marking it condemned, the building is accessible. Step through the rotting door whose panes of glass have long since been shattered by vandals and take the tour described by the *Saturday Globe* in its 1893 autobiography.[21] Although the front of the building is marred by a faded yet intrusive "Horrocks-Ibbotson Co." sign and the floor is littered with business records of the defunct fishing-equipment company, you can still hear, if you try hard enough, the excited hum of the newsroom and roar of the Campbell and Cottrell presses, smell the sickly scent of printers' ink and envision the constant flurry of activity.

Take a short walk to the center of Bagg's Square. Union Station is still there, but on most days there are more grizzled old men hanging around the barber shop than passengers waiting for Amtrak to whisk them to Albany or Buffalo. Bagg's Square is now a feeble, nearly comatose, and largely forgotten part of town. Once the nerve center of a thriving city, the square is now strangely silent. Drive along Broad Street from Bagg's Square to the city line, near the railroad tracks, where you flirt with the border of Herkimer County. This is the oldest part of Utica. Read the names of the once prosperous, now defunct, businesses on the walls of the crumbling, eerie edifices. Broad Street Hardware Corp. Heber dry goods store. Roberts Hardware Co., which a faded, obscure sign proudly notes was "established 1820." They read like a death knell for the entire northeast end of the city. The fortunes of Utica have changed since the boom years of the late nineteenth and early twentieth centuries, and probably because of that, so too has the complexion changed. The center of town has moved half a league hence, leaving the desolate, historic Bagg's Square area in its wake much as an ocean typhoon leaves flotsam. Although the *Saturday Globe* commanded an international audience, it is a shining example of how a newspaper's fortunes are inextricably linked to its host city's economy.

Walk along the quiet, cracked streets of the old downtown area—Water, Main, Post, Catherine streets—and listen carefully. If you let go for a moment you can still hear the cry of aggressive newsboys like Tom Dodge or the Lee brothers. "Extree! Extree! Mystery of the headless body solved! Read all about it in the *Saturday Globe*!" But blink and it's gone. You might gaze back wistfully at the imposing, decaying *Saturday Globe* building, your eyes meeting those of the ever-youthful, sandstone newsboy on the building's cornice, his mouth open in the hawker's cry and his arm waving a newspaper. He is the only remaining symbol of the faded glory of a newspaper which has long since nestled into the bosom of obscurity.

What might have been, had the *Saturday Globe* survived, is

anyone's guess. *USA Today* exists as a glitzy, precocious philosophical successor to the *Saturday Globe*, capitalizing irreverently on its legacy, making truckloads of money along the path the *Saturday Globe* blazed a century before. Not only has *USA Today* invested heavily (and successfully) in its artwork, graphics, use of color, and quality of printing just as the *Saturday Globe* did, it also has adopted a similar readership philosophy. "USA Today's secret is very simple," Gannett Co. chairman Allen Neuharth told an audience. "It communicates with the reader on a personal level . . . in an upbeat, exciting, positive environment." Neuharth noted proudly, "It's the most widely imitated newspaper in the USA."[22]

Yet from the arcane grave of dead newspapers the *Saturday Globe* has a lesson to teach the brash and colorful successor to the national-newspaper throne. Just as the *Saturday Globe* was choked off and eventually buried by stifling competition that capitalized on its innovations, so too may pass *USA Today*, as weather maps and front-page pictures in dailies across the country burst forth in all the colors of the rainbow (history does repeat itself), and well-crafted news stories are mutilated to meet the reading habits of a fast-food public. *USA Today* shouldn't be too smug in welcoming the design mimics to the world of gaily-colored newspapers. The *Saturday Globe* has been there before.

The *Saturday Globe* is long gone, and with it passed an era of vivid writing and stunning illustrations. The old newspaper lives on in the minds of a few survivors from those halcyon days. "One of my most vivid memories from my childhood was visiting my grandfather in Herkimer. He used to sit out on the porch, put his feet up and open that *Saturday Globe*. He used to like it a lot," Betty Carroll remembered. "The front page was very colorful," Cornelia Springer added. "They always had these big pictures on the front page. I remember it was quite sensational." Loyal *Saturday Globe* newsboy Tom Dodge said he still misses the old weekly. "The *Globe* was a fine paper," he said. "They don't make 'em that way anymore, which is too bad. There will never be another one like it."[23]

Afterword

Marietta von Bernuth

The *Saturday Globe* was founded by my grandfather, William T. Baker, and his brother, Thomas F. Baker. Its demise took place when I was eight years old. My parents and my siblings lived with my grandfather, "Pa Bakes," as we called him. He was a genial and agreeable man, fond of children, and so we ran in and out of his quarters in the house freely. He kept a generous supply of gum and Life Savers in his room, and we were encouraged to help ourselves at any time. Every Sunday he gave each of us a quarter, which seemed to us like a fortune. He also passed out quarters to other children who visited our house. This was at a time when John D. Rockefeller, said to be the richest man in the world, received a good deal of publicity for giving out dimes.

We enjoyed talking to our grandfather, but like most children we were more interested in the present than in the past, and so we never talked with him about the *Saturday Globe*. Pa Bakes was a loyal citizen of Utica and a member of a group called the Utica Boosters, which was dedicated to bringing industry to Utica and spreading the word of its advantages as a place to live. My grandfather was a firm believer in Utica's future and invested in its industries as a matter of civic duty.

The newspaper that he and his brother founded became nationally and even internationally known. Ralph Frasca has done a wonderful job in recording its rise and fall. My family and I are grateful to him for his appreciation of the *Saturday Globe*'s founders and their contribution to American journalism.

Appendix

This appendix lists all available circulation data on the *Saturday Globe* during its fourty-three-year existence. Some entries include a notation regarding a major story, a significant event occurring at the time, or, in the case of circulation data gleaned from a newspaper directory, whether the figure given is a sworn statement or unattested.

Utica Saturday Globe Circulation Data

Month & Year	*Circulation*	*Average or Peak*	*Notes*	*Sources*
21 May 1881	700	peak	The first issue	Utica Saturday Globe 27 May 1893, p. 1.
11 June 1881	1,345	average		Utica Saturday Globe 15 June 1889, p. 4.
2 July 1881	3,000	peak	President Garfield shot	Utica Daily Press, 15 February 1924, p. 1.
9 July 1881	10,000	peak	Page-one woodcut of Garfield	The Courier Magazine, October 1953, p. 22.
April 1882	7,500	average		Utica Daily Press
1 May 1882	8,000	average		Utica Saturday globe, 27 May 1893, p. 1.
3 June 1882	7,835	average		Utica Saturday Globe, 15 June 1889, p. 4.
1 July 1882	22,000	peak	Guiteau executed	Utica Saturday Globe, 27 May 1893, p. 1.
May 1883	15,000	average		The Courier Magazine, p. 22.
9 June 1883	15,840	average		Utica Saturday Globe, 15 June 1889, p. 4.
May 1884	25,000	average		Utica Saturday Globe, 27 May 1893, p. 1.
14 June 1884	26,808	average		Utica Saturday Globe, 15 June 1889, p. 4.
May 1885	35,000	average		Utica Saturday Globe, 27 May 1893, p. 1.
13 June 1885	36,780	average		Utica Saturday Globe, 15 June 1889, p. 4.

Month & Year	*Circulation*	*Average or Peak*	*Notes*	*Sources*
1 January 1886	45,000	average	Move into new home on Whitesboro Street	Utica Saturday Globe, 27 May 1893, p. 1.
April 1886	44,000	average		Utica Daily Press.
12 June 1886	47,116	average		Utica Saturday Globe, 15 June 1889, p. 4.
December 1886	55,000	average		Utica Saturday Globe, 27 May 1893, P. 1.
6 March 1887	121,087	peak	Roxalana Druse execution	Utica Saturday Globe, 27 May 1893, p. 1.
Late March 1887	80,000	average		Utica Observer, 22 March 1887, p. 1.
April 1887	87,880	average		Utica Daily Press
11 June 1887	85,218	average		Utica Saturday Globe, 15 June 1889, p. 4.
Summer 1887	80,000–90,000	average		Utica Saturday Globe, 27 May 1893, p. 1.
April 1888	128,900	average		Utica Daily Press
May 1888	115,000	average		Utica Saturday Globe
9 June 1888	108,850	average		Utica Saturday Globe, 15 June 1889, p. 4.
16 March 1889	186,347	peak	Hartford Hotel explosion	The Courier Magazine, p. 36.
May 1889	160,000	average	Just prior to Johnstown Flood	Utica Saturday Globe, 27 May 1873, p. 1.
8 June 1889	205,200	peak	Johnstown Flood story on page one	Utica Saturday Globe, 15 June 1889, p. 4.
15 June 1889	268,536	peak	More on Johnstown Flood	Utica Saturday Globe, 27 May 1893, p. 1.
April 1890	194,287	average		Utica Daily Press
1890	200,000	average		History of America's Magazines, vol. 3, p. 68.
1891	165,354	average		David M. Ellis, The Upper Mohawk Country, p. 71.
1893	180,000	average		Utica Saturday Globe, 27 May 1893, p. 1.
1896	150,000	average		Pettingill's Newspaper Directory, p. 237.
20 March 1897	294,000	peak	Corbett-Jeffries fight	Paul Williams, "Utica's Newspapers since 1900," p. 8.
1912	112,368	average	Sworn statement	Ayer American Newspaper Annuals and Directory, 1912, p. 665.
1915	100,000	average	Unattested statement	Ayer, 1915, p. 692.
22 July 1916	80,589	average	Advertisement	Editor and Publisher, July 1916, p. 19.
1919	100,000	average	Unattested statement	Ayer, 1919, p. 698.

Month & Year	*Circulation*	*Average or Peak*	*Notes*	*Sources*
1921	100,000	average	Unattested statement	Ayer, 1921, p. 705
16 February 1924	Less than 50,000	average	The last issue	Utica Observer-Dispatch, 15 Feburary 1924, p. 1.

Notes

Preface

1. Marietta von Bernuth to Ralph Frasca, 4 August 1989. Personal files of Ralph Frasca.

2. G. Thomas Tanselle, "Thoughts on Research in Printing History," *Printing History* 9 (no. 2, 1987), pp. 24–25.

3. Robert Jones Shafer, *A Guide to Historical Method*, 3d ed. (Homewood, Ill.: Dorsey, 1980), pp. 12–13.

4. Some example include Jim Allee Hart, *A History of the St. Louis Globe-Democrat* (Columbia: University of Missouri Press, 1961); Roy Hoopes, *Ralph Ingersoll: A Biography* (New York: Atheneum, 1985); Richard Kluger, *The Paper: The Life and Death of the New York Herald Tribune* (New York: Knopf, 1986); Julian S. Rammelkamp, *Pulitzer's Post-Dispatch, 1878–1883* (Princeton: Princeton University Press, 1967); Nancy L. Roberts, *Dorothy Day and the Catholic Worker* (Albany: State University of New York Press, 1984).

Chapter 1. The Genesis

1. J. A. Leo Lemay and P. M. Zall, eds., *The Autobiography of Benjamin Franklin: A Genetic Text* (Knoxville: University of Tennessee Press, 1981), pp. 93–94.

2. John J. Walsh, *Vignettes of Old Utica* (Utica, New York: Utica Public Library, 1982), p. 322.

3. W. J. Rorabaugh, *The Craft Apprentice: From Franklin to the Machine Age in America* (New York: Oxford University Press, 1986); Milton W. Hamilton, *The Country Printer* (New York: Columbia University Press, 1936), pp. 4344. On the correlation between apprenticeships and class hierarchy, see John Clapham, *A Concise Economic History of Britain* (Cambridge: Cambridge University Press, 1951), p. 133. On apprenticeships in the eighteenth-century printing trade, see Ralph Frasca, "From Apprentice to Journeyman to Partner: Benjamin Franklin's Workers and the Growth of the Early-American Printing Trade," *Pennsylvania Magazine of History and Biography* 114 (April 1990): pp. 229–48.

4. *Utica Daily Press*, 15 February, 1920.

5. *Saturday Globe*, 24 January, 1920.

6. Henry J. Cookinham, *History of Oneida County, New York* (Chicago: Clarke, 1912), pp. 287–88; *Utica Daily Press*, 15 February 1924; Walsh, unpublished manuscript that was the first draft of *Vignettes of Old Utica*, p. 366. On Sunday newspapers, see Michael Schudson, *Discovering the News: A Social History of American Newspapers* (New York: Basic, 1978), p. 99.

7. Hamilton, *The Country Printer*, pp. 216–20; *Dutchess Observer*, 1 October 1817; Moses M. Bagg, *Memorial History of Utica, New York* (Syracuse, N.Y.: Mason, 1892), p. 486.

8. Samuel Durant, *History of Oneida County, New York* (Philadelphia: Everts and Fariss, 1878), p. 304; Bagg, *Memorial History of Utica*, p. 486.

9. Walsh, unpublished manuscript, p. 366.

10. The 1880 census was 33,914, according to Douglas M. Preston and David M. Ellis, "The Ethnic Dimension," in a *The History of Oneida County* (Utica, N.Y. Hutson, 1977), p. 66.

11. Gary B. Nash, *The Urban Crucible* (Cambridge: Harvard University Press, 1979), p. 55; Walsh, *Vignettes of Old Utica*, p. 1; *Oneida County Gazetteer and Business Directory* (Utica, N.Y.: Gaffney, 1902), p. 122.

12. Walsh, *Vignettes of Old Utica*, p. 1.

13. George E. Condon, *Stars in the Water: The Story of the Erie Canal* (Garden City, N.Y.: Doubleday, 1974).

14. John F. Stover, *American Railroads* (Chicago: University of Chicago Press, 1961), p. 264–69; Walsh, *Vignettes of Utica*, p. 120; *Oneida Whig*, 9 August 1836; F. Daniel Larkin, "Three Centuries of Transportation," in *The History of Oneida County* (Utica, N.Y.: Hutson, 1977), p. 34.

15. Larkin, "Three Centuries of Transportation," p. 32.

16. *Western Centinel* 23 September 1795.

17. *Utica Patriot*, 11 January 1811.

18. Walsh, *Vignettes of Old Utica*, pp. 15, 167; *Oneida County Gazetteer and Business Directory*, p. 124.

19. Walsh, *Vignettes of Old Utica*, p. 255.

20. *Utica Herald*, 15 September 1863.

21. Virgil C. Crisafulli, "Agriculture," *The History of Oneida County*, p. 49.

22. Walsh, *Vignettes of Old Utica*, p. 258–59; *Utica Daily Press*, 10 April 1934.

23. T. Wood Clarke, *Utica for a Century and a Half* (Utica, N.Y.: Widtman, 1952), pp. 73, 81.

24. Robert E. Park and Ernest W. Burgess, *The City* (Chicago: University of Chicago Press, 1967), p. 1.

25. Quoted in Preston and Ellis, "The Ethnic Dimension," p. 59.

26. On the Oneida Community, see Maren Lockwood Carden, *Oneida: Utopian Community to Modern Corporation* (Baltimore: Johns Hopkins University Press, 1969); Ira L. Mandelker, *Religion, Society, and Utopia in Nineteenth-Century America* (Amherst: University of Massachusetts Press, 1984); Robert Allerton Parker, *A Yankee Saint: John Humphrey Noyes and the Oneida Community* (New York: G. P. Putnam's Sons, 1935).

27. Douglas B. Adams, "The Booster Press Reconsidered: Toward Redefinition," paper presented at the Association for Education in Journalism and Mass Communication Big Ten Conference, Minneapolis, Minn., April 1988, p. 12; Lemay and Zall, *The Autobiography of Benjamin Franklin*; E. P. Thompson, "Time, Work-Discipline, and Industrial Capitalism," *Past and Present* 38 (December 1967), pp. 56–97; Paul G. Faler, *Mechanics and Manufacturers in the Early Industrial Revolution: Lynn, Massachusetts, 1780–1860* (Albany: State University of New York Press, 1981), pp. 103–5; Paul E. Johnson, *A Shopkeeper's Milennium: Society and Revivals in Rochester, New York, 1815–1837* (New York: Hill & Wang, 1978).

28. *Evangelical Magazine and Gospel Advocate*, 12 May 1832, 12 February 1831.

Numerous religious newspapers and pamphlets were published in this era. For the argument that the rise of evangelism led to mass printing of religious tracts, see David Paul Nord, "The Evangelical Origins of Mass Media in America, 1815–1835," *Journalism Monographs* 88 (May 1984).

29. Dwight McDonald, "A Theory of Mass Culture," *Diogenes* 3 (Summer 1953), pp. 1–17.

30. It is important to note that this legacy of independence and the concomitant public-service ideology were not inherent in the American press from its humble seventeenth-century beginnings, but evolved gradually, emerging in the mid-eighteenth century. For the argument that, "As colonial America slowly developed its own independent national character, printers and social leaders recognized the value of a free press to an increasingly self-governing people and developed an ideology of active public service which transgressed boundaries of placid neutrality and clinging dependence on government," see Ralph Frasca, "The Professionalization of American Colonial Journalism," paper presented at the American Journalism Historians Association Convention, Atlanta, Ga., October 1989.

31. *Long Island Star*, 8 June 1809; *Suffolk County Recorder*, 8 August 1817; *Watertown Censor*, 13 April 1830; prospectus of the *Evening Post*, 16 November 1801.

32. I have made this point elsewhere about the press of a slightly earlier era. See Ralph Frasca, "Benjamin Franklin's Printing Network," *American Journalism* 5 (3, 1988): pp. 145–58.

33. Frank Luther Mott, *American Journalism* (New York: Macmillan, 1950), p. 169; Hamilton, *The Country Printer*, especially pp. 95–135.

34. *Western Spectator*, 19 April 1831.

35. Bernard A. Weisberger, *The American Newspaperman* (Chicago: University of Chicago Press, 1961), p. 89.

36. Clarence S. Brigham, *History and Bibliography of American Newspapers, 1690–1820* (Worcester, Mass.: American Antiquarian Society, 1947); Winifred Gregory, *American Newspapers 1821–1936* (New York: Wilson, 1937); Edward C. Lathem, *Chronological Tables of American Newspapers, 1690–1820* (Worcester, Mass.: American Antiquarian Society, 1972).

37. *Utica Daily Gazette*, 2 February 1846.

38. Donald L. Shaw, "News Bias and the Telegraph: A Study of Historical Change," *Journalism Quarterly* 44 (Spring 1967): pp. 3–12, 31; Richard A. Schwarzlose, "The Nation's First Wire Service: Evidence Supporting A Footnote," *Journalism Quarterly* 57 (Winter 1980): p. 555. For a view that rejects the notion that "the practice of the Associated Press became the ideal of journalism in general," see Schudson, *Discovering the News*, pp. 4–5.

39. Walter Lippman, *Liberty and the News* (New York: Harcourt, Brace and Howe, 1920), p. 71.

40. *Watertown Censor*, 13 April 1830; Anon., *Alton Trials* ... (New York: J. F. Trow 1838; reprint ed., Miami, Fla.: Mnemosyne, 1969).

41. Quoted in Sean Wilentz, *Chants Democratic: New York City and the Rise of the American Working Class, 1788–1850* (New York: Oxford University Press, 1984), p. 131.

42. Lemay and Zall, *The Autobiography of Benjamin Franklin* p. 70; "Poor Richard, 1744," in Leonard W. Labaree et al., eds., *The Papers of Benjamin Franklin* (New Haven: Yale University Press, 1959) 9: 396.

43. *Oneida County Gazetteer and Business Directory*, pp. 123–24.

Chapter 2. The *Globe* Begins to Turn

1. "The Utica Saturday Globe," *The Courier Magazine*, October 1953: p. 20. In an "Editor's Note," it is revealed that the anonymous author relied on "pertinent letters pertaining to the Globe," provided by a George Town of Utica. Neither Town nor this correspondence has been found, despite an exhaustive search.
2. Preston and Ellis, "The Ethnic Dimension," p. 66.
3. "The Utica Saturday Globe," p. 20.
4. *Utica Daily Press*, 15 February 1924.
5. *Saturday Globe*, 27 May 1893.
6. Ibid.; *Saturday Globe*, 21 May 1881.
7. On boosterism, see Carl Abbott, *Boosters and Businessmen* (Westport, Conn.: Greenwood, 1981); Daniel J. Boorstin, *The Americans: The National Experience* (New York: Random House, 1965), pp. 113–68; Robert R. Dykstra, *The Cattle Towns* (New York: Knopf, 1971); Michael Emery and Edwin Emery, *The Press and America: An Interpretive History of the Mass Media*, 6th ed. (Englewood Cliffs, N. J.: Prentice-Hall, 1988), pp. 89–114; Patrick F. Palermo, "Boosterism, Politics and the Community: An Interactionist Interpretation of the Turner Thesis," paper presented at the Organization of American Historians Convention, Cincinnati, Ohio, April 1983.
8. Schudson, *Discovering the News*, pp. 58–60, 121–22. For community and relationships in the eighteenth century, see Carl Bridenbaugh, *Cities in the Wilderness: The First Century of Urban Life in America, 1625–1742* and *Cities in Revolt: Urban Life in America, 1743–1776* (New York: Knopf, 1955); J. C. Furnas, *The Americans: A Social History of the United States, 1587–1914* (New York: Putnam's, 1971); Nash, *The Urban Crucible*.
9. *Saturday Globe*, 21 May 1881.
10. Ibid.
11. Frasca, "American Colonial Journalism," pp. 16–21.
12. For more information on the Federalist-Republican newspaper war, see Donald H. Stewart, *The Opposition Press of the Federalist Period* (Albany: State University of New York Press, 1969); Leonard W. Levy, ed., *Freedom of the Press from Zenger to Jefferson* (Indianapolis: Bobbs-Merrill, 1966); Ray Boston, "The Impact of 'Foreign Liars' on the American Press (1790–1800)," *Journalism Quarterly* 50 (Winter 1973): p. 722. On the political climate of the early republic, see Daniel Sisson, *The American Revolution of 1800* (New York: Knopf, 1974); James M. Smith, *Freedom's Fetters: The Alien and Sedition Acts and American Civil Liberties* (Ithaca, N.Y.: Cornell University Press, 1956). On thc political and economic relationships between parties and the press in the nineteenth century, see Culver H. Smith, *The Press, Politics and Patronage* (Athens: University of Georgia Press, 1977); Gerald J. Baldasty, "The Press and Politics in the Age of Jackson," *Journalism Monographs* 89 (August 1984).
13. Alfred Lawrence Lorenz, "Harrison Reed: An Editor's Trials on the Wisconsin Frontier," *Journalism Quarterly* 53 (Autumn 1976): p. 417; Mott, *American Journalism*, p. 216; *Geneva Gazette*, 24 August 1813.
14. James F. Babcock to Elihu Geer, 24 August 1843, 8 September 1843, Correspondence Collection, Connecticut Historical Society, Hartford, Conn.
15. World War I brought about the need to better understand propaganda and its effects on populations. The "hypodermic needle" theory holds that a mass communicator need only shoot messages at an audience to receive preplanned and universal effects, in the belief that all people think and act similarly when

confronted with mass communication. Harold Lasswell, *Propaganda Technique and the World War* (New York: Knopf, 1927).

16. [Philadelphia] *Aurora* 28 July 1797; [Boston] *Independent Chronicle* 30 June 1800; [Philadelphia] *Gazette of the United States*, 2 September 1800; [Richmond] *Recorder*, 17 November 1802. More examples of vituperation in the early nineteenth century may be found in William David Sloan, "Scurrility and the Party Press, 1798–1816," paper presented at the American Journalism Historians Association Convention, St. Paul, Minn., October 1987. Cleveland's paternity was revealed in the Buffalo *Evening Telegraph*, 21 July 1884.

17. *New York Times*, 22 March 1860; *New York Tribune*, 4 May 1870.

18. Schudson, *Discovering the News*, p. 7; Mott, *American Journalism*, pp. 385, 389–90, 411–12. For more information on the rise of objectivity in the middle decades of the nineteenth century, see Dan Schiller, "An Historical Approach to Objectivity and Professionalism in American News Reporting," *Journal of Communication* 29 (Autumn 1974): pp. 46–57.

19. *Saturday Globe*, 21 May 1881; 27 May 1893.

20. *Saturday Globe*, 24 January 1920.

21. *Saturday Globe*, 21 May 1881.

22. *Saturday Globe*, 24 January 1920.

23. Ibid; Mott, *American Journalism*, p. 294.

24. *Saturday Globe*, 27 May 1893.

25. *Utica Observer-Dispatch*, 15 February 1924; "The Utica Saturday Globe," p. 21.

26. *Pennsylvania Gazette*, 1 January 1746.

27. *Cayuga Republican*, 8 January 1820.

28. *New England Galaxy*, 1 January 1825.

29. Mott, *American Journalism*, p. 60; Hamilton, *The Country Printer*, p. 143; *The New York Times*, 31 December 1987, p. 17.

30. Mott, *American Journalism*, p. 314; as quoted in "The Utica Saturday Globe," p. 21.

31. Interview with Thomas Dodge, Utica, N.Y., 9 January 1986.

32. Interview with Ed Lee and Gilbert Lee, Utica, N.Y., 8 January 1986.

33. Frank L. Mott, *A History of American Magazines*, 5 vols. (Cambridge: Harvard University Press, 1930–1957) 3:691.

34. Ibid., 4:67–68.

35. Ibid., 3:53–54; 4:18, 68.

36. Ibid., 4:68–69. It is probably no coincidence that *Grit* courted the same target readership which was then proving so successful for the *Saturday Globe*, which by 1884 circulated throughout Pennsylvania.

37. "The Utica Saturday Globe," p. 21; Mott, *A History of American Magazines*, 4:680–82.

38. Mott, *A History of American Magazines*, 4:686; Paul B. Williams, "Utica's Newspapers Since 1900," paper presented to the Oneida Historical Society, Utica, N.Y., 10 November 1958, p. 12. It is unclear why Bok was sent to Utica and not the *Saturday Evening Post*'s editor, William G. Jordan. For more information on the *Saturday Evening Post*, see John Tebbel, *George Horace Lorimer and the Saturday Evening Post* (Garden City, N.Y.: Doubleday, 1948).

39. *The Saturday Evening Post* 171 (10 December 1898), p. 376; Edward Bok, *The Americanization of Edward Bok: An Autobiography* (New York: Charles Scribner's Sons, Pocket Books, 1973), pp. 170–72; Mott, *A History of American Magazines* 4:18, pp. 689–91.

40. *Saturday Globe*, 2 July 1881.
41. *Saturday Globe*, 24 January 1920; *Utica Observer-Dispatch* 4 February 1957, p. 8. It is unknown how many copies of this issue were purchased. The *Utica Press*, 15 February 1924, reported that the *Saturday Globe* sold 3,000 copies, while *The Courier*'s article on the *Saturday Globe* claims 10,000 were sold.
42. *Saturday Globe*, 2 July 1881.
43. Ibid. On the relationship between telegraph dispatches and the format of news stories, see Daniel J. Czitrom, *Media and the American Mind* (Chapel Hill: University of North Carolina Press, 1982), pp. 14–21.
44. Other newspapers did this also. See, e.g., Rammelkamp, *Pulitzer's Post-Dispatch*, p. 123.
45. *Saturday Globe*, 9 July 1881.
46. Ibid.
47. *St. Louis Post-Dispatch*, 8 August 1881; Rammelkamp, *Pulitzer's Post-Dispatch* pp. 173–75.
48. *Saturday Globe*, 24 September 1881.
49. *Saturday Globe*, 24 January 1920.
50. *Saturday Globe*, 3 September 1881.
51. Ibid; *The Beautiful Victim of the Elm City Tragedy* (New York: Ivers, 1881; Thomas McDade, *The Annals of Murder: A Bibliography of Books and Pamphlets on Murders from Colonial Times to 1900* (Norman: University of Oklahoma Press, 1961), p. 197.
52. "The Utica Saturday Globe," p. 22.
53. Edmund Pearson, *Dime Novels* (Boston: Little, Brown, 1929), pp. 13–14.
54. Ibid., pp. 8, 45, 222; Michael Denning, *Mechanic Accents* (London: Verso, 1987), p. 4.
55. Pearson, *Dime Novels*, pp. 139, 149.
56. *Saturday Globe*, 27 May 1893.

Chapter 3. Murders, Mass Distribution, and the Rise to National Prominence

1. *Saturday Globe*, 27 May 1893.
2. *The United States v. Charles J. Guiteau* (Washington: Government Publication Office, 1882; reprint ed., New York: Arno, 1973); Allan Peskin, *Garfield* (Kent, Ohio: Kent State University Press, 1978), pp. 582–613. For debates about Guiteau's sanity, see Charles J. Rosenberg, *The Trial of the Assassin Guiteau: Psychiatry and Law in the Gilded Age* (Chicago: University of Chicago Press, 1968).
3. *Utica Saturday Globe*, 27 May 1893; "The Utica Saturday Globe," p.22.
4. "The Utica Saturday Globe," p. 22.
5. For the rise of literacy in the nineteenth century, see Mott, *American Journalism*, pp. 304, 507. Schudson disparages Mott's "reflexlike" view that schooling and widespread literacy stimulated the demand for newspapers in the nineteenth century, but offers no more plausible contention. Schudson, *Discovering the News*, pp. 35–39, 198.
6. Lemay and Zall, *The Autobiography of Benjamin Franklin*, pp. 93–94.
7. *New York Journal*, 8 November 1896.
8. *Saturday Globe*, 29 May 1886; 10 March 1888; 3 September 1904.
9. Mott, *American Journalism*, p. 442.

10. Emery and Emery, *The Press and America*, pp. 115–43; Hamilton, *The Country Printer*, p. 143; Schudson, *Discovering the News*, p. 95.

11. *New York Times*, 7 February 1897; 28 March 1898; and Conde B. Pallen, "Newspaperism," *Lippincott's Monthly* 38 (November 1866): p. 476.

12. Czitrom, *Media and the American Mind*, pp. 19–20; Josiah Royce, *Race Questions, Provincialism and other American Problems* (New York: Macmillan, 1908), p. 77.

13. Mott, *American Journalism*, p. 442; John P. Ferre, "Journalism Ethics and Media Effects: The Nineteenth-Century Heritage," paper presented to the American Journalism Historians Association Convention, St. Paul, Minn., October 1987, pp. 7–8, 17.

14. On Hearst, see W. A. Swanberg, *Citizen Hearst* (New York: Scribner's, 1961). On Pulitzer, see George Juergens, *Joseph Pulitzer and the New York World* (Princeton, N.J.: Princeton University Press, 1966); Rammelkamp, *Pulitzer's Post Dispatch*.

15. *Saturday Globe*, 20 May 1916.

16. *Saturday Globe*, 4 December 1886.

17. *Saturday Globe*, 16 October 1886.

18. *Saturday Globe*, 22 January 1887.

19. Walsh, *Vignettes of Old Utica*, p. 323; *Saturday Globe*, 27 May 1983; John J. Walsh, *From Frontier Outpost to Modern City: A History of Utica 1784–1920* (Utica, N.Y.: Oneida Historical Society, 1978), p. 396.

20. *Saturday Globe*, 27 May 1893.

21. On railroads in the nineteenth century, see James A. Ward, *Railroads and the Character of America, 1820–1887* (Knoxville: University of Tennessee Press, 1986); John F. Stover, *The Life and Decline of the American Railroad* (New York: Oxford University Press, 1970); Patrick O'Brien, *The New Economic History of the Railways* (New York: St. Martin's, 1977).

22. Interview with Thomas Dodge, Utica, N.Y., 9 January 1986.

23. *Saturday Globe*, 27 May 1893.

24. Ibid.; T. Wood Clarke, *Utica for a Century and a Half*, p. 63.

25. *Utica Observer*, 22 March 1887.

26. *Saturday Globe*, 27 May 1893.

27. *Saturday Globe*, 4 December 1886.

28. *Saturday Globe*, 1 January 1887. On capital punishment for women, see Hugo Adam Bedau, ed., *The Death Penalty in America: An Anthology* rev. ed. (Garden City, N.Y. Doubleday, 1967), pp. i–xxii; Bernard O'Connell, *Should Women Hang?* (London: Allen, 1956).

29. *Saturday Globe*, 12 February 1887.

30. Ibid.

31. *Saturday Globe*, 26 February 1887.

32. *Saturday Globe*, 27 May 1893.

33. *Utica Observer*, 22 March 1887.

34. That the *Saturday Globe* could boast of international circulation is, in some ways, less important than its national circulation, because many newspapers along the northern and southern borders of the United States can make the same claim. Its circulation "as far south as Florida, west to California and Oregon, [and] east to Maine" is a more reliable measure of the geographic breadth of its circulation than the fact that it circulated "north into Canada," which is as close as 110 miles from Utica.

On the circulation of Greeley's and Bennett's papers, see Willard G. Bleyer, *Main*

Currents in the History of American Journalism (Boston: Houghton Mifflin, 1927), pp. 184–85, 224, 228; Emery and Emery, *The Press and America*, p. 127.

Beginning in 1886, New York and Chicago Sunday newspapers began concerted efforts to circulate in outlying cities, but still in their geographic region, by cooperating to secure fast, night mail trains. The *San Francisco Examiner* followed suit the next year, with the crosstown rival *San Francisco Chronicle* close behind. The *Boston Herald* adopted the same technique to serve New England cities in 1891. Mott, *American Journalism*, p. 508.

35. Charles Horton Cooley, "The Process of Social Change," *Political Science Quarterly* 12 (1978): pp. 77–88.

36. For more information, see Robert Wiebe, *The Search for Order, 1877–1920* (New York: Hill & Wang, 1968).

37. George M. Beard, *American Nervousness* (New York: Putnam's 1881), quoted in Czitrom, *Media and the American Mind*, pp. 20–21.

38. Clifford Geertz, *The Interpretation of Cultures* (New York: Basic, 1973), p. 453.

39. On the values of high circulation, see Frank W. Rucker, *Newspaper Circulation* (Ames: Iowa State College Press, 1958), pp. 1–7.

40. The 15 February 1924 *Utica Press* reported an April circulation of 128,900. The twelve-year history printed in the 27 May 1893 *Saturday Globe* noted a 115,000 circulation had been attained by its seventh birthday, which was 21 May.

41. *Saturday Globe*, 18 February 1888.

42. *Saturday Globe*, 16 March 1889; "The Utica Saturday Globe," p. 36.

43. "The Utica Saturday Globe," p. 37.

44. Schudson links the development of commuter reading to the rise of yellow journalism, especially the use of illustrations and large headlines. *Discovering the News*, pp. 102–3.

Chapter 4. "The Demon Flood": Tragedy in Johnstown

1. *Saturday Globe*, 8 June 1889.

2. Paula and Carl Degen, *The Johnstown Flood of 1889* (New York: Eastern Acorn Press, 1984), p. 19.

3. David G. McCullough, *The Johnstown Flood* (New York: Simon and Schuster, 1968), pp. 82–83, 98.

4. Quoted in McCullough, *The Johnstown Flood*, p. 100.

5. *The Johnstown Tribune*, quoted in McCullough, *The Johnstown Flood*, pp. 149–50.

6. *Saturday Globe*, 1 June 1889.

7. *Saturday Globe*, 8 June 1889.

8. *New York Times*, 8 June 1889.

9. *Saturday Globe*, 8 June 1889. McCullough asserts that the "Paul Revere" story was a myth. See McCullough, *The Johnstown Flood*, pp. 222–23.

10. *Saturday Globe*, 8 June 1889.

11. *Saturday Globe*, 15 June 1889.

12. Ellis Baldwin, "Big Dick of the Globe," in *The Way to Wealth* 6 (Utica, N.Y.: Utica Savings Bank, 1935), p. 17.

13. *New York Daily Graphic*, 13 June 1889.

14. McCullough, *The Johnstown Flood*, p. 223.

15. "The Utica Saturday Globe" p. 37; *Saturday Globe*, 24 January 1920; Rammelkamp, *Pulitzer's Post-Dispatch* p. 192; Warren T. Francke, "Sensationalism and the Development of 19th-Century Reporting," *Journalism History* 12 (Autumn–Winter 1985): pp. 80–85.

16. "The Utica Saturday Globe," p. 37; Baldwin, "Big Dick of the Globe," p. 16.

17. *Saturday Globe*, 15 June 1889; 22 June 1889. The 15 June issue of the *Saturday Globe* reports the exact number was 205,130 and elsewhere in the same issue claims 205,200. The following week's issue escalated the circulation to 205,400, but this may be the result of back-issue sales.

18. *Saturday Globe*, 15 June 1889.

19. "The Utica Saturday Globe," p. 37; *Saturday Globe*, 15 June 1889.

20. *Saturday Globe*, 22 June 1889.

21. Ibid.; *Saturday Globe*, 29 June 1889.

22. *Saturday Globe*, 6 July 1889.

23. *Saturday Globe*, 27 July 1889.

24. Baldwin, "Big Dick of the Globe," p.16.

25. Newbell N. Pickett, *Folk Beliefs of the Southern Negro* (Chapel Hill: University of North Carolina Press, 1926), p. 15; Lawrence W. Levine, *Black Culture and Black Consciousness* (New York: Oxford University Press, 1977), pp. 56, 80.

26. *Saturday Globe*, 23 November 1889.

27. Ibid.

28. Ibid.

29. St. Clair Drake, *Black Folk Here and There* (Los Angeles: Center for Afro-American Studies, University of California at Los Angeles, 1987), pp. 25–30; Eric Foner, ed., *America's Black Past* (New York: Harper & Row, 1970), p. 142.

30. Baldwin, "Big Dick of the Globe," p. 16.

31. Paul Williams, "Utica's Newspapers Since 1900," paper presented to the Oneida Historical Society, Utica, N.Y., November 1958, p. 11; *Utica Observer-Dispatch*, 15 February 1924.

32. Mott, *American Journalism*, pp. 312, 547.

33. Arthur J. Kaul, "The Washington Institute: Printers and the Radicalization of an Urban Labor Network," paper presented to the Social Science History Association Convention, Chicago, November 1988. For more information on the tradition of printing apprenticeships, see Frasca, "From Apprenticeship to Journeyman to Partner."

34. Williams, "Utica's Newspapers Since 1900," pp. 11–12.

35. Ibid., p. 12; Baldwin, "Big Dick of the Globe," p. 17; Mott, *American Journalism*, p. 488. Dickinson's request that a death-row convict accelerate the time of his execution is reminiscent of an identical episode in the award-winning stage play and movie *The Front Page*. See Ben Hecht and Charles MacArthur, *The Front Page* (New York: Covici-Friede, 1928).

36. Baldwin, "Big Dick of the Globe," p. 17.

37. *Utica Observer-Dispatch*, 18 October 1934; *Elmira Daily Gazette*, 10 February 1890.

38. *Saturday Globe*, 25 July 1891.

39. John J. Lane, *The Life, Trial and Confession of Frank C. Almy* (Laconia, N. H.: John J. Lane, circa 1892), pp. 4–5; *Saturday Globe* 25 July 1891.

40. *Saturday Globe*, 25 July 1891.

41. Ibid.

42. Lane, *The Life, Trial and Confession of Frank C. Almy*, pp. 10, 18.
43. Ibid., pp. 11, 19, 29; Baldwin, "Big Dick of the Globe," p. 17.
44. *Saturday Globe*, 12 December 1891.

Chapter 5. The Halcyon Days

1. *Utica Daily Press*, 9 April 1934.

2. Walsh, *Vignettes of Old Utica*, pp. 323–24; "The Utica Saturday Globe," p. 37; *Saturday Globe*, 27 May 1893; Emery and Emery, *The Press and America*, pp. 140–41; Bleyer, *Main Currents in the History of American Journalism* (Boston: Houghton Mifflin, 1927), p. 394; Erastus Geer to Elihu Geer, 15 December 1875, Correspondence Collection, Connecticut Historical Society, Hartford, Conn.

3. Williams, "Utica's Newspapers Since 1900," p. 13; Clarke, *Utica for a Century and a Half*, p. 63; *Saturday Globe*, 27 May 1893.

4. *Saturday Globe*, 27 May 1893. The *Saturday Globe*'s circulation never exceeded 300,000. The 1 million figure surely refers to total readership via in-home and pass-on circulation.

5. *Saturday Globe*, 17 October 1896. A synthesis of several sources suggests this 200,000 estimate. In his *History of American Magazines*, Mott wrote on p. 68 that the *Saturday Globe*'s 1890 circulation was 200,000. The 15 February 1924 *Utica Daily Press* reported an April 1890 circulation of 194,287. The 1891 average was 165,354, according to David M. Ellis, *The Upper Mohawk Country* (Woodland Hills, Ca.: Windsor, 1982), p. 71. In *Utica for a Century and a Half*, Clarke suggested that the 1893 circulation was about 180,000. The *Saturday Globe*'s own estimate in 1893 is similar to these. Reporting that circulation dropped somewhat after the Johnstown flood had become yesterday's news, the newspaper noted, "From that time to the present the sales of the Globe have varied from about 160,000 in the heated season to over 200,000 in winter, with frequent jumps far above the latter number whenever there were happenings of especial importance to excite the interest of the public." *Saturday Globe*, 27 May 1893. For a graphic representation of these and other circulation figures, see the appendix.

6. *Saturday Globe*, 1 December 1894; *Saturday Globe*, 21 August 1897; *Saturday Globe*, 25 July 1891; *Saturday Globe*, 12 October 1895; *Saturday Globe*, 16 March 1895; *Saturday Globe*, 21 August 1897.

7. *Saturday Globe*, 22 April 1893; *Saturday Globe*, 27 May 1893.

8. Williams, "Utica's Newspapers Since 1900," p. 2, 12; "The Utica Saturday Globe," p. 37; *Utica Daily Press*, 15 February 1924.

9. Williams, "Utica's Newspapers Since 1900," p. 7.

10. *The Continuation of Our Weekly Newes*, 1 February 1626; Bleyer, *Main Currents in the History of American Journalism*, p. 38; *Catholick Intelligence: or Infallible News both Domestick and Forreign*, 8 March 1680.

11. [Goshen, N.Y.] *Orange County Patriot* 1 July 1810; Schudson, *Discovering the News*, pp. 18–19.

12. Schudson, *Discovering the News*, pp. 93–94; *Philadelphia Public Ledger*, 23 September 1836; *Boston Daily Times*, 11 October 1837.

13. *New York Tribune*, 30 April 1841; *New York Daily Times*, 21 November 1851.

14. Quoted in Hamilton, *The Country Printer*, p. 50.

15. Wiebe, *A Search for Order*; William S. Rossiter, "Printing and Publishing," *U.S. Census Reports* 9 (12th Census), 1902, pp. 1041–42; Charles Edward Russell,

These Shifting Scenes (New York: George H. Doran, 1914), p. 309; Oswald Garrison Villard, *Some Newspapers and Newspaper-Men* (New York: Knopf, 1923), p. 40.

16. Linda Lawson, "Advertisements Masquerading as News in Turn-of-the-Century American Periodicals," *American Journalism* 5 (2, 1988): pp. 81–96.

17. Bleyer, *Main Currents in the History of American Journalism*, p. 595.

18. Lynda M. Maddox and Eric J. Zanot, "The Image of the Advertising Practitioner as Presented in the Mass Media, 1900–1972," *American Journalism* 2 (1985): pp. 118; Quentin J. Schultze, "'An Honorable Place': The Quest for Professional Advertising Education, 1900–1917," *Business History Review* 56 (Spring 1982): pp. 16–32; Idem, "Professionalism in Advertising: The Origin of Ethical Codes," *Journal of Communication* 31 (Spring 1981): pp. 64–71. On professional traits, see Douglas Birkhead, "Presenting the Press: Journalism and the Professional Project," (Ph.D. diss., University of Iowa, 1982); Frasca, "American Colonial Journalism."

19. Mott, *American Journalism*, p. 593; Emery and Emery, *The Press and America*, p. 220.

20. Mott, *History of American Magazines* 4, p. 15; *Epoch* 10 (11 December 1891).

21. Emery and Emery, *The Press and America*, p. 224.

22. *Saturday Globe*, 24 January 1920; "The Utica Saturday Globe," p. 37; Williams, "Utica's Newspapers Since 1900," p. 12.

Regarding assertions about the *Saturday Globe*'s printing of illustrations, several sources used in this book—Clarke's *Utica for a Century and a Half*, Ellis's *The Upper Mohawk Country* and the 15 February 1924 *Utica Observer-Dispatch*—contend in error that the *Saturday Globe* was the first newspaper to print halftones on a rotary press. Mott, *American Journalism*, p. 501 and Bleyer, *Main Currents in the History of American Journalism*, p. 396, both note that the first halftones printed on a rotary press were produced by the *Boston Journal* in its Sunday edition, 6 May 1894. Although similar to the rotary press, the cylinder press used by the *Saturday Globe* was different in that it did not provide the continuous feed that a rotary press allows.

23. Williams, "Utica's Newspapers Since 1900," p. 13.

24. Ibid.; *Saturday Globe*, 4 December 1886.

25. Emery and Emery, *The Press and America*, p. 115; Mott, *American Journalism*, p. 598.

26. Theodore Peterson, "The Social Responsibility Theory of the Press," in Fred S. Siebert, Theodore Peterson, Wilbur Schramm, *Four Theories of the Press* (Urbana: University of Illinois Press, 1956), pp. 73–75; Ferre, "Journalism Ethics and Media Effects: The Nineteenth-Century Heritage." On the public-service ideology, see Harold L. Wilensky, "The Professionalization of Everyone?" *The American Journal of Sociology* 70 (September 1964): p. 37.

27. Emery and Emery, *The Press and America*, p. 115.

28. William Peter Hamilton in the *Wall Street Journal*, quoted in Peterson, "The Social Responsibility Theory of the Press," in Siebert, Peterson, Schramm, *Four Theories of the Press*, p. 73.

29. *Pettingill's Newspaper Directory, 1896* (New York: S. M. Pettingill, 1896), p. 237. For circulation estimates of the *Saturday Globe* in the 1890s, see note 5.

30. *New York Journal*, 28 February 1897.

31. *The World Almanac and Book of Facts, 1988* (New York: Pharos, 1988), p. 886.

32. *Saturday Globe*, 20 March 1897.

33. Ibid.
34. Ibid.
35. Ibid.; Williams, "Utica's Newspapers Since 1900," p. 13; *Utica Observer-Dispatch*, 15 February 1924. The *Observer-Dispatch* erred by referring to the incorrect fight. It printed that the peak of circulation was reached at the time of the Corbett-Jeffries fight, in the early 1890s. Corbett and Jeffries did fight, but it was in 1903. Circulation was well below 294,000 by then, and this fight did not receive nearly as much coverage as the 1897 bout.
36. *Saturday Globe*, 20 March 1897; *The World Almanac and Book* of *Facts, 1988*, p. 886.

Chapter 6. Adherence to the Formula

1. David F. Trask, *The War with Spain in 1898* (New York: Macmillan, 1981), pp. 1–31. See also G. J. A. O'Toole, *The Spanish War: An American Epic* (New York: Norton, 1984).
2. *Saturday Globe*, 21 August 1897.
3. Mott, *American Journalism*, p. 528; W. A. Swanberg, *Citizen Hearst*, pp. 113, 152.
4. *Saturday Globe*, 4 December 1897.
5. Trask, *The War with Spain*, pp. 52–59; Lewis L. Gould, *The Presidency of William McKinley* (Lawrence: The Regents Press of Kansas, 1980), pp. 87–90. On the press' ability to mold public opinion, see Charles H. Brown, *The Correspondents' War* (New York: Scribner's, 1967).
6. Trask, *The War with Spain*, pp. 95–107; *Saturday Globe*, 7 May 1898.
7. Emery and Emery, *The Press and America*, p. 241.
8. *Saturday Globe*, 7 May 1898.
9. Ibid.
10. Trask, *The War with Spain*, pp. 257–69, 286–319.
11. *Saturday Globe*, 24 September 1898; Trask, *The War with Spain*, pp. 445–72.
12. *Saturday Globe*, 15 September 1900.
13. Swanberg, *Citizen Hearst*, pp. 187–88.
14. *Saturday Globe*, 29 September 1900.
15. Baldwin, "Big Dick of the Globe," p. 17.
16. *Saturday Globe*, 29 September 1900.
17. Frasca, "American Colonial Journalism," pp. 12–25; Lincoln Steffens, *The Autobiography of Lincoln Steffens* (New York: Harcourt, Brace, 1931), p. 375; Schudson, *Discovering the News*, pp. 71–87.
18. Herbert Asbury, *Carry Nation* (New York: Knopf, 1929), pp. 30–35; Robert Smith Bader, *Prohibition in Kansas* (Lawrence: University Press of Kansas, 1986), pp. 134–35; *Saturday Globe*, 9 February 1901.
19. Asbury, *Carry Nation*, pp. 35; Bader, *Prohibition in Kansas*, pp. 133–55; *Saturday Globe*, 9 February 1901.
20. Asbury, *Carry Nation*, pp. 164, 257–58; *Saturday Globe*, 2 March 1901.
21. *Saturday Globe*, 22 June 1901.
22. *Saturday Globe*, 19 September 1908; Carleton Beales, *Cyclone Carry* (New York: Chilton, 1962), p. 344. Bader, *Prohibition in Kansas*, p. 154, downplays Nation's role in the creation of national prohibition.
23. On Czolgosz, the best source is A. Wesley Johns, *The Man Who Shot*

McKinley (South Brunswick, N. J.: Barnes, 1970), who on pp. 18–49 details Czolgosz's early life, employment, and involvement in anarchism. The shooting is described on pp. 89–100.

24. *Saturday Globe*, 14 September 1901.

25. Ibid.

26. Johns, *The Man Who Shot McKinley*, pp. 109, 112, 168.

27. New York *Evening Journal*, 10 April 1901; *New York Journal*, 4 February 1900. The quatrain was written by Ambrose Bierce, perhaps best known as the author of *The Devil's Dictionary*.

28. *Saturday Globe*, 14 September 1901; *New York Times*, 14 December 1890; New York *Tribune* 4 December 1901.

29. New York *Journal* 19 September 1901; Swanberg, *Citizen Hearst*, pp. 191–94, 209–14.

30. Johns, *The Man Who Shot McKinley*, pp. 202–48.

31. *Saturday Globe*, 2 November 1901.

32. *Saturday Globe*, 8 August 1903; 15 August 1903.

33. Eric Saul and Donald P. DeNevi, *The Great San Francisco Earthquake and Fire, 1906* (Millbrae, Ca.: Celestial, 1981), pp. 21, 24, 112; [Newark, N. J.] *Sunday Star Ledger*, 13 April 1986, p. 25.

34. Swanberg, *Citizen Hearst*, p. 240; Interview with Sally Luther, Jacksonville, Florida, 3 April 1986.

35. *Utica Daily Press*, 12 August 1946; January 1947; Sally Luther to Ralph Frasca, 8 April 1986. Personal files of Ralph Frasca.

36. *Saturday Globe*, 15 August 1903.

37. Ibid.

38. *Saturday Globe*, 29 August 1908.

39. *Saturday Globe*, 24 September 1908.

Chapter 7. Increasing Competition and Declining Fortunes

1. Bleyer, *Main Currents*, p. 390.

2. Steffens, *Lincoln Steffens*, p. 150; Schudson, *Discovering the News*, pp. 71–73; Frasca, "American Colonial Journalism."

3. Lemay and Zall, eds., *The Autobiography of Benjamin Franklin*, p. 18; Frasca, "From Apprentice to Journeyman to Partner." For an example of the apprentice's obligations, see Samuel Richardson, *The Apprentice's Vade Mecum* (London: Samuel Richardson, 1734; reprint ed., Los Angeles: Augustan Reprint Society, 1975), pp. 2–20. On the menial nature of some tasks, see O. Jocelyn Dunlop and Richard D. Denman, *English Apprenticeship and Child Labor: A History* (London: Unwin, 1912), pp. 19–20; Sharon V. Salinger, *"To Serve Well and Faithfully": Labor and Indentured Servants in Pennsylvania, 1682–1800* (Cambridge: Cambridge University Press, 1987), p. 7. On beatings endured by printing apprentices, see W. J. Rorabaugh, *The Craft Apprentice: from Franklin to the Machine Age in America*, pp. 11, 43, 93, 103, 193.

4. Burton J. Bledstein, *The Culture of Professionalism* (New York: Norton, 1976), pp. 289, 326–27; Alexander M. Carr-Saunders and Paul A. Wilson, *The Professions* (Oxford, England: Oxford University Press, 1933; reprint ed., London: Frank Cass, 1964), p. 310.

5. Anthony Smith, "Is Objectivity Obsolete?" *Columbia Journalism Review*

(May/June 1980): p. 61; Gaye Tuchman, "Objectivity as Strategic Ritual: An Examination of Newsmen's Notions of Objectivity," *American Journal of Sociology* 77 (January 1972): p. 660; Schudson, *Discovering the News*, p. 7.

6. Tuchman, "Objectivity as Strategic Ritual," pp. 665–70.

7. Ralph Frasca, "Journalism, Social Science and the 'Objectivity Standard': An Overview and a New Paradigm," *Social Science Perspectives Journal* 2 (1988): pp. 138–49; Tuchman, "Objectivity as Strategic Ritual," pp. 665–70. John McCormally, former editor and publisher of the *Burlington Hawk Eye*, an Iowa newspaper, disparaged the ritual of quoting sources just to have conflicting assertions. "Our worst failure has been the practice, under the pretense of objectivity, of publishing the unchallenged statements of public officials, of succumbing, all too subjectively, to the patriotic, religious, racial and economic myths and stereotypes of the country." John McCormally, "Editor Bites Back," speech presented in the Professional Journalist Series at the School of Journalism, University of Iowa, Iowa City, 20 February, 1973.

8. Schudson, *Discovering the News*, p. 145.

9. Walter Lippman, *Liberty and the News*, p. 72.

10. Mott, *American Journalism*, p. 496.

11. Schudson, *Discovering the News*, p. 89.

12. Williams, "Utica's Newspapers Since 1900," p. 13.

13. Mott, *American Journalism*, pp. 546–49; S. N. D. North, *History and Present Condition of the Newspaper and Periodical Press in the United States* (Washington: Government Printing Office, 1884), p. 65. There are approximately 1,750 daily newspapers as of this writing—about 500 fewer than in 1914, despite the fact that the nation's population has more than doubled since then.

14. Emery and Emery, *The Press and America*, pp. 187–88; Mott, *American Journalism*, p. 598.

15. Mott, *American Journalism*, p. 512; Emery and Emery, *The Press and America*, p. 222.

16. Steffens, *The Autobiography of Lincoln Steffens*, pp. 358, 393; Harold S. Wilson, *McClure's Magazine and the Muckrakers* (Princeton, N. J.: Princeton University Press, 1970). For more information on muckrakers, see David M. Chalmers, *The Social and Political Ideas of the Muckrakers* (New York: Citadel, 1964); Judson A. Grenier, "Muckraking and the Muckrakers: An Historical Definition," *Journalism Quarterly* 37 (Autumn 1960): p. 552; Harry H. Stein, "American Muckrakers and Muckraking: The 50-Year Scholarship," *Journalism Quarterly* 56 (Spring 1979): p. 9.

17. Sidney Kobre, "The Sociological Approach in Newspaper Research," *Journalism Quarterly* 22 (Spring 1966): p. 43; Wiebe, *The Search for Order*.

18. Mott, *American Journalism*, p. 589; Donald Abramoske, "Victor Lawson and the Chicago Weekly News: A Defeat," *Journalism Quarterly* 43 (Spring 1966): p. 43.

19. *Utica Daily Press*, 9 April 1934; *Saturday Globe*, 20 May 1916; *Utica Observer-Dispatch*, 18 October 1934; Williams, "Utica's Newspapers Since 1900," p. 13.

20. *American Newspaper Annuals and Directory* (Philadelphia: Ayer, 1912), p. 665; Ibid., 1915, p. 691; advertisement in *Editor and Publisher*, 22 July 1916, p. 19.

21. *Saturday Globe*, 20 May 1916.

22. Ibid.

23. Williams, "Utica's Newspapers Since 1900," p. 32.

24. Interview with Marietta von Bernuth, Utica, New York, 21 February 1986; Williams, "Utica's Newspapers Since 1900," p. 33.

Chapter 8. The *Morning Telegram*: A Short-Lived Sister

1. Mott, *American Journalism*, p. 508.
2. Williams, "Utica's Newspapers Since 1900," pp. 33, 39. The information about the *Morning Telegram* in this paper consists of unpublished information supplied by Gerrit Hyde, the *Morning Telegram*'s day city editor. As a result of Hyde's contribution, this paper is the best of the few sources on the *Morning Telegram*, and I have used it extensively.
3. Williams, "Utica's Newspapers Since 1900," p. 39.
4. Ibid., pp. 40–42.
5. Ibid., pp. 39–40.
6. Ibid., pp. 39, 43–44.
7. Ibid., pp. 39–42, 44.
8. Ibid., pp. 38–39.
9. Ibid., pp. 41–42.
10. *Morning Telegram*, 1 July 1920.
11. Ibid.
12. Hamilton, *The Country Printer*, p. 183; [Cooperstown, N.Y.] *Otsego Herald*, 18 March 1809; *Catskill Recorder*, 5 January 1807; *Poughkeepsie Journal Extra*, 23 September 1795.
13. Williams, "Utica's Newspapers Since 1900," pp. 36–37.
14. *Morning Telegram*, 1 July 1920.
15. *Morning Telegram*, 27 July 1920; 6 July 1920.
16. *Morning Telegram*, 28 July 1920; Williams, "Utica's Newspapers Since 1900," p. 35.
17. Williams, "Utica's Newspapers Since 1900," p. 38.
18. Ibid., pp. 38, 43.
19. Ibid., pp. 35–36.
20. Ibid., pp. 36–37.
21. *Morning Telegram*, 17 December 1921.
22. "The Utica Saturday Globe," p. 37; Williams, "Utica's Newspapers Since 1900," pp. 44–45.
23. Emery and Emery, *The Press and America*, p. 337.
24. *American Newspaper Annuals and Directory* (Philadelphia: N. W. Ayer and Son, 1923), p. 741; Emery and Emery, *The Press and America*, pp. 334–35.
25. *American Newspaper Annuals and Directory*, p. 741.
26. Williams, "Utica's Newspapers Since 1900," pp. 45–46.
27. *Morning Telegram*, 11 January 1922.
28. "Utica Telegram Suspends," *Editor & Publisher*, 14 January 1922, p. 26; Williams, "Utica's Newspapers Since 1900," p. 3.
29. Williams, "Utica's Newspapers Since 1900," pp. 38, 40–44.
30. Interview with Thomas Dodge, Utica, New York, 9 January 1986.

Chapter 9. A Demise and a Legacy

1. *American Newspaper Annuals and Directory*, 1923, p. 741.
2. Williams, "Utica's Newspapers Since 1900," p. 13; *Utica Observer-Dispatch*, 15 February 1924.
3. Interview with Florentine Slyer, Troy, N.Y., 2 April 1986.

4. *Saturday Globe*, 27 May 1922.
5. Ibid.
6. Ibid.
7. *Utica Observer-Dispatch*, 15 February 1924.
8. *Utica Daily Press*, 15 February 1924; U.S. Bankruptcy Court, Northern District of New York, Utica, N.Y., record of bankruptcy proceedings against Globe-Telegram Co., Case No. 10816, filed 7 June 1924.
9. *Utica Daily Press*, 15 February 1924.
10. "'Thirty' for Utica Globe," *Editor and Publisher*, 23 February 1924, p. 17.
11. U.S. Bankruptcy Court, record of bankruptcy proceedings against Globe-Telegram Co.; Marietta von Bernuth to Ralph Frasca, 4 August 1989. Personal files of Ralph Frasca.
12. *Utica Daily Press*, 10 April 1934; obituary for William T. Baker, *Editor and Publisher*, 14 April 1934, p. 33.
13. Interview with Marietta von Bernuth, Utica, New York, 21 February 1986.
14. Marietta von Bernuth to Ralph Frasca, 8 November 1989. Personal files of Ralph Frasca.
15. Clarke, *Utica for a Century and a Half*, p. 278.
16. *Utica Observer-Dispatch*, 18 October 1934.
17. Subrata N. Chakravarty and Carolyn Torcellini, "Citizen Kane Meets Adam Smith," *Forbes*, 20 February 1989, p. 82.
18. Walter Lippman, *Liberty and the News*, pp. 37–38.
19. *Toledo Blade*, 7 June 1904; the *Minneapolis Tribune* slogan appeared daily on the masthead beginning in 1908; Canfield delivered a speech to the Colgate University Press Club which was reported in the 12 February 1897 *New York Times*.
20. *Saturday Globe*, 24 January 1920.
21. See the imaginary tour of the *Saturday Globe* plant, *Saturday Globe*, 27 May 1893, described in Chapter 4.
22. Allen Neuharth, quoted in Peter Prichard, *The Making of McPaper* (Kansas City: Andrews, McMeel & Parker, 1987), p. 340.
23. Interview with Betty Carroll, Utica, N.Y., 22 February 1986; interview with Cornelia Springer, Utica, N.Y., 22 February 1986; interview with Thomas Dodge, Utica, N.Y., 9 January 1986.

Bibliography

Abbott, Carl. *Boosters and Businessmen*. Westport, Conn.: Greenwood, 1981.

Abramoske, Donald. "Victor Lawson and the Chicago Weekly News: A Defeat." *Journalism Quarterly* 43 (Spring 1966): 43–48.

Adams, Douglas B. "The Booster Press Reconsidered: Toward Redefinition." Paper presented at the Association of Education in Journalism and Mass Communication Big Ten Conference, Minneapolis, Minn., April 1988.

Alton Trials .... New York: J. F. Trow, 1838. Reprint. Miami, Fla.: Mnemosyne, 1969.

American Newspaper Annuals and Directory. Philadelphia: Ayer, 1912.

Asbury, Herbert. *Carry Nation*. New York: Knopf, 1929.

Aurora, 28 July 1797.

Bader, Robert Smith. *Prohibition in Kansas*. Lawrence: University Press of Kansas, 1986.

Bagg, Moses M. *Memorial History of Utica, New York*. Syracuse, N.Y.: Mason, 1892.

Baldasty, Gerald J. "The Press and Politics in the Age of Jackson." *Journalism Monographs* 89 (August 1984).

Baldwin, Ellis. "Big Dick of the Globe." In *The Way to Wealth* 6 Utica, N.Y.: Utica Savings Bank, 1935.

Beales, Carlton. *Cyclone Carry*. New York: Chilton, 1962.

Beard, George M. *American Nervousness*. New York: Putnam's, 1881.

The Beautiful Victim of the Elm City Tragedy. New York: Ivers, 1881.

Bedau, Hugo Adam, ed. *The Death Penalty in America: An Anthology*. Rev. ed. Garden City, N.Y.: Doubleday, 1967.

Birkhead, Douglas. "Presenting the Press: Journalism and the Professional Project." Ph.D. diss., University of lowa, 1982.

Bledstein, Burton J. *The Culture of Professionalism*. New York: Norton, 1976.

Bleyer, Willard G. *Main Currents in the History of American Journalism*. Boston: Houghton Mifflin, 1927.

Bok, Edward. *The Americanization of Edward Bok: An Autobiography*. New York: Charles Scribner's Sons, Pocket Books, 1973).

Boorstin, Daniel J. *The Americans: The National Experience*. New York: Random House, 1965.

Boston Daily Times 11 October 1837.

Boston, Ray. "The Impact of 'Foreign Liars' on the American Press (1790–1800)." *Journalism Quarterly* 50 (Winter 1973): 722–30.

Bridenbaugh, Carl. *Cities in Revolt: Urban Life in America, 1743–1776*. New York: Knopf, 1955.

———. *Cities in the Wilderness: The First Century of Urban Life in America, 1625–1742*. New York: Knopf, 1955.

Brigham, Clarence S. *History and Bibliography of American Newspapers, 1690–1820*. Worcester, Mass.: American Antiquarian Society, 1947.

Brown, Charles H. *The Correspondents' War*. New York: Scribner's, 1967.

Carden, Maren Lockwood. *Oneida: Utopian Community to Modern Corporation*. Baltmore: Johns Hopkins University Press, 1969.

Carr-Saunders, Alexander M. and Paul A. Wilson. *The Professions*. Oxford, England: Oxford University Press, 1933. Reprint. London: Frank Cass, 1964.

Carroll, Betty. Interview with author. Utica, N.Y., 22 February 1986.

Catholick Intelligence: Or Infallible News both Domestick and Forreign. 8 March 1680.

Catskill Recorder. 5 January 1807.

Cayuga Republican. 8 January 1820.

Chakravarty, Subrata N. and Carolyn Torcellini. "Citizen Kane Meets Adam Smith." *Forbes* 20 February 1989: 82–85.

Chalmers, David M. *The Social and Political Ideas of the Muckrakers*. New York: Citadel, 1964.

Clapham, John. *A Concise Economic History of Britain*. Cambridge: Cmabridge University Press, 1951.

Clarke, T. Wood. *Utica for a Century and a Half*. Utica, N.Y.: Widtman, 1952.

Condon, George E. *Stars in the Water: The Story of the Erie Canal*. Garden City, N.Y.: Doubleday, 1974.

The Continuation of Our Weekly Newes, 1 February 1626.

Cookinham, Henry J. *History of Oneida County, New York*. Chicago: Clark, 1912.

Cooley, Charles Horton. "The Process of Social Change." *Political Science Quarterly* 12 (1897): 63–81.

Crisafulli, Virgil C. "Agriculture." In *The History of Oneida County*. Utica. N.Y.: Hutson, 1977.

Czitrom, Daniel J. *Media and the American Mind*. Chapel Hill: University of North Carolina Press, 1982.

Degen, Paula and Carl. *The Johnstown Flood of 1889*. New York: Eastern Acorn Press, 1984.

Denning, Michael. *Mechanic Accents*. London: Verso, 1987.

Dodge, Thomas. Interview with author. Utica, N.Y., 9 January 1986.

Drake, St. Clair. *Black Folk Here and There*. Los Angeles: Center for Afro-American Studies, University of California at Los Angeles, 1987.

Dunlop, O. Jocelyn and Richard D. Denman. *English Apprenticeship and Child Labor: A History*. London: Unwin, 1912.

Durant, Samuel. *History of Oneida County, New York*. Philadelphia: Everts and Fariss, 1878.

Dykstra, Robert R. *The Cattle Towns*. New York: Knopf, 1971.

Dutchess Observer, 1 October 1817.

Editor and Publisher. 22 July 1916; 14 January 1922; 23 February 1924; 14 April 1934.

Ellis, David M. *The Upper Mohawk Country*. Woodland Hills, Ca.: Windsor, 1982.

Elmira Daily Gazette. 10 February 1890.

Emery, Michael and Edwin Emery. *The Press and America: An Interpretive History of the Mass Media*. 6th ed. Englewood Cliffs, N.J.: Prentice-Hall, 1988.

Epoch. 10 (11 December 1891).

Evangelical Magazine and Gospel Advocate. 12 February 1831; 12 May 1832.

Evening Post (prospectus). 16 November 1801.

Evening Telegraph. 21 July 1884.

Faler, Paul G. *Mechanics and Manufacturers in the Early Industrial Revolution: Lynn, Massachusetts, 1780–1860*. Albany: State University of New York Press, 1981.

Ferre, John P. "Journalism Ethics and Media Effects: The Nineteenth-Century Heritage." Paper presented to the American Journalism Historians Association Convention, St. Paul, Minn., October 1987.

Foner, Eric, ed. *America's Black Past*. New York: Harper & Row, 1970.

Francke, Warren T. "Sensationalism and the Development of 19th-Century Reporting." *Journalism History* 12 (Autumn-Winter 1985): 80–85.

Frasca, Ralph. "From Apprentice to Journeyman to Partner: Benjamin Franklin's Workers and the Growth of the Early American Printing Trade." *Prennsylvania Magazine of History and Biography* 114 (April 1990): 229–48.

———. "Benjamin Franklin's Printing Network." *American Journalism* 5 (3, 1988): 145–58.

———. "Journalism, Social Science and the 'Objectivity Standard': An Overview and a New Paradigm." *Social Science Perspectives Journal* 2 (1988): 138–49.

———. "The Professionalization of American Colonial Journalism." Paper presented at the American Journalism Historians Association Convention, Atlanta, Ga., October 1989.

Furnas, J. C. *The Americans: A Social History of the United States, 1587–1914*. New York: Putnam's, 1971.

Gazette of the United States. 2 September 1800.

Geertz, Clifford. *The Interpretation of Cultures*. New York: Basic, 1973.

Geneva Gazette. 24 August 1813.

Gould, Lewis L. *The Presidency of William MacKinley*. Lawrence: The Regents Press of Kansas, 1980.

Gregory, Winifred. *American Newspapers 1821–1936*. New York: Wilson, 1937.

Grenier, Judson. "Muckraking and the Muckrakers: An Historical Definition." *Journalism Quarterly* 37 (Autumn 1960): 552–58.

Hamilton, Milton W. *The Country Printer*. New York: Columbia University Press, 1936.

Hart, Jim Allee. *A History of the St. Louis Globe-Democrat*. Columbia: University of Missouri Press, 1961.

Hartford, Conn. Connecticut Historical Society. Correspondence Collection. James F. Babcock to Elihu Geer, 24 August 1843, 8 September 1843; Erastus Geer to Elihu Geer, 15 December 1875.

Hecht, Ben and Charles MacArthur. *The Front Page*. New York: Covici-Friede, 1928.

Hoopes, Roy. *Ralph Ingersoll: A Biography*. New York: Atheneum, 1985.

Independent Chronicle. 30 June 1800.

Johns, A. Wesley. *The Man Who Shot McKinley*. South Brunswick, N. J.: Barnes, 1970.

Johnson, Paul E. *A Shopkeeper's Milennium: Society and Revivals in Rochester, New York, 1815–1837*. New York: Hill & Wang, 1978.

Juergens, George. *Joseph Pulitzer and the New York World*. Princeton: Princeton University Press, 1966.

Kaul, Arthur J. "The Washington Institute: Printers and the Radicalization of an Urban Labor Network." Paper presented to the Social Science History Association Convention, Chicago, November 1988.

Kluger, Richard. *The Paper: The Life and Death of the New York Herald Tribune*. New York: Knopf, 1986.

Kobre, Sidney. "The Sociological Approach in Newspaper Research." *Journalism Quarterly* 22 (Spring 1945): 12–22.

Labaree, Leonard W. et al., eds. *The Papers of Benjamin Franklin*. 27 volumes to date. New Haven: Yale University Press, 1959–.

Lane, John J. *The Life, Trial and Confession of Frank C. Almy*. Laconia, N. H.: John J. Lane, circa 1892.

Larkin, Daniel F. "Three Centuries of Transportation." In *The History of Oneida County*. Utica, N.Y.: Hutson, 1977.

Lasswell, Harold. *Propaganda Technique and the World War*. New York: Knopf, 1927.

Lathem, Edward C. *Chronological Tables of American Newspapers, 1690–1820*. Worcester, Mass.: American Antiquarian Society, 1972.

Lawson, Linda. "Advertisements Masquerading as News in Turn-of-the-Century American Periodicals." *American Journalism* 5 (2, 1988): 81–96.

Lee, Ed and Gilbert. Interview with author. Utica, N.Y., 8 January 1986.

Lemay, J. A. Leo and P. M. Zall, eds. *The Autobiography of Benjamin Franklin: A Genetic Text*. Knoxville: University of Tennessee Press, 1981.

Levine, Lawrence W. *Black Culture and Black Consciousness*. New York: Oxford University Press, 1977.

Levy, Leonard W., ed. *Freedom of the Press from Zenger to Jefferson*. Indianapolis: Bobbs-Merrill, 1966.

Lippman, Walter. *Liberty and the News*. New York: Harcourt, Brace and Howe, 1920.

Long Island Star, 8 June 1809.

Lorenz, Alfred Lawrence. "Harrison Reed: An Editor's Trials on the Wisconsin Frontier." *Journalism Quarterly* 53 (Autumn 1976): 417–22, 462.

Luther, Sally. Interview with author. Jacksonville, Fla., 3 April 1986.

———. Letter to author, 8 April 1986.

McCormally, John. "Editor Bites Back." Speech presented in the Professional Journalist Series at the School of Journalism, University of Iowa, Iowa City, 20 February 1973.

McCullough, David G. *The Johnstown Flood*. New York: Simon and Schuster, 1968.

McDade, Thomas. *The Annals of Murder: A Bibliography of Books and Pamphlets*

On Murders from Colonial Times to 1900. Norman: University of Oklahoma Press, 1961.

McDonald, Dwight. "A Theory of Mass Culture." *Diogenes* 3 (Summer 1953): 1–17.

Maddox, Lynda M. and Zanot, Eric J. "The Image of the Advertising Practitioner as Presented in the Mass Media, 1900–1972." *American Journalism* 2 (2, 1985): 117–29.

Mandelker, Ira L. *Religion, Society, and Utopia in Nineteenth-Century America*. Amherst: University of Massachusetts Press, 1984.

Morning Telegram. 1 July 1920–11 January 1922.

Mott, Frank Luther. *American Journalism*. New York: Macmillan, 1950.

———. *A History of American Magazines*. 5 vols. Cambridge, Mass: Harvard University Press, 1930–57.

Nash, Gary B. *The Urban Crucible*. Cambridge, Mass.: Harvard University Press, 1979.

New England Galaxy, 1 January 1825.

New York Daily Graphic, 13 June 1889.

New York Daily Times, 21 November 1851.

New York Evening Journal, 10 April 1901.

New York Journal, 8 November 1896; 28 February 1897; 4 February 1900; 19 September 1901.

New York Times, 22 March 1860; 14 December 1890; 7 February 1897; 12 February 1897; 28 March 1898; 31 December 1987.

New York Tribune, 30 April 1841; 4 May 1870; 4 December 1901.

Nord, David Paul. "The Evangelical Origins of Mass Media in America, 1815–1835." *Journalism Monographs* 88 (May 1984).

North, S. N. D. *History and Present Condition of the Newspaper and Periodical Press in the United States*. Washington: Government Printing Office, 1884.

O'Brien, Patrick. *The New Economic History of the Railways*. New York: St. Martin's, 1977.

O'Connell, Bernard. *Should Women Hang?* London: Allen, 1956.

Oneida County Gazetteer and Business Directory. Utica, N.Y.: Gaffney, 1902.

Oneida Whig. 9 August 1836.

Orange County Patriot, 1 July 1810.

O'Toole, G. J. A. *The Spanish War: An American Epic*. New York: Norton, 1984.

Otsego Herald. 18 March 1809.

Palermo, Patrick F. "Boosterism, Politics and the Community: An Interactionist Interpretation of the Turner Thesis." Paper presented at the Organization of American Historians Convention, Cincinnati, Ohio, April 1983.

Pallen, Conde B. "Newspaperism." *Lippincott's Monthly* 38 (November 1868): 470–77.

Park, Robert E. and Ernest W. Burgess. *The City*. Chicago: University of Chicago Press, 1967.

Parker, Robert Allerton. *A Yankee Saint: John Humphrey Noyes and the Oneida Community*. New York: G. P. Putnam's Sons, 1935.

Pearson, Edmund. *Dime Novels*. Boston: Little, Brown, 1929.

Pennsylvania Gazette. 1 January 1746.

Peskin, Allan. *Garfield*. Kent, Ohio: Kent State University Press, 1978.

Peterson, Theodore. "The Social Responsibility Theory of the Press." In Fred S. Siebert, Theodore Peterson, Wilbur Schramm, *Four Theories of the Press*. Urbana: University of Illinois Press, 1956.

Pettingill's Newspaper Directory, 1896. New York: S. M. Pettingill, 1896.

Philadelphia Public Ledger. 23 September 1836.

Pickett, Newbell N. *Folk Beliefs of the Southern Negro*. Chapel Hill: University of North Carolina Press, 1926.

Poughkeepsie Journal Extra. 23 September 1795.

Preston, Douglas M. and David M. Ellis. "The Ethnic Dimension." In *The History of Oneida County*. Utica, N.Y.: Hutson, 1977.

Prichard, Peter. *The Making of McPaper*. Kansas City: Andrews, McMeel & Parker, 1987.

Rammelkamp, Julian S. *Pulitzer's Post-Dispatch, 1878-1883*. Princeton: Princeton University Press, 1967.

Recorder. 17 November 1802.

Richardson, Samuel. *The Apprentice's Vade Mecum*. London: Samuel Richardson, 1734. Reprint. Los Angeles: Augustan Reprint Society, 1975.

Roberts, Nancy L. *Dorothy Day and the Catholic Worker*. Albany: State University of New York Press, 1984.

Rorabaugh, W. J. *The Craft Apprentice: from Franklin to the Machine Age in America*. New York: Oxford University Press, 1986.

Rosenberg, Charles J. *The Trial of the Assassin Guiteau: Psychiatry and Law in the Gilded Age*. Chicago: University of Chicago Press, 1968.

Rossiter, William S. "Printing and Publishing." In *U.S. Census Reports* 9 (12th Census), 1902: 1039-1119.

Royce, Josiah. *Race Questions, Provincialism and Other American Problems*. New York: Macmillan, 1908.

Rucker, Frank W. *Newspaper Circulation*. Ames: Iowa State College Press, 1958.

Russell, Charles Edward. *These Shifting Scenes*. New York: George H. Doran, 1914.

St. Louis Post-Dispatch 8 August 1881.

Salinger, Sharon V. *"To Serve Well and Faithfully": Labor and Indentured Servants in Pennsylvania, 1682-1880*. Cambridge: Cambridge University Press, 1987.

Saturday Evening Post. 171 (10 December 1898): 376.

Saturday Globe. 21 May 1881-16 February 1924.

Saul, Eric and Donald P. DeNevi. *The Great San Francisco Earthquake and Fire, 1906*. Millbrae, Ca.: Celestial, 1981.

Schaefer, Robert Jones. *A Guide to Historical Method*. 3d ed. Homewood, Ill.: Dorsey, 1980.

Schiller, Dan. "An Historical Approach to Objectivity and Professionalism in American News Reporting." *Journal of Communication* 29 (Autumn 1974): 46-57.

Schudson, Michael. *Discovering the News: A Social History of American Newspapers*. New York: Basic, 1978.

Schultze, Quentin J. "'An Honorable Place': The Quest for Professional Advertising Education, 1900-1917." *Business History Review* 56 (Spring 1982): 16-32.

———. "Professionalism in Advertising: The Origin of Ethical Codes." *Journal of Communication* 31 (Spring 1981): 64-71.

Schwarzlose, Richard A. "The Nation's First Wire Service: Evidence Supporting a Footnote." *Journalism Quarterly* 57 (Winter 1980): 555-62.

Shaw, Donald L. "News Bias and the Telegraph: A Study of Historical Change." *Journalism Quarterly* 44 (Spring 1967): 3-12, 31.

Sisson, Daniel. *The American Revolution of 1800.* New York: Knopf, 1974.

Sloan, William David. "Scurrility and the Party Press, 1798-1816." Paper presented at the American Journalism Historians Association Convention, St. Paul, Minn., October 1987.

Slyer, Florentine. Interview with author. Troy, N.Y., 2 April 1986.

Smith, Anthony. "Is Objectivity Obsolete?" *Columbia Journalism Review* 19 (May/June 1980): 61-65.

Smith, Culver H. *The Press, Politics and Patronage.* Athens: University of Georgia Press, 1977.

Smith, James M. *Freedom's Fetters: The Alien and Sedition Acts and American Civil Liberties.* Ithaca, N.Y.: Cornell University Press, 1956.

Springer, Cornelia. Interview with author. Utica, N.Y., 22 February 1986.

Steffens, Lincoln. *The Autobiography of Lincoln Steffens.* New York: Harcourt, Brace, 1931.

Stein, Harry H. "American Muckrakers and Muckraking: The 50-Year Scholarship." *Journalism Quarterly* 56 (Spring 1979): 9-17.

Stewart, Donald H. *The Opposition Press of the Federalist Period.* Albany: State University of New York Press, 1969.

Stover, John F. *American Railroads.* Chicago: University of Chicago Press, 1961.

———. *The Life and Decline of the American Railroad.* New York: Oxford University Press, 1970.

Suffolk County Recorder. 8 August 1817.

Sunday Star-Ledger. 13 April 1986.

Swanberg, W. A. *Citizen Hearst.* New York: Scribner's, 1961.

Tanselle, G. Thomas. "Thoughts on Research in Printing History." *Printing History* 9 (2, 1987): 24-25.

Tebbel, John. *George Horace Lorimer and the Saturday Evening Post.* Garden City, N.Y.: Doubleday, 1948.

Thompson, E. P. "Time, Work-Discipline, and Industrial Capitalism." *Past and Present* 38 (December 1967): 56-97.

Toledo Blade. 7 June 1904.

Trask, David F. *The War with Spain in 1898.* New York: Macmillan, 1981.

Tuchman, Gaye. "Objectivity as Strategic Ritual: An Examination of Newsmen's Notions of Objectivity." *American Journal of Sociology* 77 (January 1972): 660-79.

U.S. Bankruptcy Court, Northern District of New York, Utica, N.Y. Record of of bankruptcy proceedings against Globe-Telegram Co. Case No. 10816, filed 7 June 1924.

The United States v. Charles J. Guiteau. Washington: Government Publication Office, 1882. Reprint. New York: Arno, 1973.

Utica Daily Gazette 2 February 1846.

Utica Daily Press 15 February 1924; 9 April 1934; 10 April 1934; 12 August 1946; January 1947.

Utica Herald 15 September 1863.

Utica Observer 22 March 1887.

Utica Observer-Dispatch 15 February 1924; 18 October 1934; 4 February 1957.

Utica Patriot 11 January 1811.

Utica Press 15 February 1924.

"The Utica Saturday Globe." *The Courier Magazine*, October 1953: 20-22, 36-37.

Villard, Oswald Garrison. *Some Newspapers and Newspaper-Men.* New York: Knopf, 1923.

von Bernuth, Marietta. Interview with author. Utica, N.Y., 21 February 1986.

———. Letters to author, 4 August 1989; 8 November 1989.

Walsh, John J. *From Frontier Outpost to Modern City: A History of Utica, 1784-1920.* Utica, N.Y. Oneida Historical Society, 1978.

———. *Vignettes of Old Utica.* Utica, N.Y.: Utica Public Library, 1982.

Ward, James A. *Railroads and the Character of America, 1820-1887.* Knoxville: University of Tennessee Press, 1986.

Watertown Censor. 13 April 1830.

Weisberger, Bernard A. *The American Newspaperman.* Chicago: University of Chicago Press, 1961.

Western Centinel. 23 September 1795.

Western Spectator. 19 April 1831.

Wiebe, Robert. *The Search for Order, 1877-1920.* New York: Hill & Wang, 1968.

Wilensky, Harold L. "The Professionalization of Everyone?" *The American Journal of Sociology* 70 (September 1964): 137-58.

Wilentz, Sean. *Chants Democratic: New York City and the Rise of the American Working Class, 1788-1850.* New York: Oxford University Press, 1984.

Williams, Paul B. "Utica's Newspapers Since 1900." Paper presented to the Oneida Historical Society, Utica, N.Y., November 1958.

Wilson, Harold S. *McClure's Magazine and the Muckrakers.* Princeton: Princeton University Press, 1970.

The World Almanac and Book of Facts, 1988. New York: Pharos, 1988.

Index